IMAGES
of America

THE MUSIC HALL, PORTSMOUTH

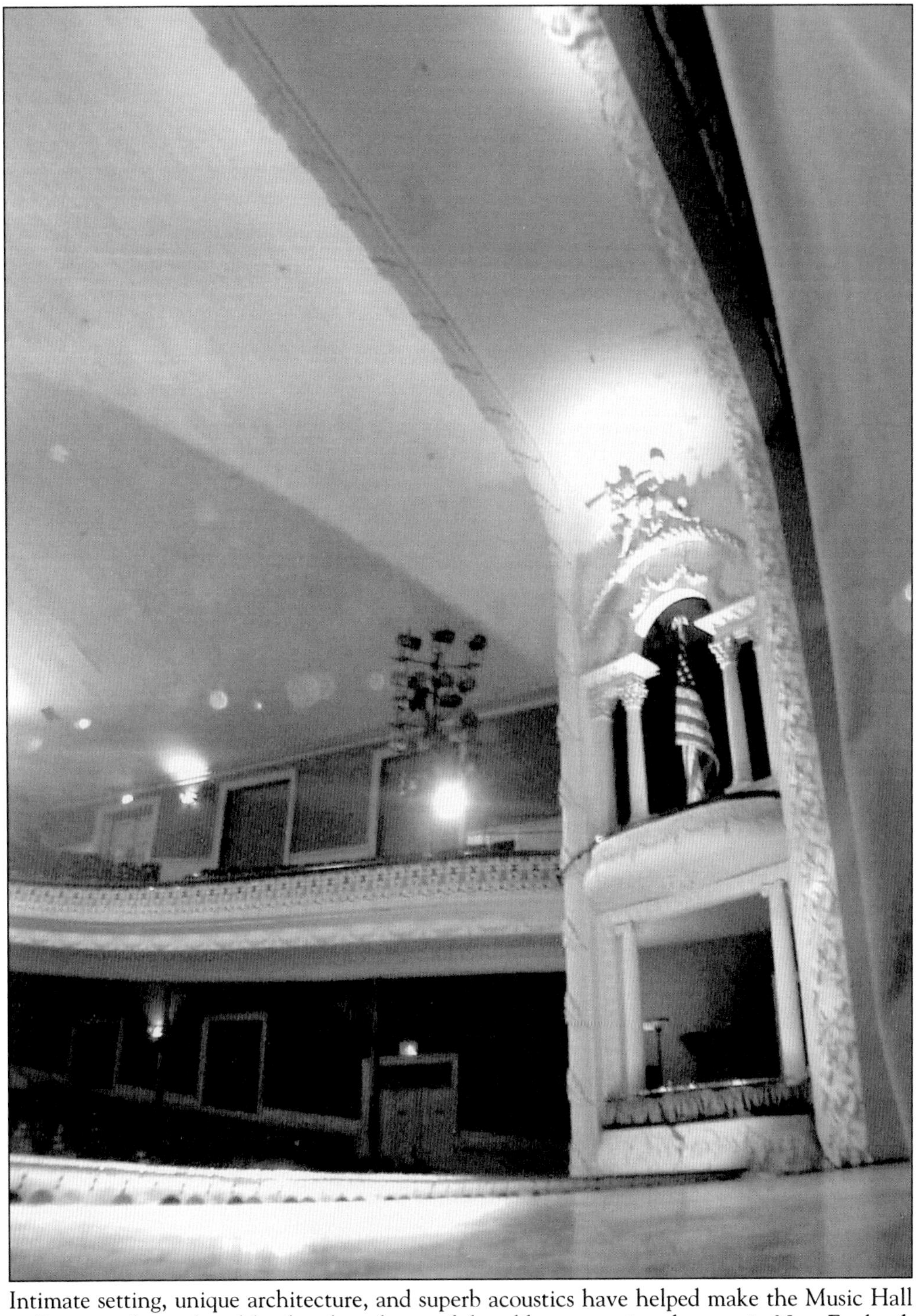

Intimate setting, unique architecture, and superb acoustics have helped make the Music Hall in Portsmouth a cultural landmark and one of the oldest operating theaters in New England. Presenting the finest entertainments of stage and screen from all over the globe and serving as a common ground for people of all ages to come together in appreciation of arts of all kinds, the Music Hall now celebrates over 125 years of standing ovations.

IMAGES
of America

The Music Hall, Portsmouth

Zhana Morris and Trevor F. Bartlett
on behalf of the Friends of the Music Hall

ARCADIA
PUBLISHING

ISBN 978-0-7385-1249-5

Published by Arcadia Publishing
Charleston, South Carolina

Printed in the United States of America

Library of Congress Catalog Card Number: 2003107898

For all general information contact Arcadia Publishing at:
Telephone 843-853-2070
Fax 843-853-0044
E-mail sales@arcadiapublishing.com
For customer service and orders:
Toll-Free 1-888-313-2665

Visit us on the Internet at www.arcadiapublishing.com

Contents

ACKNOWLEDGMENTS

The Friends of the Music Hall would graciously like to thank all those who contributed old photographs, new photographs, anecdotes, research, and pure hard work to support the production of this book: Jameson French, David Choate, Richard Smith, the Portsmouth Athenaeum, Strawbery Banke, Portsmouth Public Library, Mark Forder, Sarah Crawford, Clark Knowles, James A. Cannavino Library, George Barker, Ralph Morang, Nancy Horton, Chris Smith, the Press Room, Buffalo Bill Historical Center, Bill Nelson, Harriet Beecher Stowe Center, the State Library of Tasmania, Jerry Ohlinger, Sharon Flaherty, Portsmouth (Virginia) Public Library, Nora Studley, Drika Overton, Bob Pierce, Joseph Johnson, Mark James Morreale, Claudia Valenzuela, Nicole Clutier, Rebecca Taylor, and the Music Hall staff, board, and volunteers.

INTRODUCTION

Portsmouth can now claim having a building devoted exclusively to entertainments, not only substantial in its structure and containing all of the modern improvements, but in the general arrangements and decoration of its interior rivaling any other of its size in New England.

This description in an 1878 newspaper caught our attention as we began the research for *The Music Hall, Portsmouth* because of the obvious pride indicated in this simple statement. Music Hall ("the" was not part of its official name in the early days) was brought back to life after the previous building (also a theater) burned to the ground in 1876. On the cusp of major industrial breakthroughs, electricity, the telephone, automobiles, and more, the Music Hall was the focus for all of Portsmouth.

The land now occupied by the Music Hall had originally been designated as Puritan church lands, pasture that could be used to support the salary of a minister. For the next 100 years, the land was indeed used in this manner, but as the town grew, it became apparent that the property was more valuable as a building site. In the 18th century, the property held the country's first almshouse and, later, Portsmouth's second prison. In 1806, the First Christian Society in Portsmouth built a church later called the Temple, which, in the same article as the quote above, was described as "not so elaborate in structure and decoration as the building of the same name at Jerusalem, yet the title was not inappropriate, as like the other it was a place where all classes met."

The Temple continued to be a place of worship throughout the middle of the 19th century, when it made a slow transition to more secular activities. A balcony was added to the main floor, and the area of the pulpit was replaced with a stage to facilitate dramatic entertainments. A "bowling saloon" was added as well.

Portsmouth seems to have been plagued through the years by Christmas fires. In 1802, 1806, and 1813, major fires destroyed large parts of the downtown area during the holidays. In 1876, the Temple burned to the ground—by some reports on Christmas Eve, by others on Christmas Day.

The land was sold to members of the Peirce family, who owned the adjacent property on Congress Street. The Peirce family had a long history in Portsmouth as businessmen, politicians, and philanthropists. Almost every generation was connected to at least one other wealthy and influential local family. The Wentworths, Sheafes, and Sises were all related through the Peirce name.

Led by William Augustus Peirce (whose descendants still reside in the Seacoast area), the five siblings, William Augustus, Joseph Wentworth, Ann Wentworth, Robert Cutts, and Sarah Coffin, and Sarah's husband, William Kennard, began the process of building a new hall in 1877.

The brick building was 75 feet across the front and 103 feet along the side. There were 24 windows between the front and side, all ornamented with gothic arches. (The north side, facing Congress Street, butted up against another Peirce building, the Kearsarge Hotel.) Between the orchestra section, the balcony, and the gallery, the theater could seat 1,214 people. In 1870, there were fewer than 10,000 people residing in Portsmouth; in just over a week, the entire population could have visited the hall at least once.

As an indication of the times, most newspaper articles written about the opening of the new hall describe in great detail not only the decorative features but also the mechanical ones. The gas lights are described as using between 2,000 and 3,000 feet of gas pipe to supply 230 lights, including 80 in the chandelier and 16 in the footlight trough. The boiler is described in detail as well, a $25^2/_3$-horsepower machine requiring only four pounds of steam to heat the entire building.

On January 29, 1878, the Honorable W.H.Y. Hackett, mayor of Portsmouth and father-in-law of one of the Peirce brothers, congratulated the citizens of Portsmouth on "the completion and opening of this beautiful, commodious, much needed and long-expected Music Hall" in his opening speech. He added, "We meet this evening somewhat like a family that had lost house and home by fire, and after camping out for a year are first re-united in their new and spacious mansion, while some are admiring its architecture and the general arrangements, others selecting their rooms, and all are about to enjoy the first feast in their new home."

That opening night, a Tuesday, the Music Hall was crowded with the community's finest, a live orchestra, performers from the Boston Museum Company, and a finely dressed, smiling staff ready to assist.

For the next few decades, the Music Hall presented countless entertainments. The hall was, as it remains today, a place for the community to join together in common causes or to support local groups. The Temperance Society held regular meetings at the hall, and Portsmouth High School held graduation ceremonies there until just prior to World War II.

The driving force behind the early years of the Music Hall was a man named Fernando W. Hartford. His first connection to the Music Hall was as manager, initially under the Peirce family and then under his good friend Frank Jones, the beer mogul who owned the theater in the last few years of his life. Hartford would also become the owner of the *Portsmouth Herald* and seven-time mayor, in addition to purchasing the building upon Jones's death.

The Music Hall's history is full of people such as Hartford who have strived to keep the hall operational in a growing downtown that seemed determined to diminish the hall's importance to the community.

The second of these owners was Guy Tott of Kittery, Maine. Tott purchased the building at auction during World War II, in a time when three other theaters were operating downtown and the Music Hall was regulated primarily to the lecture circuit. Off the main street and without the modern amenities of the new movie houses owned by the likes of Paramount and E.M. Loew, this purchase was a risk, even at the lowest accepted bid of $10,000.

Tott managed to upgrade the hall and ran it as a second-run movie house for a number of years, until E.M. Loew, who owned the Colonial Theater in Market Square, started booking the films in 1947 and purchased it in 1971.

Although it is unlikely that E.M. Loew ever actually set foot in the theater, he can be considered the third of the great owners. It was during this time that the Music Hall regained some prestige in the community, becoming a first-run movie house. Unfortunately, Loew eventually decided that the Colonial would be a better place for these movies, and the Music Hall was once again "demoted" to second place. It is quite possible that it is because of this decision, however, that the Music Hall stands today. In 1982, E.M. Loew sold the building, as it was no longer making money for him. This sale led to the last two series of owners, who began the process of restoration that would enable the hall to outlast all three of the other larger theaters.

In the mid-1980s, a group of area residents, headed by Lewis Shaw, purchased the hall and financed an ambitious cleanup and restoration. Work was done in almost every area of the theater to bring the building up to modern standards. In the latter part of the decade, the Friends of the Music Hall was formed and, with a great amount of community support, was able to buy the building. The Friends of the Music Hall has since brought back a year-round season of live events and movies.

It is with the help of all of those people, in the recent and more distant past, that this theater has survived. For 125 years, the Music Hall has endured war, economic depression, and competition from other theaters to become the state's oldest operating theater. The purpose of this book is to celebrate those years and to look forward to a continuation of "performances that bring joy to the world, delight to the young at heart, inspiration to the world-weary, understanding to contemporary concerns, and community support to worthy causes" (Friends of the Music Hall mission statement, 2003).

One

Music Hall 1878–1899

In 1878, there were approximately 9,000 people living in Portsmouth. In a time before television and radio, meetinghouses—be they secular or religious in nature—were a central part of daily life for many people. It was in venues such as the Temple, and then the Music Hall, that political rallies, high school graduations, and Memorial Day celebrations could be seen by all ages and classes.

Through the first few decades of the Music Hall's history, people gathered there for news, entertainment, and community. In his opening night speech, Mayor W.H.Y. Hackett said of the hall, "This hall is a credit as well as a convenience to our city. A community is known to some extent by the character and place of its amusements. This place will exert a refining influence upon those who occupy it. It will serve to some extent as the place of our social reunions, for we cannot come together in a well arranged and well ordered place of amusement, without quickening our interest and deepening our sympathy with each other; we cannot, in company and sympathy enjoy music and the drama—those recreations which enliven, sweeten and lengthen life, without increasing our interest in and our respect for each other."

With this in mind, we show you pieces of these first few decades. Images of the opening night program, performers from the opening company, and artifacts from the basement to the rafters will bring you back to Portsmouth's late-19th-century community. From minstrel shows to Memorial Evening Exercises, musical conventions to actual dog and pony shows, the Music Hall brought all kinds of entertainment to Portsmouth in a time when it was most needed.

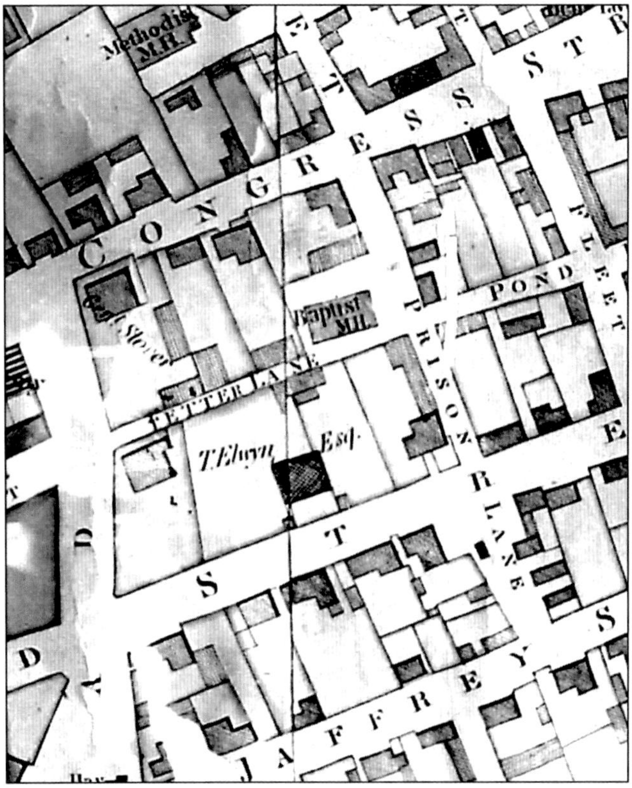

This map of Portsmouth was drawn in 1813. The Baptist meetinghouse would eventually be called the Temple. Note the names of the streets: Prison Lane and Fetter Lane, now known as Chestnut Street and Porter Street. Prior to being owned by the Baptist church, the property held the town prison and the country's first almshouse. The building shown here burned down in 1876, clearing the way for the Music Hall. (Courtesy of the Portsmouth Athenaeum.)

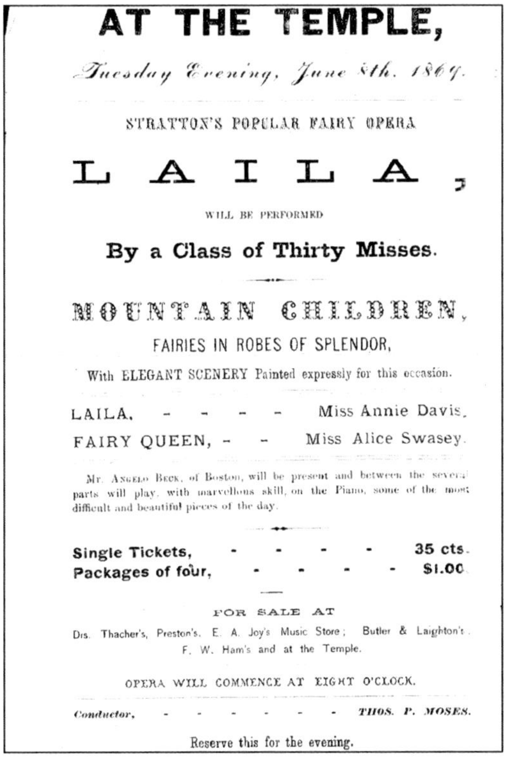
AT THE TEMPLE,

Tuesday Evening, June 8th, 1869.

STRATTON'S POPULAR FAIRY OPERA

LAILA,

WILL BE PERFORMED

By a Class of Thirty Misses.

MOUNTAIN CHILDREN,

FAIRIES IN ROBES OF SPLENDOR,

With ELEGANT SCENERY Painted expressly for this occasion.

LAILA, - - - - Miss Annie Davis.
FAIRY QUEEN, - - Miss Alice Swasey.

Mr. Angelo Beck, of Boston, will be present and between the several parts will play, with marvellous skill, on the Piano, some of the most difficult and beautiful pieces of the day.

Single Tickets, - - - - 35 cts.
Packages of four, - - - - $1.00

FOR SALE AT

Drs. Thacher's, Preston's, E. A. Joy's Music Store; Butler & Laighton's, F. W. Ham's and at the Temple.

OPERA WILL COMMENCE AT EIGHT O'CLOCK.

Conductor, - - - - - - - *THOS. P. MOSES.*

Reserve this for the evening.

This single remaining piece of Temple memorabilia in the Music Hall collection, a playbill from an opera titled *Laila*, offers some insight into the entertainment of the barely post–Civil War era. The inner pages tell us the story of a fairy queen who disguises herself as a beggar in hopes of finding a kind soul to take her in. Laila, a young mountain girl, does so and is rewarded for her generosity. Variations on well-known stories were quite common in postwar years, created in hopes of rebuilding a sense of unified morality.

PROGRAMME FOR THE OPENING NIGHT

TUESDAY EVENING, JANUARY 29th, 1878.

OVERTURE . . . . BY THE . . . . ORCHESTRA

Under the direction of

H. L. HARLOW,

At 7.30; after which an

OPENING ADDRESS

Will be delivered by the

HON. W. H. Y. HACKETT.

The performance will commence with the late T. W. Robertson's brilliant domestic Comedy, in 3 acts, entitled

CASTE

The Hon. George D'Alroy, ... Mr. J. Stuart Clarke
Captain Hawtree, ... Mr. Frank M. Warren
Old Eccles, ... Mr. Elmer Warner
Sam Gerridge, ... Mr. Edwin Milliken
Dixon, ... Mr. John R. Heard
POLLY ECCLES, ... Miss MARY CARY
Esther Eccles, ... Miss Susie Cluer
THE MARQUISE, ... Mrs. M. A. PENNOYER

The entertainment will conclude with the laughable Farce, in 1 act, of

JOHN WOPPS

JOHN WOPPS, a Policeman, . . Mr. CHAS. H. THAYER
Mr. Chopps, a butcher, ... Mr. Robert Archer
Sam Snug, from Australia, ... Mr. Elmer Warner
Tom Chaffer, ... Mr. John R. Heard
Mrs. Wopps, ... Miss Nellie Downing
Mrs. Chopps, ... Miss Susie Cluer

WEDNESDAY EVENING, JAN. 30, 1878,

Will be presented the most successful Comedy in the English language, entitled

MARRIED LIFE

Mr. Lionel Lynx, ... Mr. J. Stuart Clarke
Mr. Younghusband, ... Mr. Frank Carlos
Mr. Samuel Coddle, ... Mr. Elmer Warner
Mr. Henry Dove, ... Mr. Edwin Milliken
Mr. Dismal, ... Mr. John R. Heard
MRS. YOUNGHUSBAND, ... Miss MARY CARY
MRS. HENRY DOVE, ... Miss OLIVIA RAND
Mrs. Lynx, ... Miss Susie Cluer
MRS. CODDLE, ... Mrs. M. A. PENNOYER
Mrs. Dismal, ... Miss Nellie Downing

After which will be presented the Comic Drama of

TOODLES

TIMOTHY TOODLES, ... Mr. CHAS. H. THAYER
George Acorn, ... Mr. J. Stuart Clarke
Charles Fenton, ... Mr. Frank Carlos
Frank Acorn, ... Mr. Robert Archer
The Landlord, ... Mr. Edwin Mayo
MRS. TOODLES, ... Mrs. M. A. PENNOYER
Mary Acorn, ... Miss Grace Hall

THURSDAY EVENING, JAN. 01, 1878,

LAST NIGHT,

First production in this city of the powerful and intensely interesting Emotional Drama, founded on Dickens' novel of Bleak House, in 5 acts, by B. E. Woolf, Esq., author of the "Mighty Dollar," entitled

POOR JO

As played with Great Success at the

BOSTON MUSEUM AND UNION SQ. THEATRE, N. Y.

—(INTRODUCING)—

MISS MARY CARY,

In her marvelous Portraiture of POOR JO, the London Street Waif.

Pronounced by the press and public the most realistic performance ever witnessed on the stage.

First appearance in this city of

MRS. THOMAS BARRY,

Who will appear in her great role, LADY DEDLOCK,

As originally played by her at the Union Square Theatre, New York.

JO, "always a movin' on," . . . . Miss MARY CARY
Mr. INSPECTOR BUCKET, ... Mr. CHAS. H. THAYER
Mr. Guppy, ... Mr. Edwin Milliken
Mr. Tulkinghorn, ... Mr. Elmer Warner
Sir Leicester Dedlock, Bart., ... Mr. Robert Archer
Mercury, ... Mr. Frank M. Warren
Servant, ... Mr. Edwin Mayo
LADY DEDLOCK, ... Mrs. THOMAS BARRY
HORTENSE, ... Mrs. M. A. PENNOYER
Esther, ... Miss Grace Hall
Maid to Esther, ... Miss Fannie Browning

PRICES OF ADMISSION.

75 CTS. 50 CTS. 35 CTS.

Tickets will be sold at W. R. Preston's Drug Store.

Owing to the extreme length of the peformances they will commence precisely at 7.45. Doors open at 7.

TREASURER, ... Mr. QUINCY KILBY

NEW MUSIC HALL,

PORTSMOUTH.

BUILT UNDER THE IMMEDIATE SUPERVISION OF

WM. A. PIERCE, Esq.

WILLIAM A. ASHE, Architect.

THE FRESCO PAINTING

By W. S. HENAY & SON, of Concord

THE UPHOLSTERY,

By DEMEREST & JOYCE, Brooklyn, New York.

THE STEAM APPARATUS,

From the EXETER MACHINE WORKS, WILLIAM BURLINGHAM, Agent.

THE STAGE AND MECHANICAL APPARATUS,

Made by WELD & BOYSON, 390 Tremont Street, Boston.

THE SCENERY,

Painted expressly for this Theatre, by FRED. WELD, of Boston.

THE INITIAL PERFORMANCES

GIVEN UNDER THE MANAGEMENT OF

THAYER & TOMPKINS.

Boston Job Print, Alden Street.

There were actually a few versions of the opening night program made; this one appears to be for all three of the performances brought to Portsmouth for this auspicious event. This one piece of paper began the process of historical research into the hall. Not only are the performers listed, but the architect (William Ashe), the fresco painter (W.S. Henay), and numerous other craftsmen are given prominence on the front cover.

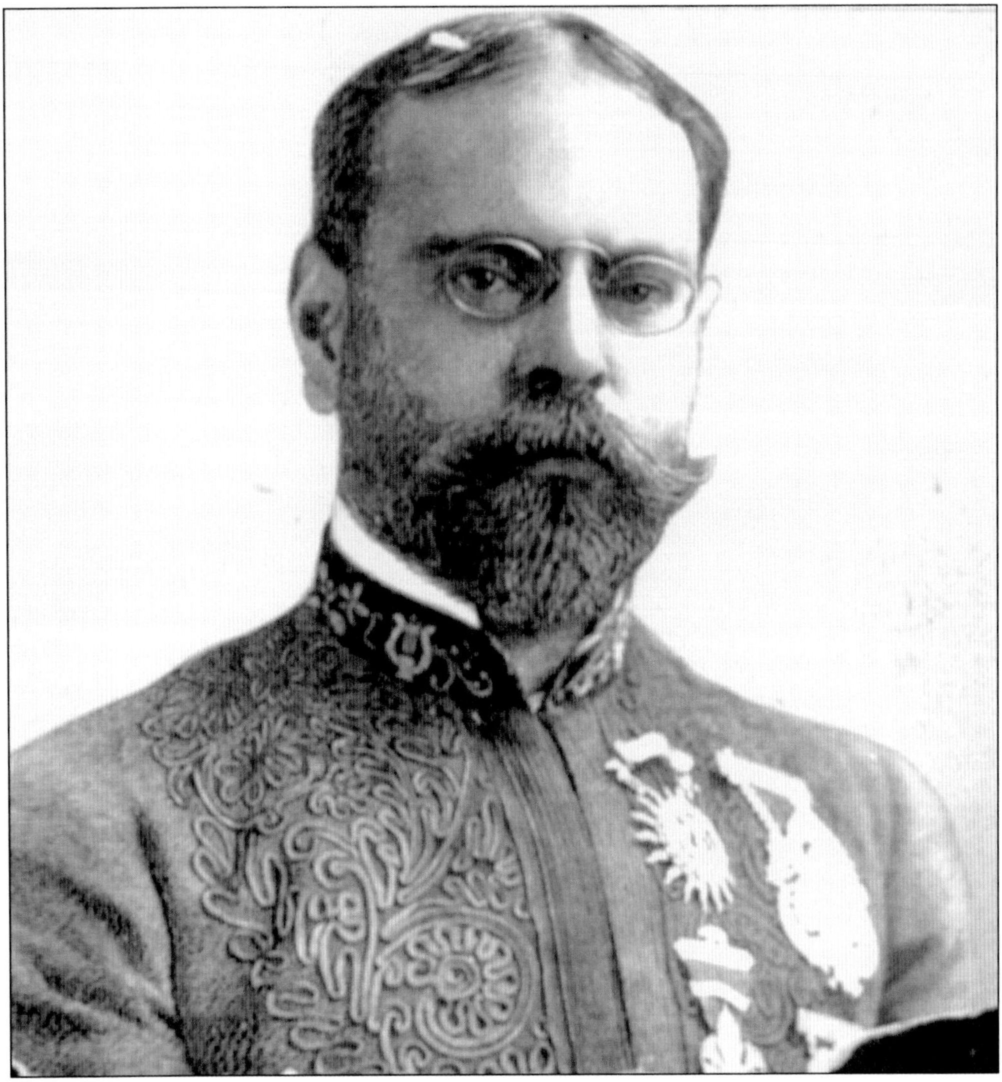

John Philip Sousa is known as the king of American marches. It is only fitting that he should appear at the Music Hall in its early years alongside great performers of the era. Sousa spent most of his early career with the U.S. Marine Band (he conducted the well-respected band through five presidents) but was also involved with traditional theater, conducting Gilbert and Sullivan's *H.M.S.Pinafore* on Broadway.

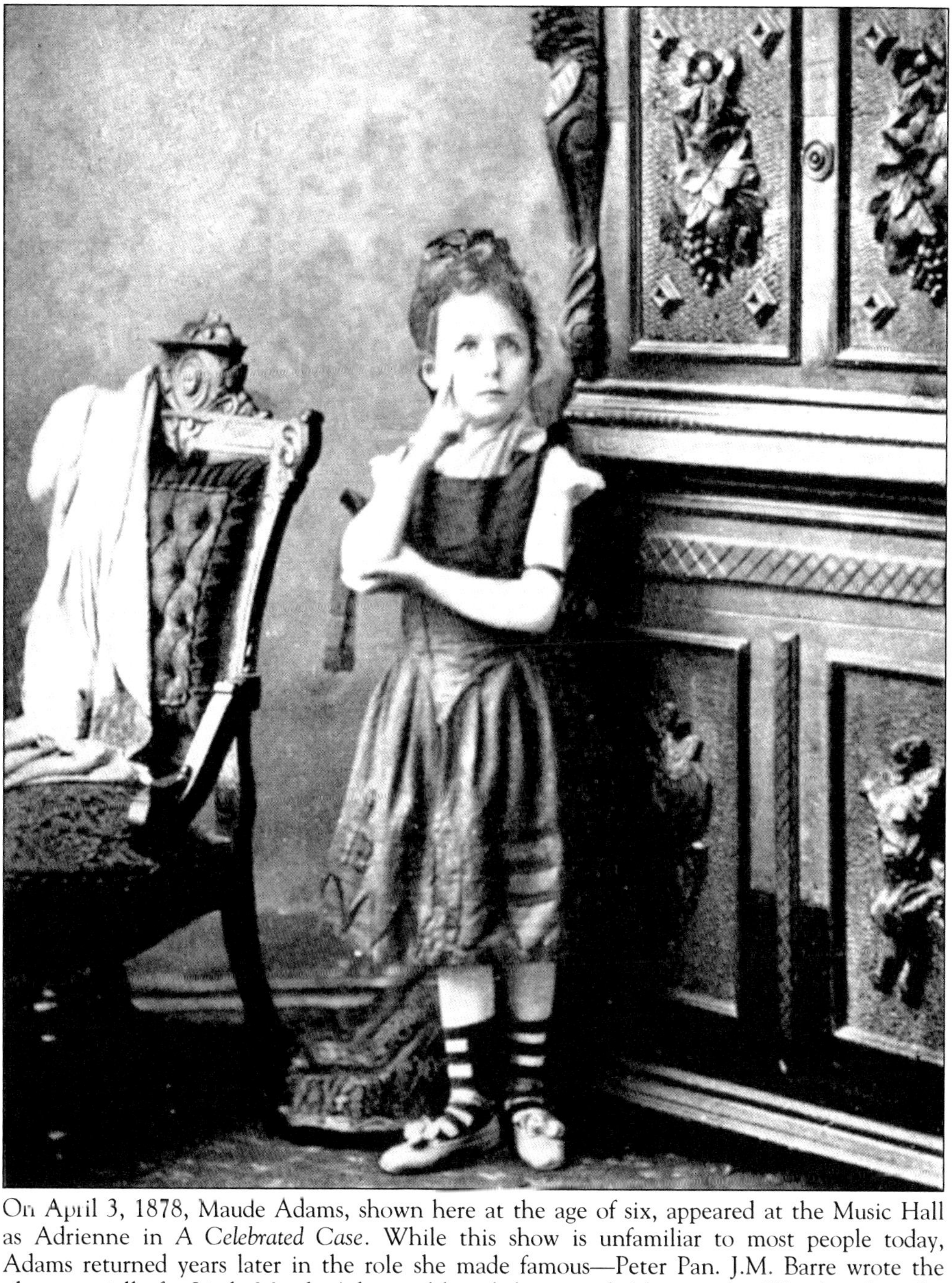

On April 3, 1878, Maude Adams, shown here at the age of six, appeared at the Music Hall as Adrienne in A *Celebrated Case*. While this show is unfamiliar to most people today, Adams returned years later in the role she made famous—Peter Pan. J.M. Barre wrote the play especially for Little Maude Adams, although he intended her to play Wendy, whom he considered the lead. After performing as Wendy in Europe, Adams premiered the title role in the United States and went on to do 1,500 performances. (*Peter Pan*, incidentally, was directed by Dion Boucicault II, the son of the playwright mentioned on page 14.) Not satisfied with limiting herself to acting, Adams also worked with General Electric Laboratories and invented an incandescent lamp that was later used in color filmmaking. (Courtesy of Sarah Crawford.)

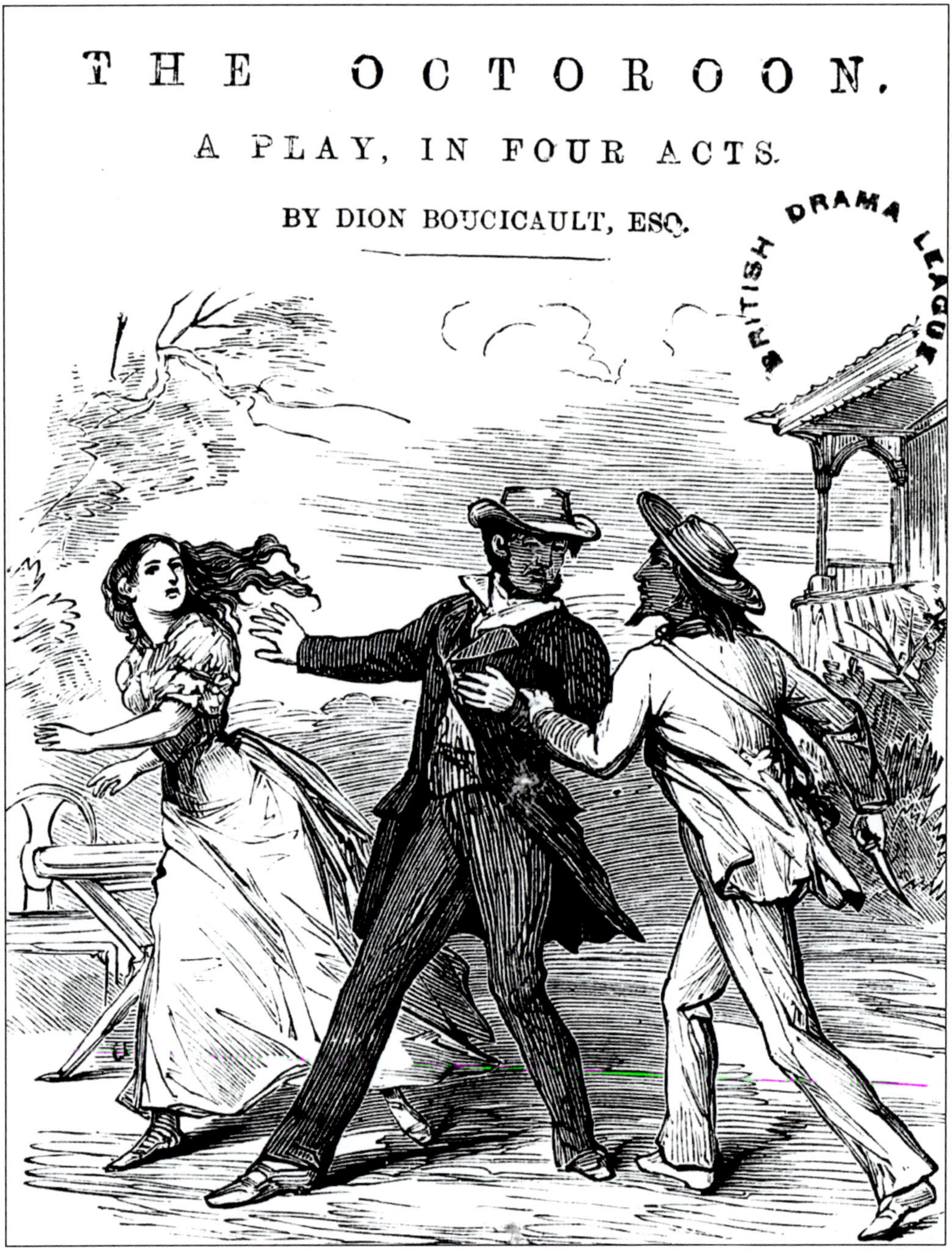

In February 1878, well-known promoter and Boston theater manager John Stetson brought to Portsmouth a revival of the antislavery drama *The Octoroon*. The play, written by Dion Boucicault, was originally produced in 1859, just prior to the American Civil War. There are conflicting stories about the play's origins, as there were several books published on the same theme. (Courtesy of the James A. Cannavino Library, Marist College)

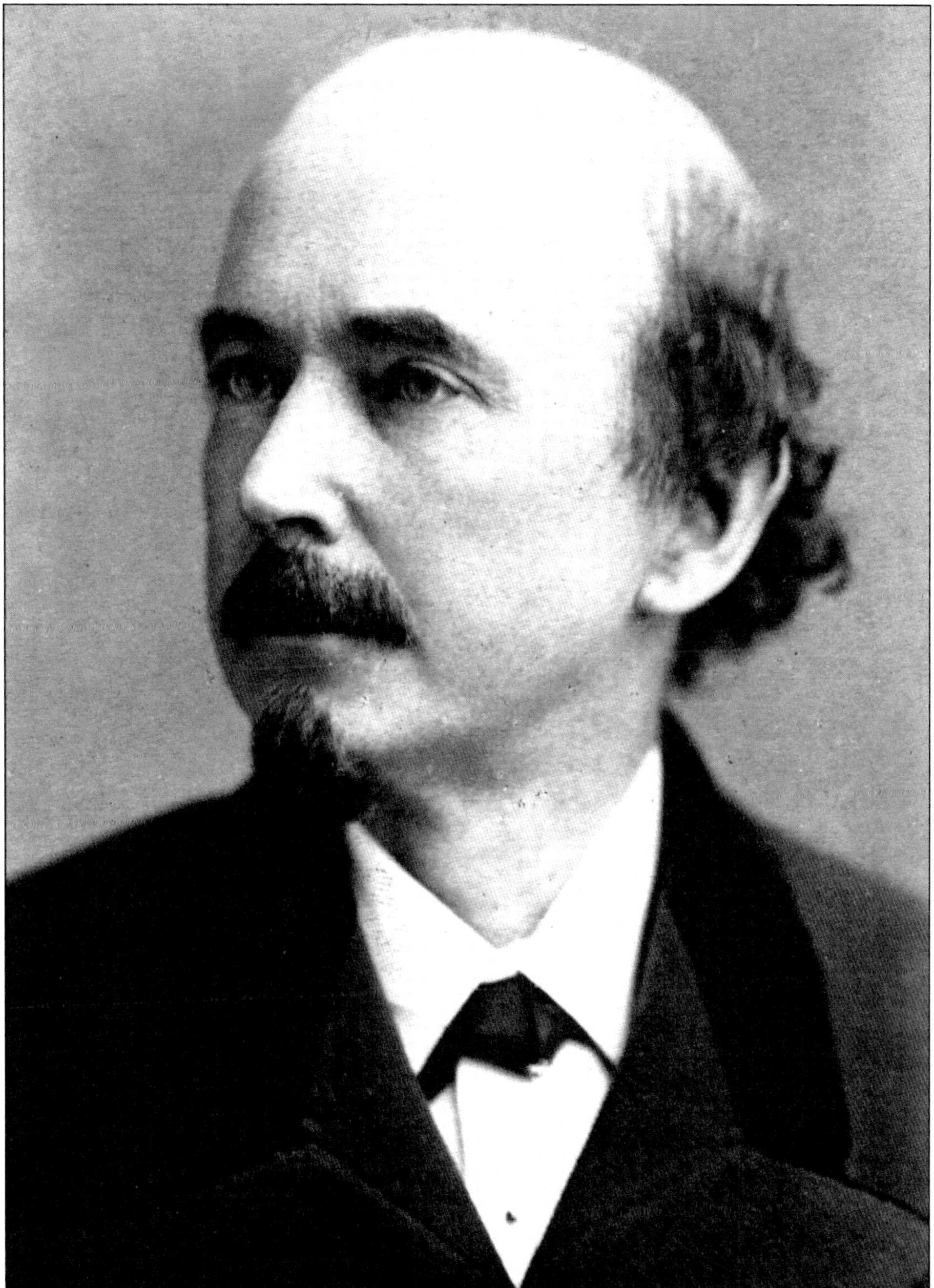

An interesting element to *The Octoroon* was the introduction of a camera to capture the antagonist in the act. While the technology was there, this was by no means a common piece of equipment. (George Eastman, founder of Kodak, was not yet five years old when the play was written.) While the show was a great success for Dion Boucicault, shown here, it did have a number of negative associations. The abolitionist John Brown was hanged just three days prior to the show's premiere, and the controversial topic was often discredited because of Boucicault's own immigrant status. (Courtesy of Bill Nelson.)

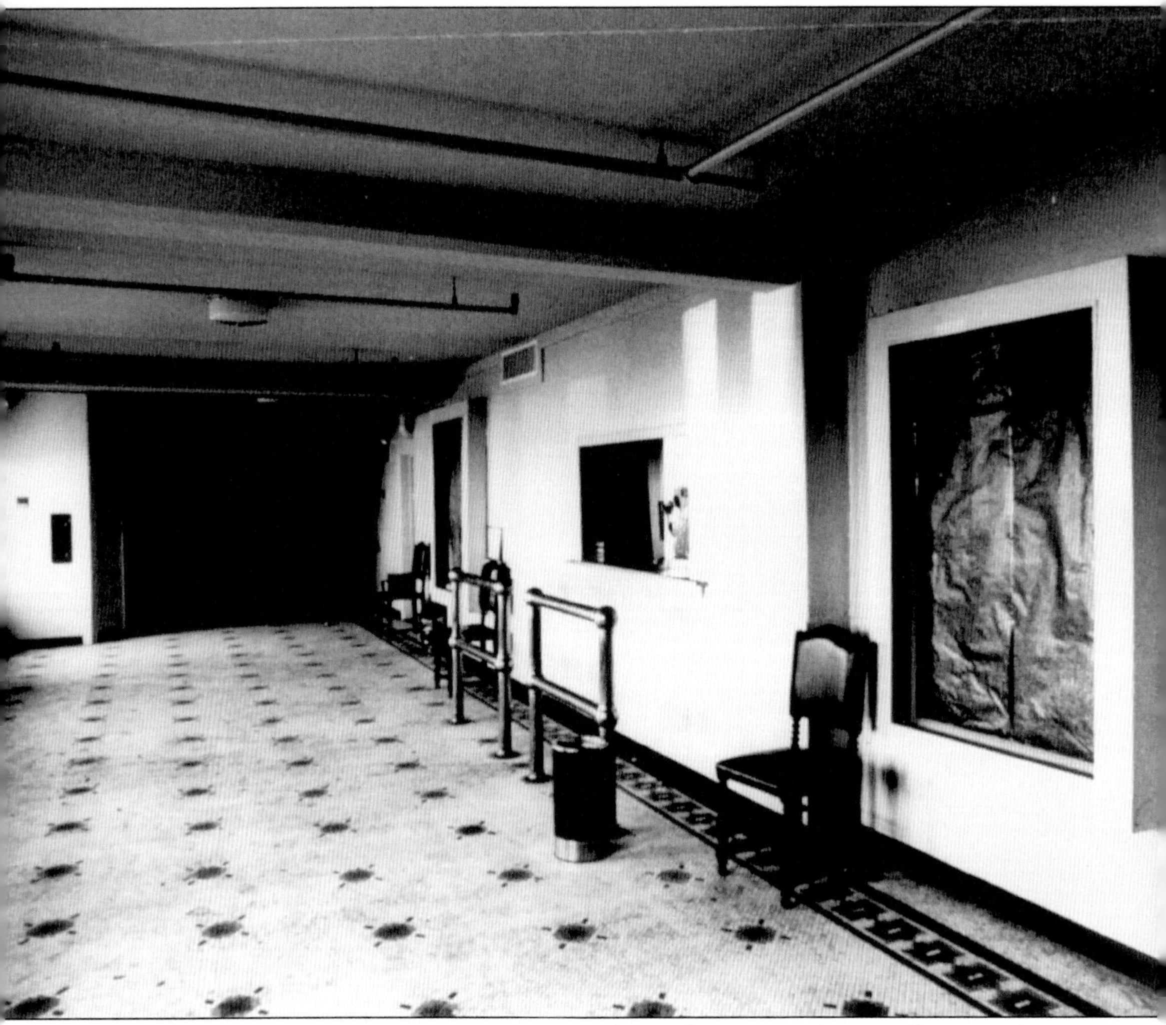

The lower lobby has had minor alterations and countless paint jobs over the years, but one of the few remaining original elements of decoration can be found on the floor. This original ceramic tile is well past its prime but is a great example of the blue, green, and dark red color scheme that was once seen throughout the entire building, including the walls and the ceiling. (Courtesy of George Barker.)

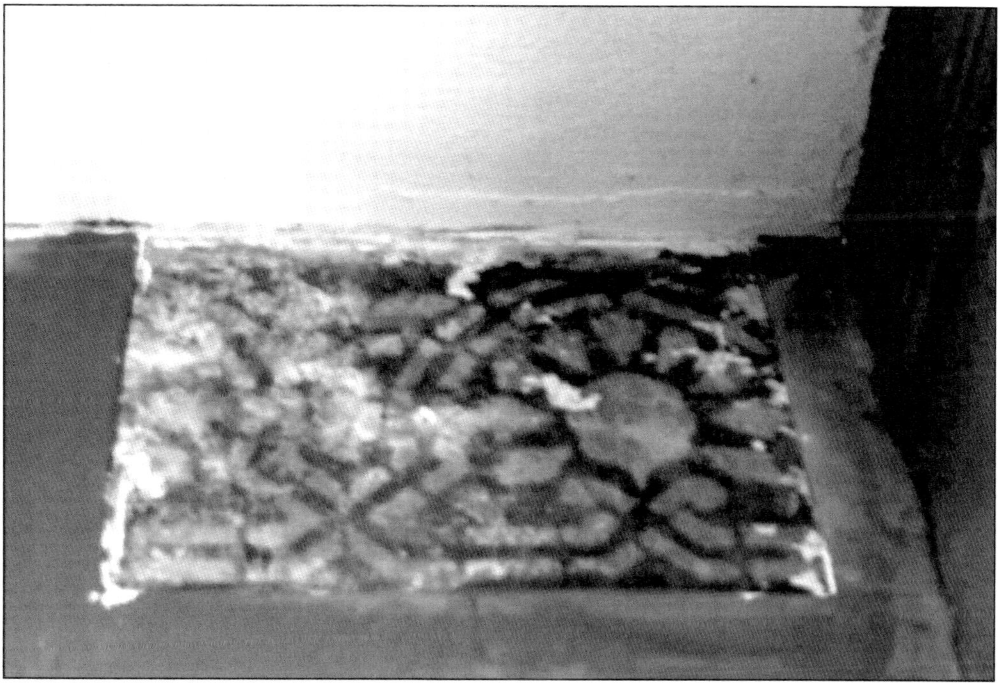

These frescos can be seen in the painted border in the lobby. Recent documentation indicates that they are indeed part of the original decoration from 1878. The lower border matches the dark red of the tiles, while the top border is resplendent in the smoky blue. (Courtesy of Rebecca Taylor.)

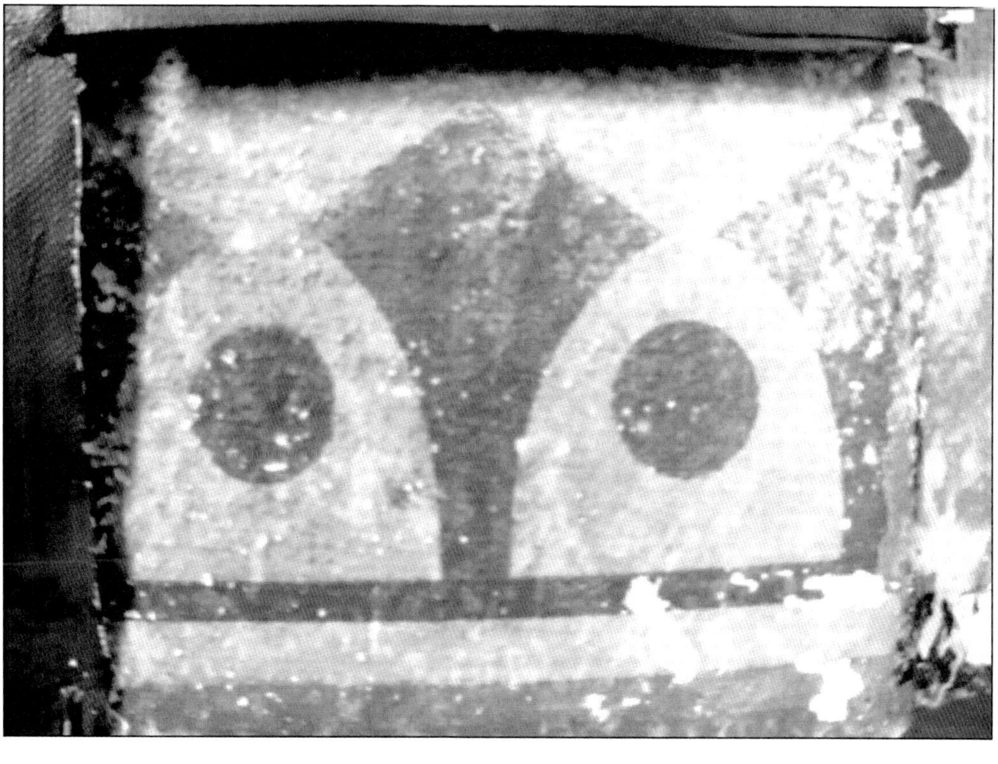

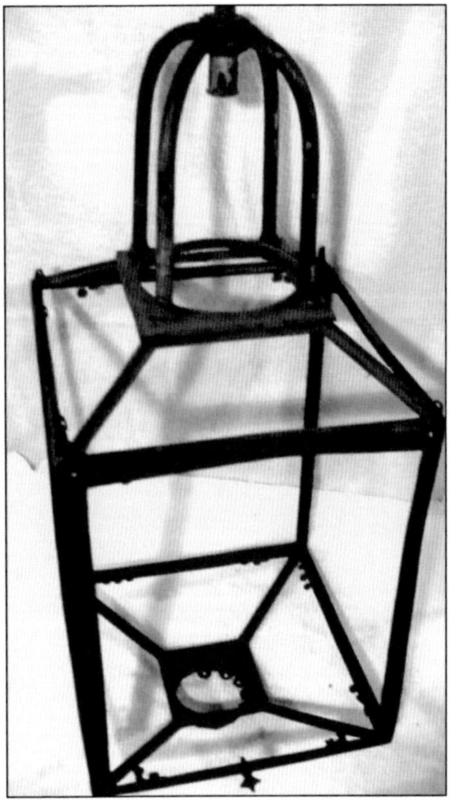

Missing its glass panes, this is one of two remaining gas lanterns that lit the exterior entrance for that first audience in 1878. Edison and Swan were still three years away from perfecting the electric lamp, and it would be a few more before the Music Hall made the switch. (Courtesy of Rebecca Taylor.)

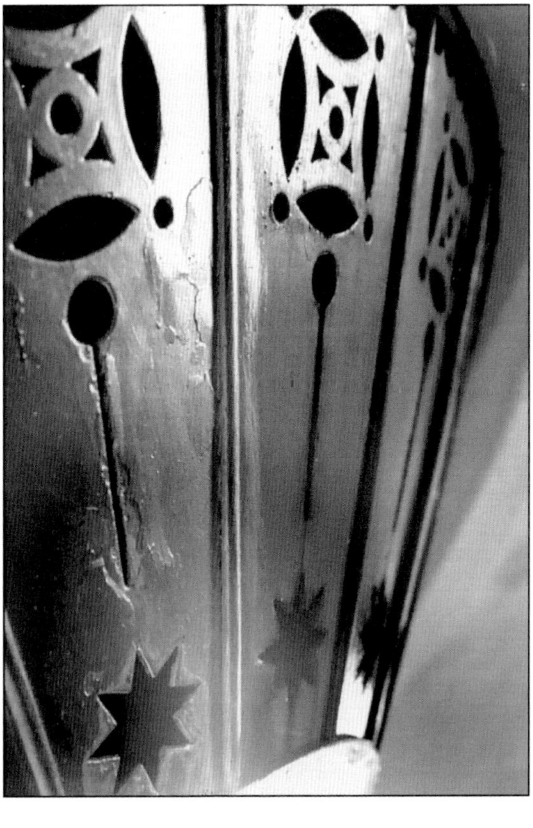

In 1878, the decorative plate shown here held a chandelier with 80 gas jets. With the upgrade to electricity, the chandelier was replaced, but both lighting units have now been missing for many years. (Courtesy of Clark Knowles.)

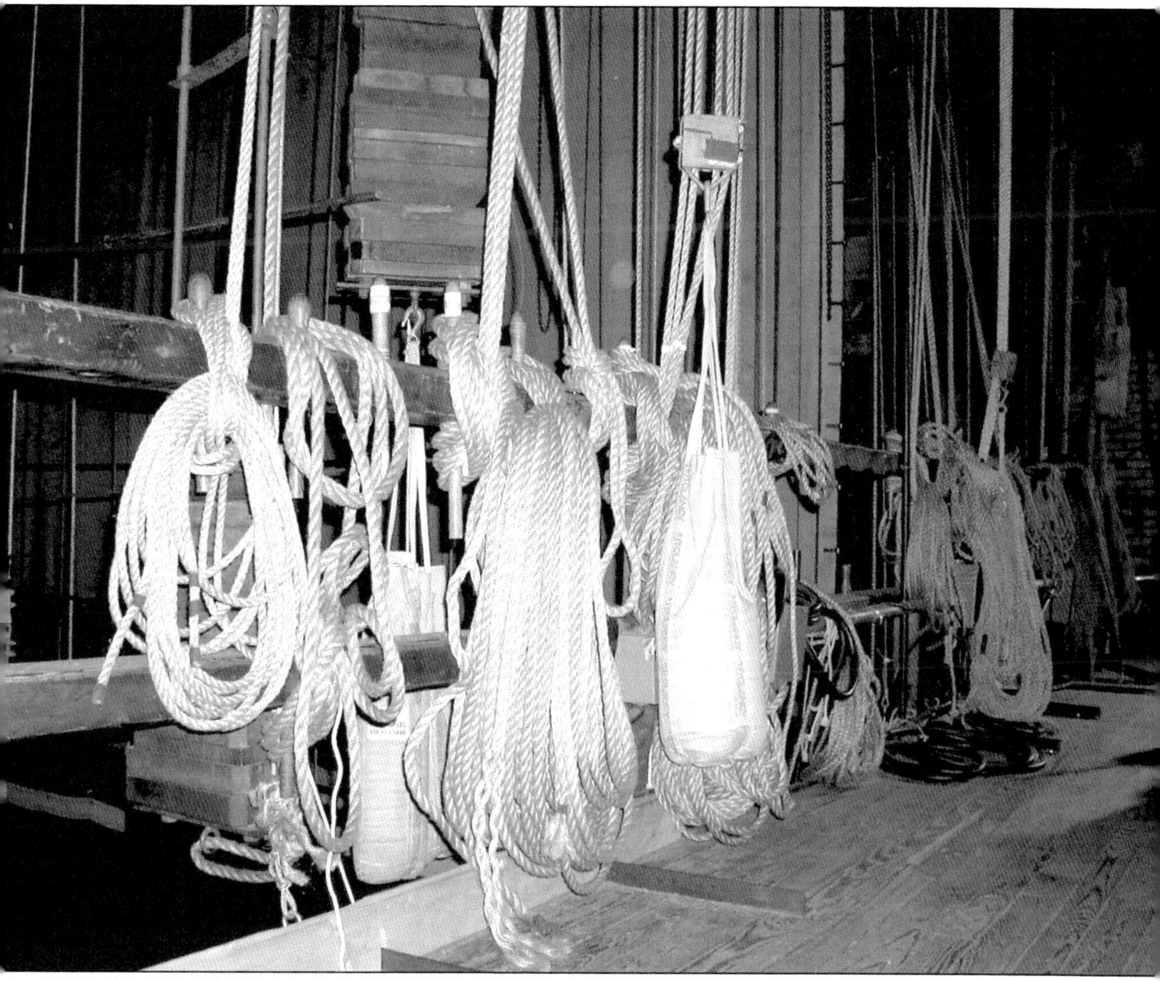

The fly rail is the unseen center of activity in any theater. From this walkway 35 feet in the air, technicians lower and raise the scenery, movie screen, and lights. Its similarity to an old wooden sailing vessel can be seen clearly in the hemp ropes and tie pins. It is quite likely that the Music Hall was built by workers from the Portsmouth Naval Shipyard, and the original stagehands would have been sailors who were already familiar with how to handle ropes. While many modernizations have been made to theatrical rigging systems, this system still seems to work in many small houses around the country to this day. (Courtesy of Chris Smith.)

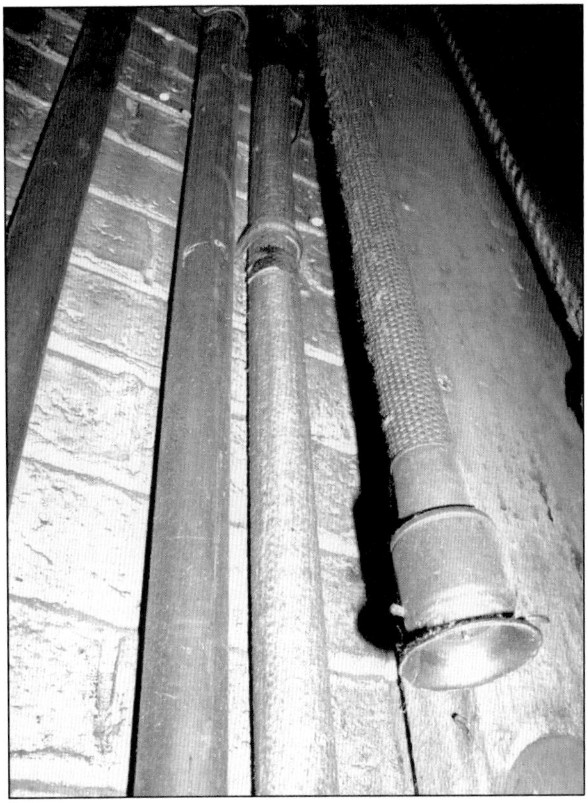

Many aspects of theaters across the globe are shared by ships of the same era. Among them was the speaking tube. The only remaining example in the hall, this tube is a coiled spring of metal covered with woven cloth. The speaking tube was used for communication among sides of the stage, the conductor, and the house manager. (Courtesy of Chris Smith.)

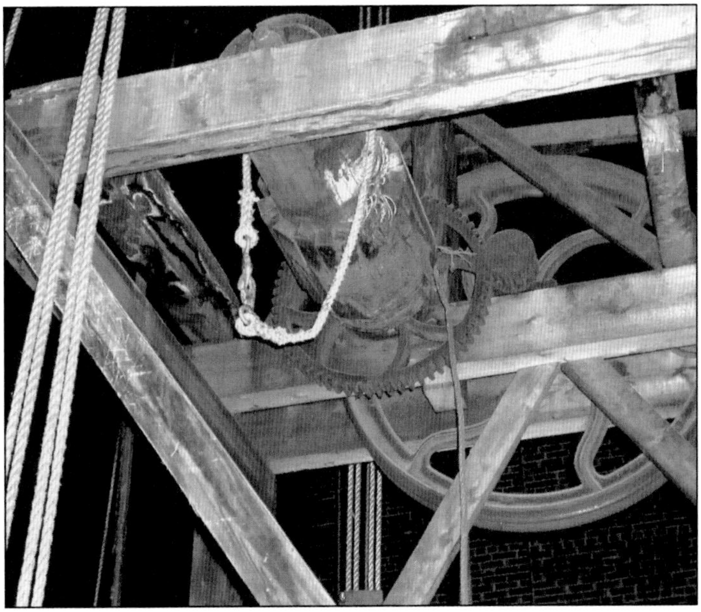

The attic of the Music Hall holds many treasures. Shown are the components of the original hand-cranked elevator that once carried opera divas to their dressing rooms three levels above the stage. The elevator car still exists in the basement, although it likely would fail a modern-day safety inspection. Made entirely of wood, the open platform was just large enough to carry one person and a trunk of costumes. (Courtesy of Chris Smith.)

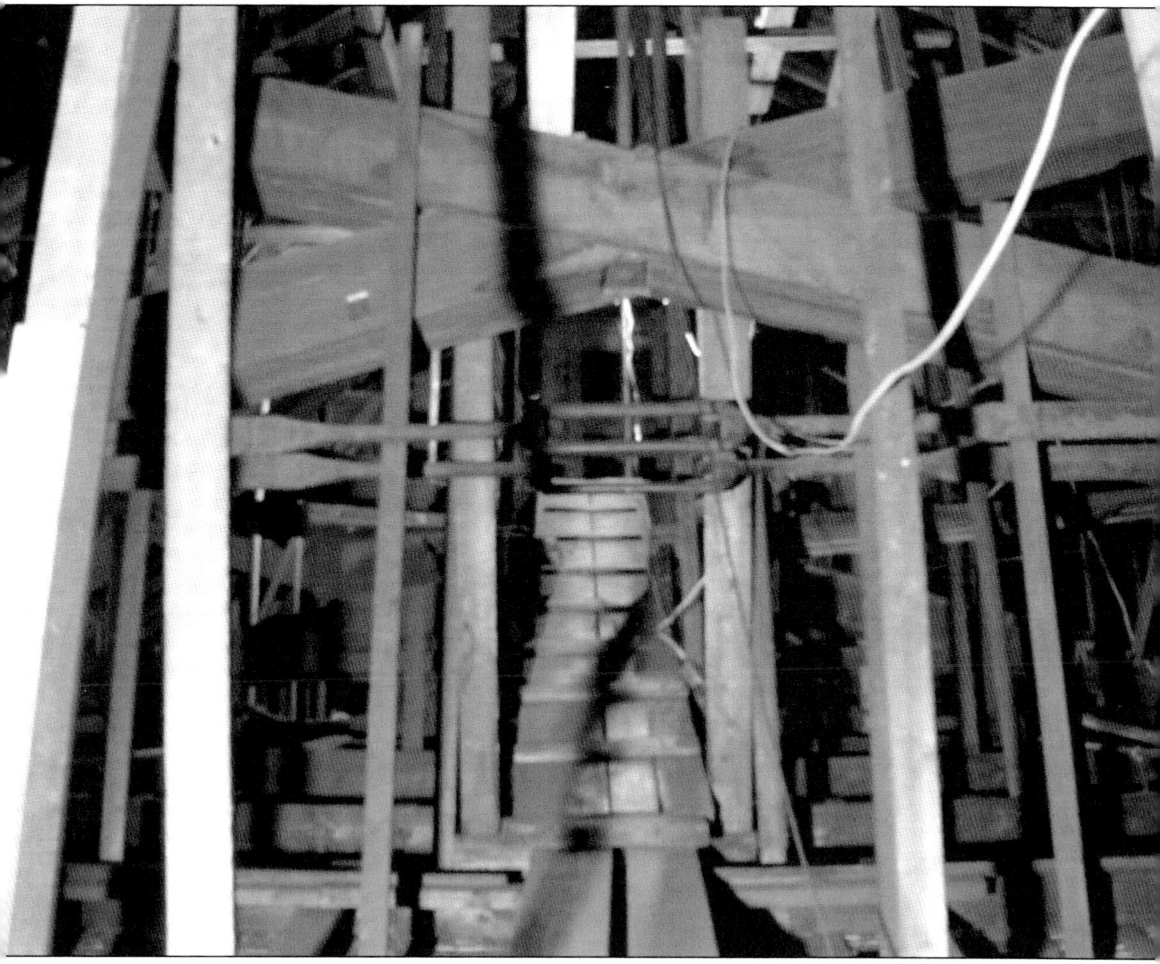

Climbing the rafters may not be for everyone, but these planks lead up to the highest point in the dome of the theater. Crafted like a wooden ship turned inside out, the ceiling of the audience chamber is actually suspended from the roof with a series of four-inch-by-four-inch boards. The large crossbeams and two-foot-long turnbuckle help pull the side walls in toward the middle to further support the ceiling. The view from the top of the plank is the underside of the decorative plate in the center of the dome. Through the decorative work, one can see the seats 60 feet below. (Courtesy of Chris Smith.)

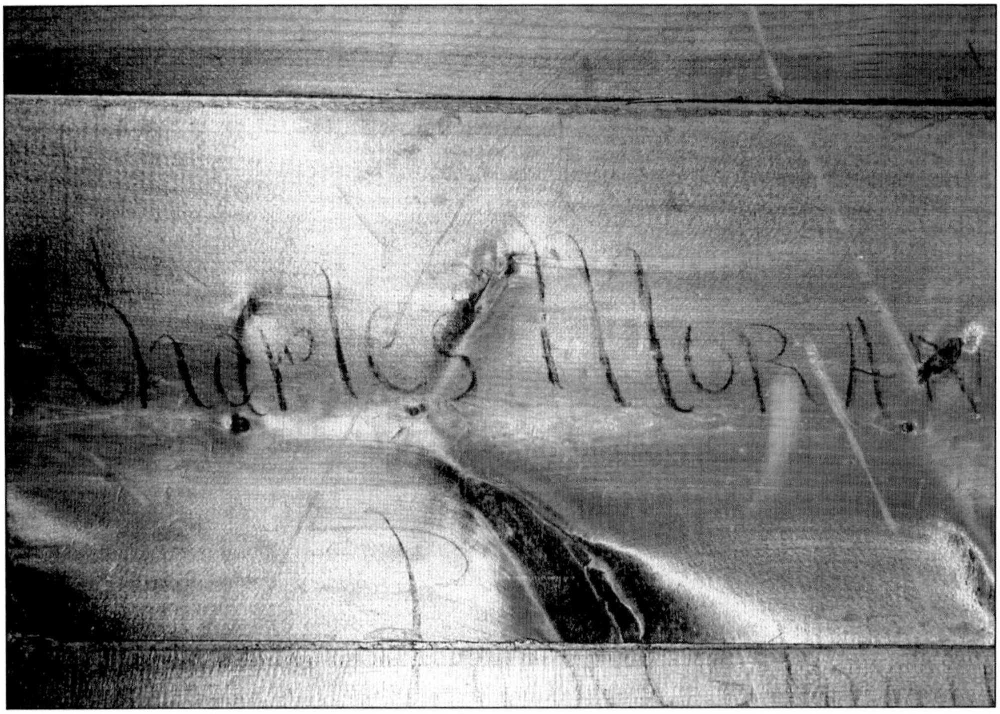

This signature was found in the attic space above the proscenium archway. Written in charcoal, it has withstood the test of time. While it has no date, the signature is in close proximity to others from the 1880s. Could Charles Moran have been a member of the famed Moran tugboat company that resides on the nearby river? (Courtesy of Chris Smith.)

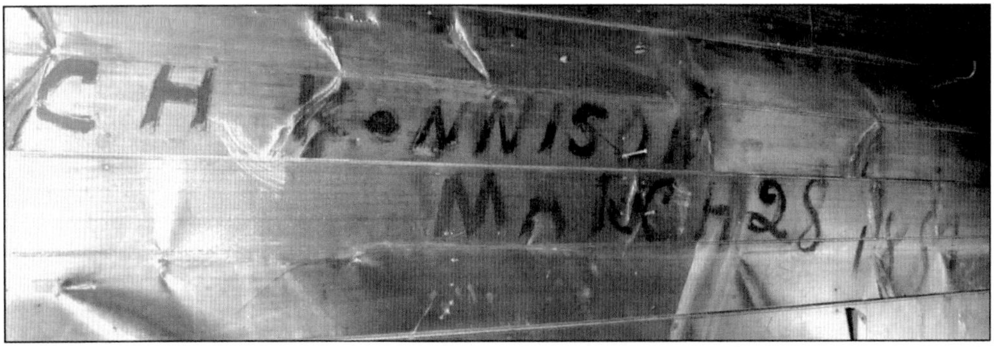

The attic is full of signatures dating from as early as 1880. Many of them can be seen only upon close inspection, as time and dust have faded the faint lead pencil and charcoal lines. This signature, however, is haphazardly painted in 12-inch letters and dated 1881. (Courtesy of Chris Smith.)

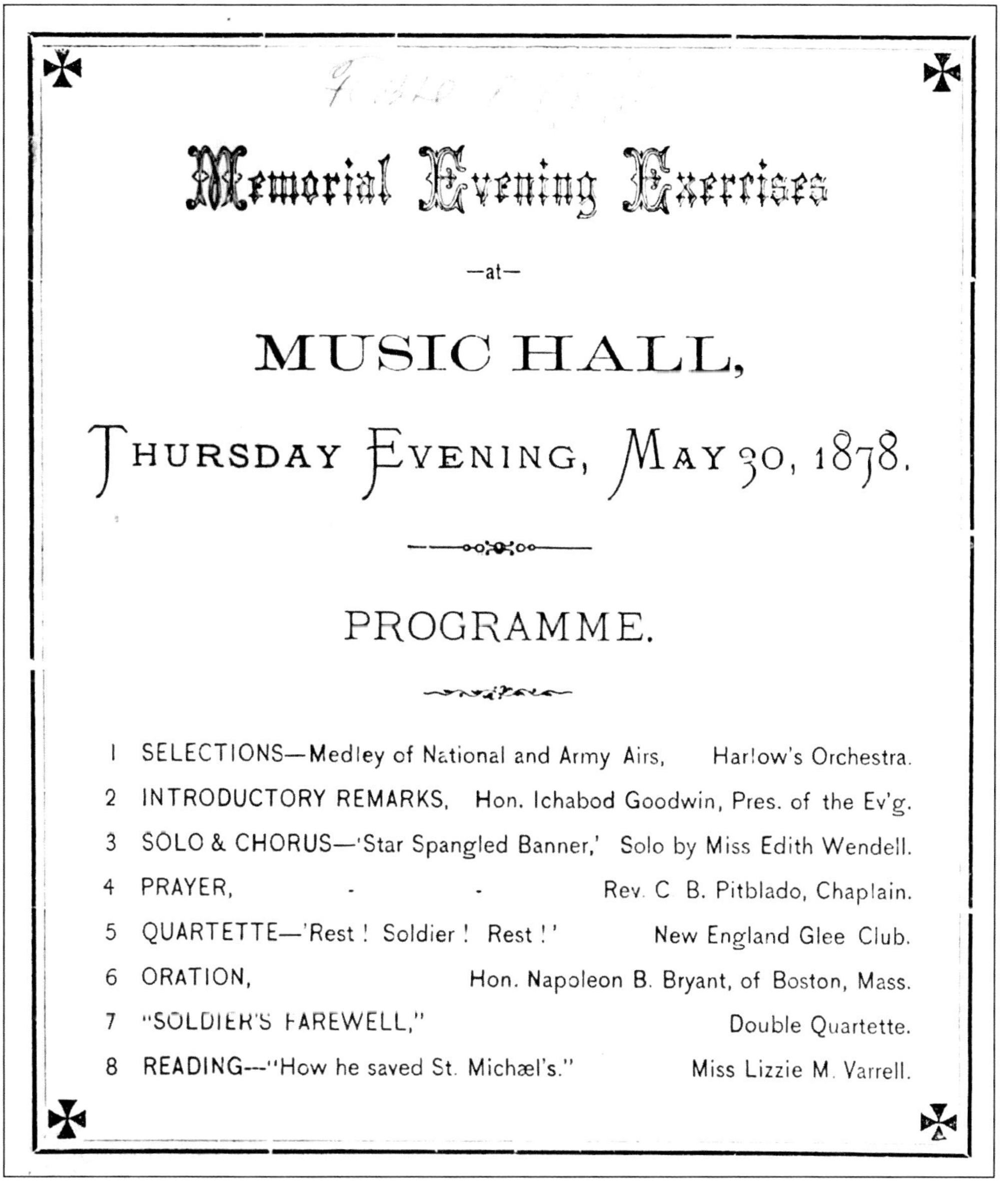

Memorial Evening Exercises

—at—

MUSIC HALL,

THURSDAY EVENING, MAY 30, 1878.

PROGRAMME.

1 SELECTIONS—Medley of National and Army Airs, Harlow's Orchestra.
2 INTRODUCTORY REMARKS, Hon. Ichabod Goodwin, Pres. of the Ev'g.
3 SOLO & CHORUS—'Star Spangled Banner,' Solo by Miss Edith Wendell.
4 PRAYER, - - Rev. C. B. Pitblado, Chaplain.
5 QUARTETTE—'Rest ! Soldier ! Rest !' New England Glee Club.
6 ORATION, Hon. Napoleon B. Bryant, of Boston, Mass.
7 "SOLDIER'S FAREWELL," Double Quartette.
8 READING---"How he saved St. Michæl's." Miss Lizzie M. Varrell.

On the 10th anniversary of the first official Memorial Day, this program was handed out to the patrons attending the Memorial Evening Exercises that would be come a staple at the Music Hall. Local bands performed patriotic songs, former governor Ichabod Goodwin presided, and Rev. C.B. Pitblado of Canada gave the prayer and benediction. The playbill asks the audience to stand for the duration of the final song, not "The Star-Spangled Banner," which would become the national anthem 50 years later, but "Marching through Georgia," written in 1864 to celebrate Gen. William Tecumseh Sherman's infamous campaign. It is said that by 1890, Sherman had heard the song so often that he requested it never be played in his presence again.

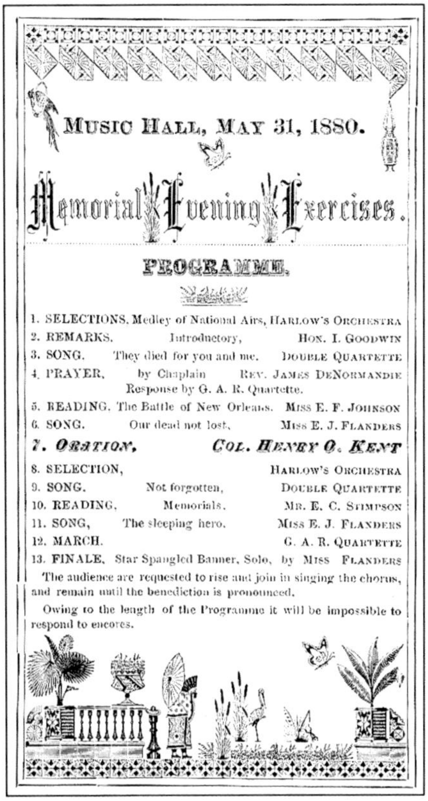

MUSIC HALL, MAY 31, 1880.

Memorial Evening Exercises.

PROGRAMME.

1. SELECTIONS, Medley of National Airs, HARLOW'S ORCHESTRA
2. REMARKS, Introductory, HON. I. GOODWIN
3. SONG. They died for you and me. DOUBLE QUARTETTE
4. PRAYER, by Chaplain REV. JAMES DENORMANDIE
Response by G. A. R. Quartette.
5. READING. The Battle of New Orleans. MISS E. F. JOHNSON
6. SONG. Our dead not lost, MISS E. J. FLANDERS
7. ORATION, COL. HENRY O. KENT
8. SELECTION, HARLOW'S ORCHESTRA
9. SONG. Not forgotten, DOUBLE QUARTETTE
10. READING, Memorials. MR. E. C. STIMPSON
11. SONG, The sleeping hero. MISS E. J. FLANDERS
12. MARCH. G. A. R. QUARTETTE
13. FINALE, Star Spangled Banner, Solo, by MISS FLANDERS

The audience are requested to rise and join in singing the chorus, and remain until the benediction is pronounced.

Owing to the length of the Programme it will be impossible to respond to encores.

The annual Memorial Evening Exercises were enjoyed by full houses in each of the four years represented by these playbills. Former governor Ichabod Goodwin presided over the exercises every year except for 1884, when Capt. J.H. Hutchinson took over. "The Star-Spangled Banner" was sung in 1880 and 1881, but the song from the first event returned, and the audience was asked to stand for "Marching through Georgia."

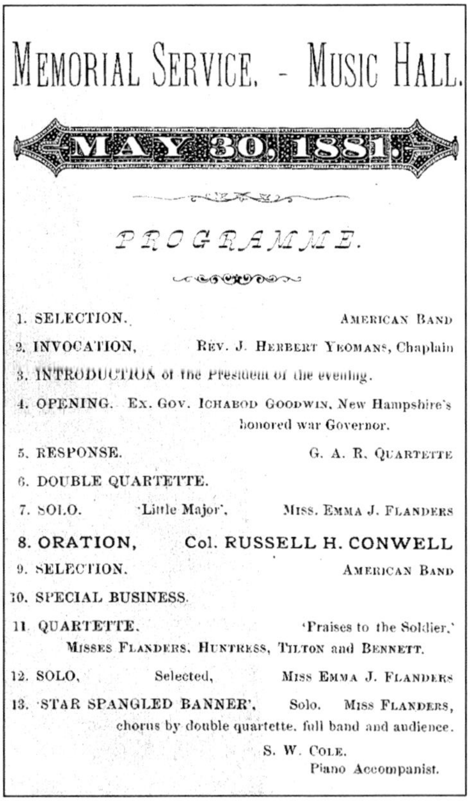

MEMORIAL SERVICE. - MUSIC HALL.

MAY 30, 1881.

PROGRAMME.

1. SELECTION. AMERICAN BAND
2. INVOCATION, REV. J. HERBERT YEOMANS, Chaplain
3. INTRODUCTION of the President of the evening.
4. OPENING. EX. GOV. ICHABOD GOODWIN, New Hampshire's honored war Governor.
5. RESPONSE. G. A. R. QUARTETTE
6. DOUBLE QUARTETTE.
7. SOLO. 'Little Major', MISS. EMMA J. FLANDERS
8. ORATION, Col. RUSSELL H. CONWELL
9. SELECTION. AMERICAN BAND
10. SPECIAL BUSINESS.
11. QUARTETTE. 'Praises to the Soldier.'
MISSES FLANDERS, HUNTRESS, TILTON and BENNETT.
12. SOLO, Selected, MISS EMMA J. FLANDERS
13. 'STAR SPANGLED BANNER', Solo. MISS FLANDERS, chorus by double quartette, full band and audience.

S. W. COLE.
Piano Accompanist.

MUSIC HALL.

PROGRAMME EVENING EXERCISES,

MEMORIAL DAY,

TUESDAY, MAY 30, 1882.

1. SELECTION, BAND.
2. INTRODUCTORY REMARKS, EX-GOV. GOODWIN, President of the Evening
3 "MARCHING THROUGH GEORGIA," BAND AND AUDIENCE.

Bring the good old bugle, boys, we'll sing another song,
Sing it with a spirit, that will start the world along,
Sing it as we used to sing it, fifty thousand strong,
While we were marching through Georgia.

Chorus:—"Hurrah! Hurrah! we bring the jubilee!
Hurrah! Hurrah! the flag that made you free!"
So we sang the chorus from Atlanta to the sea,
While we were marching through Georgia.

So we made a thoroughfare for Freedom and her train,
Sixty miles in latitude—three hundred to the main;
Treason fled before us, for resistance was in vain,
While we were marching through Georgia.

Chorus:—"Hurrah! Hurrah! we bring the jubilee, etc.

4, PRAYER, by Chaplain REV. W. A MCGINLEY.
5. QUARTETTE, G. A. R. QUARTETTE.
6. RECITATION, MISS LIZZIE M. VARRELL.
7. ORATION, Hon. CHAS. H. BURNS, of WILTON, N. H.
8. SELECTION, BAND.
9. SONG, MISS MARY MCCARTHY.
10. VIOLIN SOLO, MISS FANNIE HOYT.
11 RECITATION, MISS LIZZIE M. VARRELL.
12. "AMERICA," BAND AND AUDIENCE.
13 BENEDICTION, REV. W. A MCGINLEY.

The audience are requested to remain in their seats until after the benediction is pronounced.

Quite a few local and regional celebrities took part in these Memorial Day events. The oration in 1880 was given by Col. Henry O. Kent, soon to be a New Hampshire state senator, who was the personal military aide to Abraham Lincoln for the president's short visit to Gettysburg. In 1882, the oration was given by Col. Russell H. Conwell, the founder of Temple University, who was known all over the nation for his "Acres of Diamonds" speech regarding the wealth to be found within "our own great country."

Evening Exercises, Music Hall.

MEMORIAL DAY, MAY 30th, 1883.

MONTGOMERY'S MUSIC AND ART STORE,

No. 6 PLEASANT STREET, is the place to find

Bargains in Pianos and Organs

$215 buys a good 7-octave Piano of a well-known and reliable make, warranted to give satisfaction. $75 buys an Organ with four sets of reeds of 2 1-2 octaves each, made by one of the best makers in the country, fully warranted. *Where can you do better?* Don't fail to call before purchasing and *save your money by buying at home.*

PIANOS AND ORGANS TO RENT ON REASONABLE TERMS.

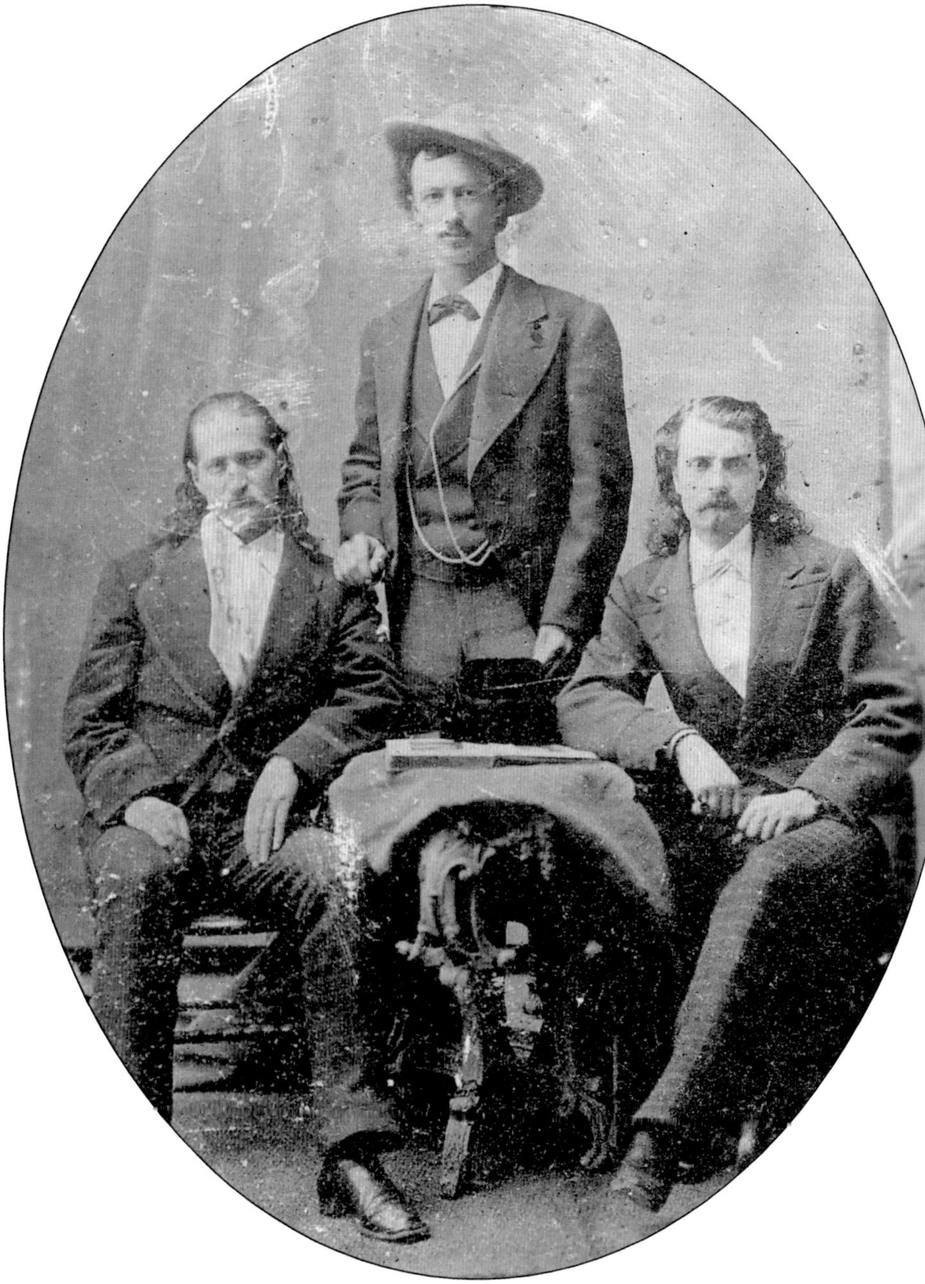

On November 15, 1880, the residents of Portsmouth were wrangled from their homes to see one of the world's greatest showmen. Buffalo Bill Cody (on the right with Wild Bill Hickok and Texas Jack Omohundro) and his famous Combination made cattle roping, sharpshooting, and blood battles with Native Americans into entertainment for the masses. While certainly the Music Hall is not large enough to stage a full battle scene, horses were included in many acts upon its deck, and the patrons who were lucky enough to see this performance likely witnessed many a trick from horseback. (Courtesy of the Buffalo Bill Historical Center, Cody, Wyoming.)

Prof. George Bartholomew took training horses to a new level with his traveling show Equine Paradox. In July 1884, he brought 20 horses into the hall and staged a series of acts, including a schoolroom in which one horse brings the teacher an apple while another solves a math problem using chalk on a board. The caption on the bottom of the playbill states, "20 educated horses do everything but talk."

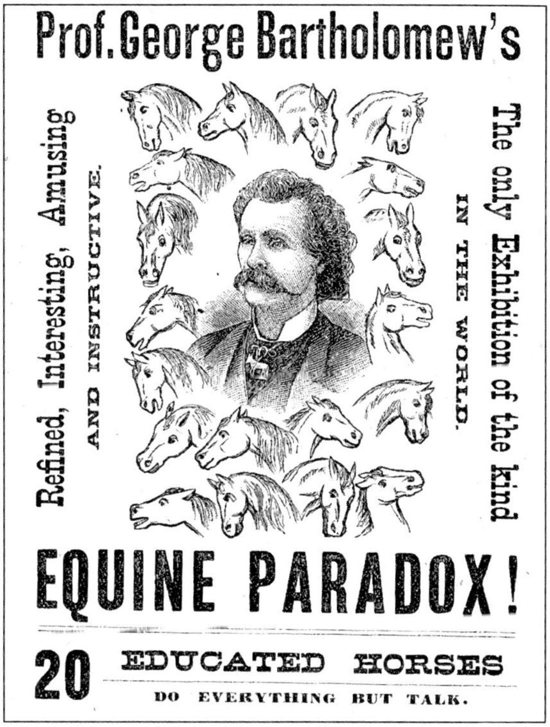

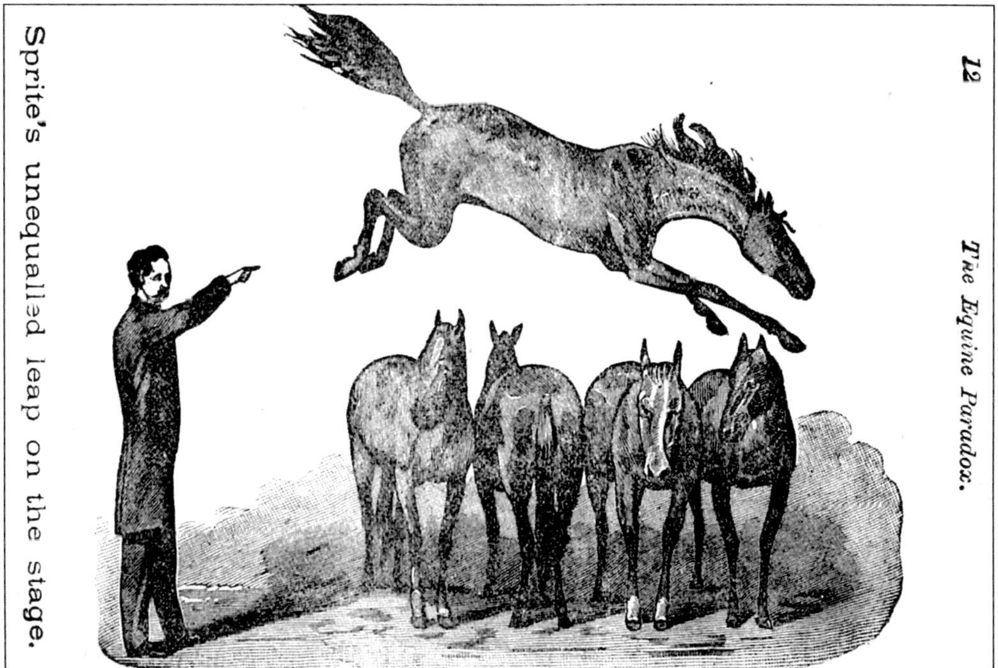

From mock courtroom scenes to equine leapfrog, these horses were trained using a method gleaned from the ornithologist John James Audubon, who, according to George Bartholomew, claimed that one did not need to beat animals into submission but rather accept and mold their innate intelligence.

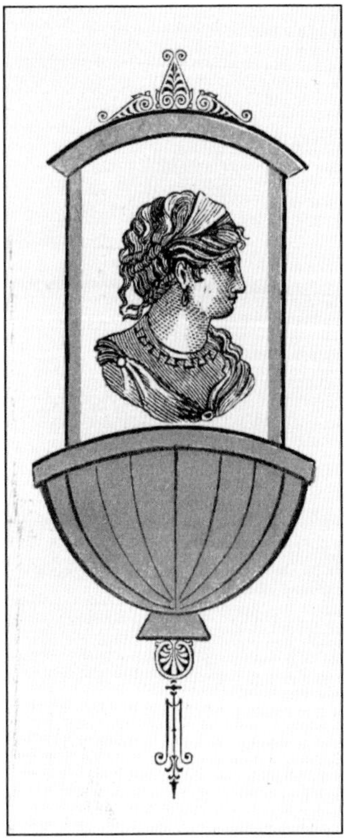

The decorative beauty of the Victorian era can be seen in this emblem from the front cover of a playbill for the second annual Course of the Rockingham Entertainments at the Music Hall in 1879. Printed in black with gold overlay, the emblem is a perfect example of the style seen on printed materials of the day.

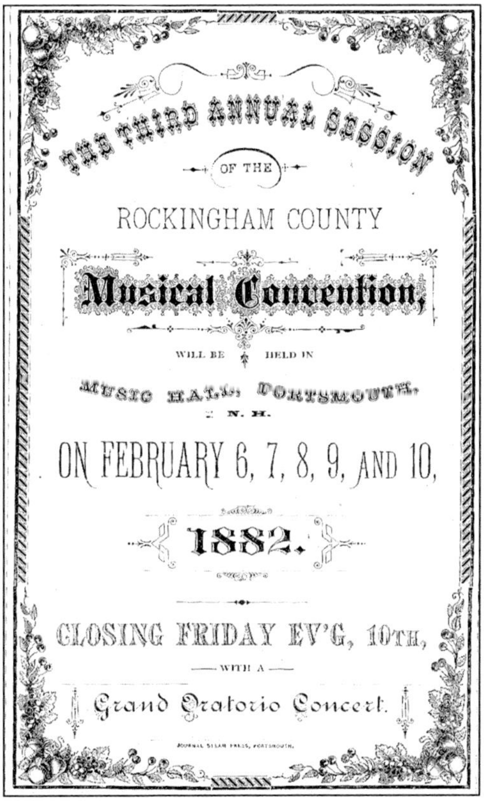

Even in its earliest incarnations, the Music Hall was host to countless community events. The annual Rockingham County Musical Convention began in 1880 and was an opportunity for numerous local musicians to demonstrate their skills. The interior of this 1882 playbill lists 15 artists, including a special appearance by Fedor Willimek, a zither soloist. Ella Cleveland Fenderson is listed as "Portsmouth's favorite singer," and an invitation is extended "to all Musical Societies, Choirs, and all lovers of music, to be present and join the chorus." The playbill also notes that hotels and boardinghouses will grant special terms to all persons attending the convention.

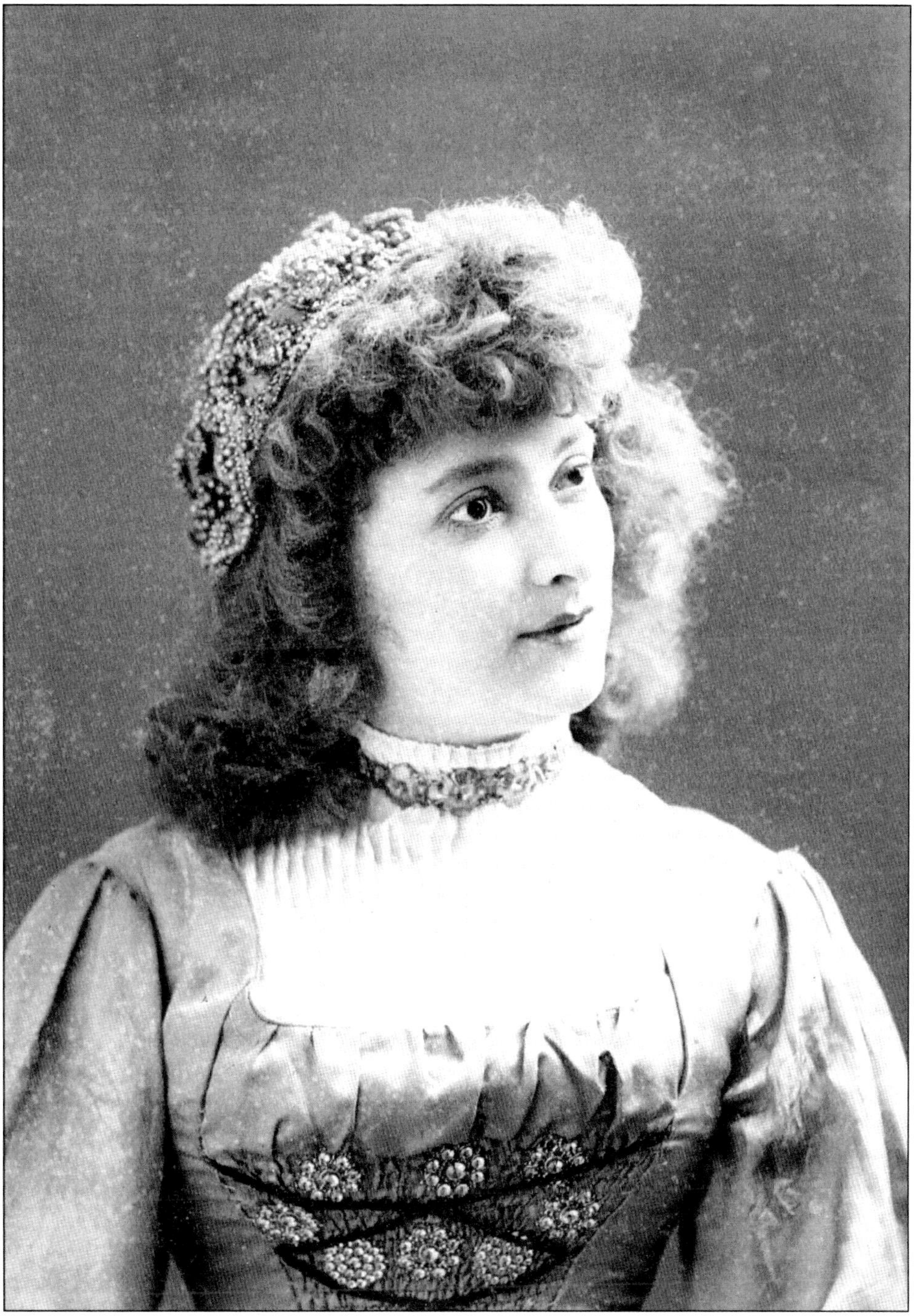

Actors and actresses from the Victorian and vaudeville eras often performed numerous times on the same stage throughout their careers. Margaret Mather is noted as performing at the Music Hall at least twice in the 1880s. Although considered one of the great Shakespearean actresses of her time, Portsmouth audiences saw her in *The Lady of Lyons* in April 1883 and *The Honeymoon* in 1887. A dramatic actress, Mather died true to form, performing on a stage, and was buried in the white gown she wore as Juliet. (Courtesy of Bill Nelson.)

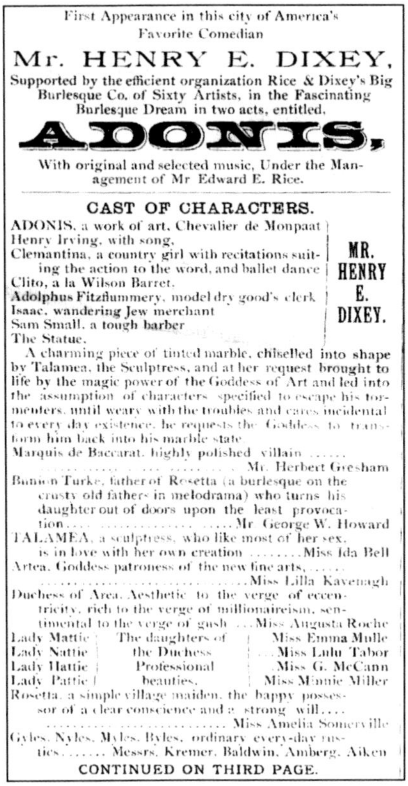

First Appearance in this city of America's Favorite Comedian

Mr. HENRY E. DIXEY,

Supported by the efficient organization Rice & Dixey's Big Burlesque Co. of Sixty Artists, in the Fascinating Burlesque Dream in two acts, entitled,

ADONIS,

With original and selected music, Under the Management of Mr Edward E. Rice.

CAST OF CHARACTERS.

ADONIS, a work of art, Chevalier de Monpaat
Henry Irving, with song,
Clemantina, a country girl with recitations suiting the action to the word, and ballet dance
Clito, a la Wilson Barret.
Adolphus Fitzflummery, model dry good's clerk
Isaac, wandering Jew merchant
Sam Small, a tough barber
The Statue.
— MR. HENRY E. DIXEY.

A charming piece of tinted marble, chiselled into shape by Talamea, the Sculptress, and at her request brought to life by the magic power of the Goddess of Art and led into the assumption of characters specified to escape his tormenters, until weary with the troubles and cares incidental to every day existence, he requests the Goddess to transform him back into his marble state.

Marquis de Baccarat, highly polished villain ...... Mr. Herbert Gresham
Banion Turke, father of Rosetta (a burlesque on the crusty old fathers in melodrama) who turns his daughter out of doors upon the least provocation ..... Mr George W. Howard
TALAMEA, a sculptress, who like most of her sex, is in love with her own creation .... Miss Ida Bell
Artea, Goddess patroness of the new fine arts, ... Miss Lilla Kavenagh
Duchess of Area, Aesthetic to the verge of eccentricity, rich to the verge of millionaireism, sentimental to the verge of gush ... Miss Augusta Roche

Lady Mattie	The daughters of	Miss Emma Mulle
Lady Nattie	the Duchess	... Miss Lulu Tabor
Lady Hattie	Professional	Miss G. McCann
Lady Pattie	beauties.	Miss Minnie Miller

Rosetta, a simple village maiden, the happy possessor of a clear conscience and a strong will.... Miss Amelia Somerville
Gyles, Nyles, Myles, Byles, ordinary every-day rustics....... Messrs. Kremer, Baldwin, Amberg, Aiken

CONTINUED ON THIRD PAGE.

Considered the first matinee idol of Broadway, Henry E. Dixey wrote and starred in this burlesque comedy about a statue brought to life. Opening in 1884, *Adonis* became the longest running show on Broadway up to that point. This 1888 tour playbill includes such descriptions as "Talamea, a sculptress, who like most of her sex, is in love with her own creation" and "Duchess of Area, Aesthetic to the verge of eccentricity, rich to the verge of millionaireism, sentimental to the verge of gush." (Courtesy of the Portsmouth Public Library.)

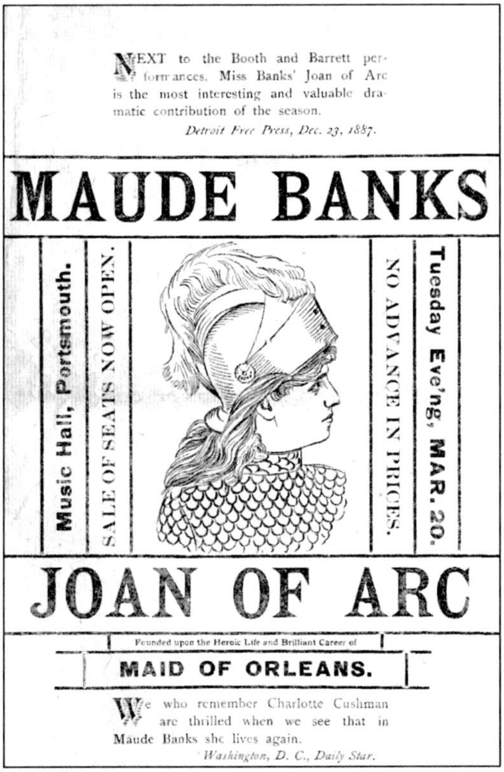

This playbill from the late 1880s seems to be an early example of nepotism. Very little has been found about Maude Banks other than the fact that she was the daughter of a Massachusetts congressman, a fact that is listed prominently on the inside of this playbill. In numerous locations, Banks is likened to Charlotte Cushman, a famous actress of the period who was known for the traditionally male roles she played, such as Hamlet and Romeo.

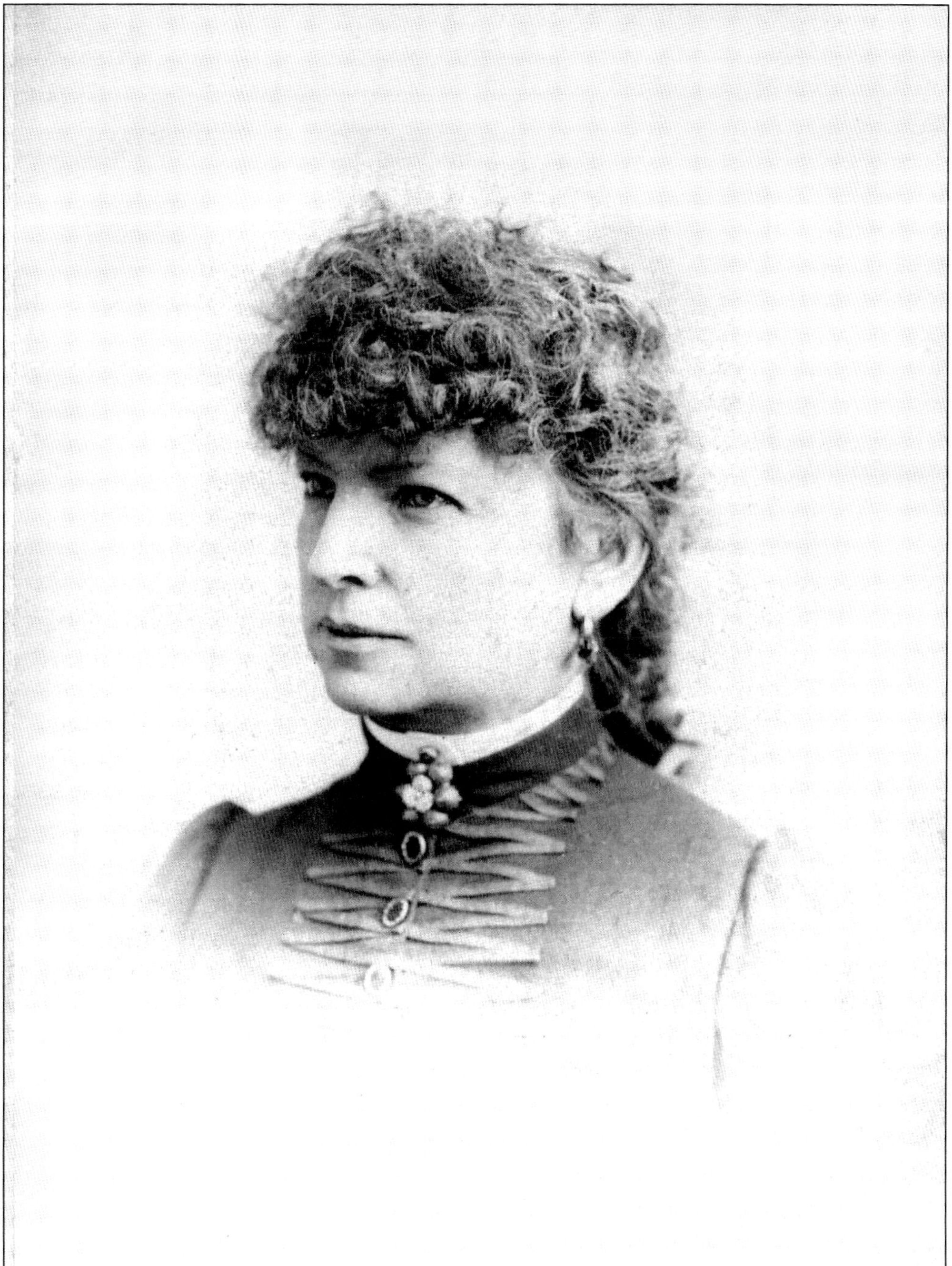

Maggie Mitchell, beloved actress and manager of her own company, was near the end of her acting career when she arrived on the Music Hall stage in the show *Little Barefoot* on April 19, 1884, but patrons of the theater would have known about the title role in *Fanchon* (meaning "cricket"), which made her famous. The play was adapted for her from the novel by George Sand, and Fanchon became her signature role for more than 30 years. (Courtesy of Bill Nelson.)

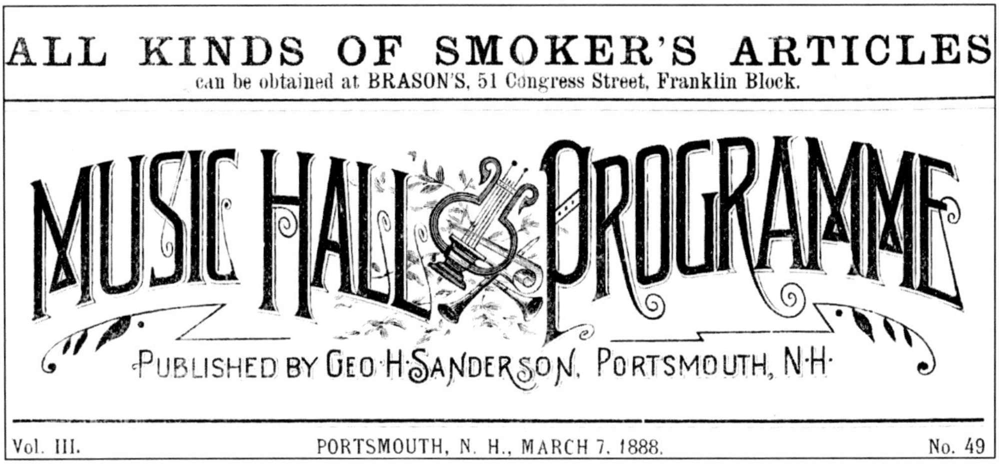

ALL KINDS OF SMOKER'S ARTICLES
can be obtained at BRASON'S, 51 Congress Street, Franklin Block.

MUSIC HALL PROGRAMME
PUBLISHED BY GEO·H·SANDERSON, PORTSMOUTH, N·H·

Vol. III. PORTSMOUTH, N. H., MARCH 7, 1888. No. 49

In the late 1990s, the Friends of the Music Hall adopted a logo once thought to be the original version used in 1878. As seen on these programs, one from March 1888 and the other from November 1889, it was a later image that was actually duplicated. The logo from 1889 (used to create the current logo) seems to have been very short-lived, as a playbill from 1890 uses the earlier one again.

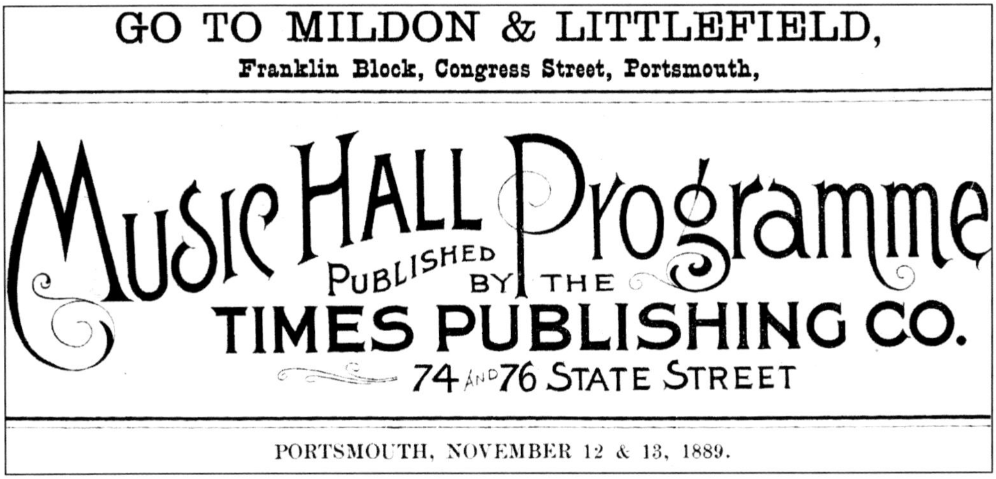

GO TO MILDON & LITTLEFIELD,
Franklin Block, Congress Street, Portsmouth,

Music Hall Programme
PUBLISHED BY THE
TIMES PUBLISHING CO.
74 AND 76 STATE STREET

PORTSMOUTH, NOVEMBER 12 & 13, 1889.

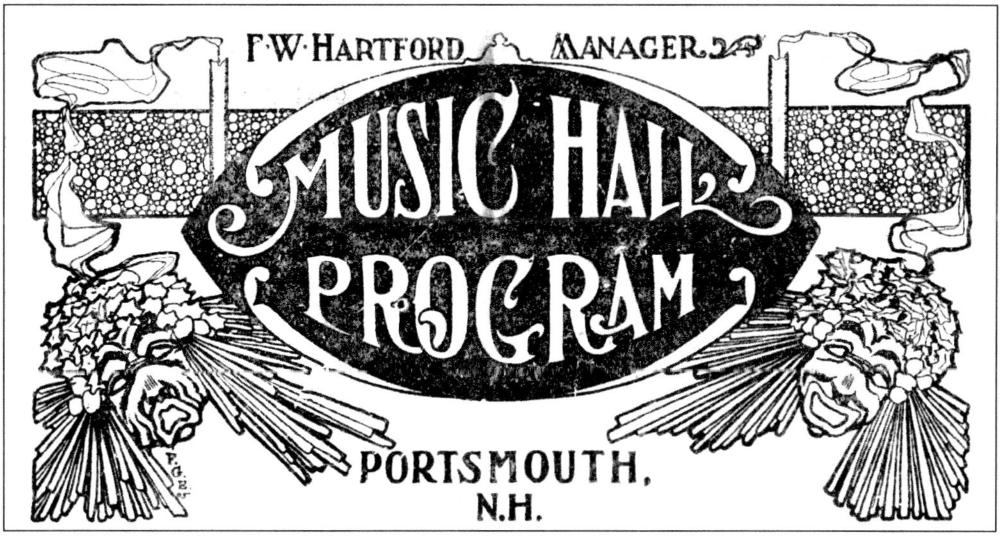

The artistic talent of program designers is clear in these Music Hall logos from 1905 and 1911. Decorative comedy and tragedy masks and griffins on either side of what appears to be a Medusa-like figure show the connection to Greek mythology ever present in the theater.

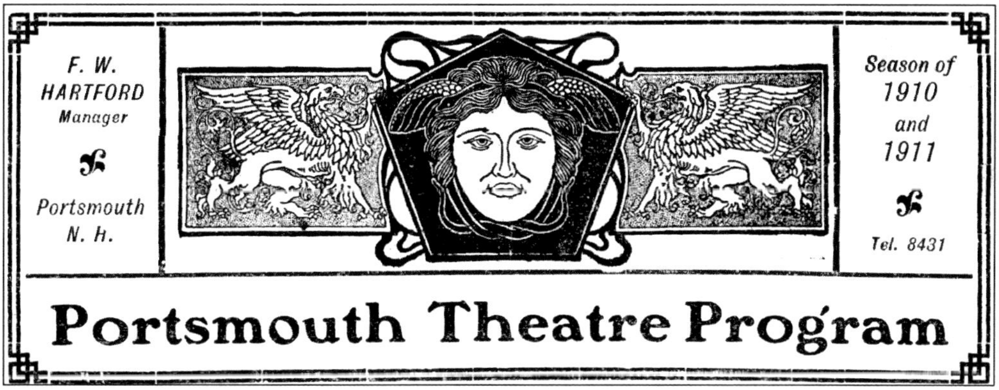

Music Hall, Friday Evening, Nov. 18, 1892.

JOHN W. SHERMAN'S

TABLEAUX PHANTASMA.

Under the auspices of the Universalist Church.

Musical Director, Mr. Harry Osgood

Soloists, Misses Tilton and Rose and Prof. G. D. Whittier.

Readers, Mrs. Della Mayhew and Mr. Henry R. Rose.

PROGRAM.

PIANO OVERTURE Mr. Harry Osgood

MYTHOLOGICAL ILLUSIONS.

Grand Mythological Groups and Participants.

MAIDENHOOD dissolving into HIGHLAND MARY
Flossie Hill Addie Newman
EGERIA dissolving into REBECCA AT THE WELL
Lucy Hill Nettie Eldredge
PURITY dissolving into HISTORY
Annie Furber Nellie Sherman
FRUIT GIRL dissolving into TOILET
Miss Garland Miss Preble
HOPE dissolving into TAMBOURINE GIRL
Miss Rugg Mrs. Herbert Paterson
PRAYER dissolving into GALATEA
Miss Marston Blanche Boynton
INNOCENCE dissolving into VESTAL VIRGIN
Mabel Shedd Minnie Green
NIGHT dissolving into MORNING
Retta Furber Barbara Vogler
HEBE dissolving into CHILD'S PRAYER
Ella Furber Nellie Walden, Rachel Tucker
RUTH AND NAOMI dissolving into FORSAKEN
Sadie Marden and Alice Rand Ella Lowd
SHEPHERD BOY, 1st Position, dissolving into TRUTH
May Whittier Miss Smart
SHEPHERD BOY, 2d Position, dissolving into BEATRICE
May Whittier Miss Sherwood

This 1892 performance of *Tableaux Phantasma* is a perfect example of the extraordinary spectacle common in theater. A closer look at the play list describes illusion after illusion, with names such as "Innocence," "Faith," and "Maidenhood." In one section called the "Pathetic Illusion," the description reads, "Introducing Illusionary Snow Storm and Realistic Scenic Effects. Real and Mythical Persons on the Stage at One and the Same Time." Another section reads, "Producing the Fascinating Effect of Dissolving Massive Crosses with Living People Through one Another, also Dissolving the 'Rock of Ages' Through the Water, Leaving The Stage Empty."

PURE COD LIVER OIL.

ODORLESS. PALATABLE.

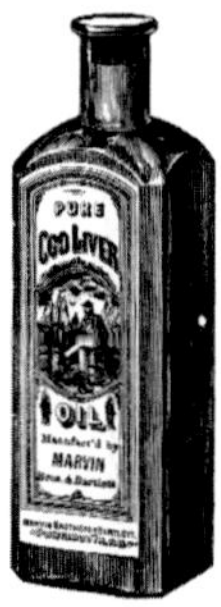

NOT VITIATED. NOT MEDICATED.

We beg to call your attention to the Cod Liver Oil, which we make from *fresh* and *selected* livers of cod-fish caught during the cold weather of our northern winters, the rigor of which the fish could not endure were their vital forces not sustained by a wonderful provision of nature which makes the livers of this species of fish reservoirs for the accumulation of *oil*, without which they could not live in the icy waters of our coast.

The great nutrient and healing qualities of Cod Liver Oil are thought to be largely due to the fact that the fish derive a large portion of their sustenance from marine plants, thus imparting properties to this oil which oils derived from land-grown animals or plants do not possess.

This larger-than-usual advertisement was found inside the playbill for *Tableaux Phantasma*. Over the course of four pages, it describes not only the benefits of cod liver oil but also the process by which it is made from the fish taken in at the Portsmouth docks. Note the use of the word "palatable" on the front page.

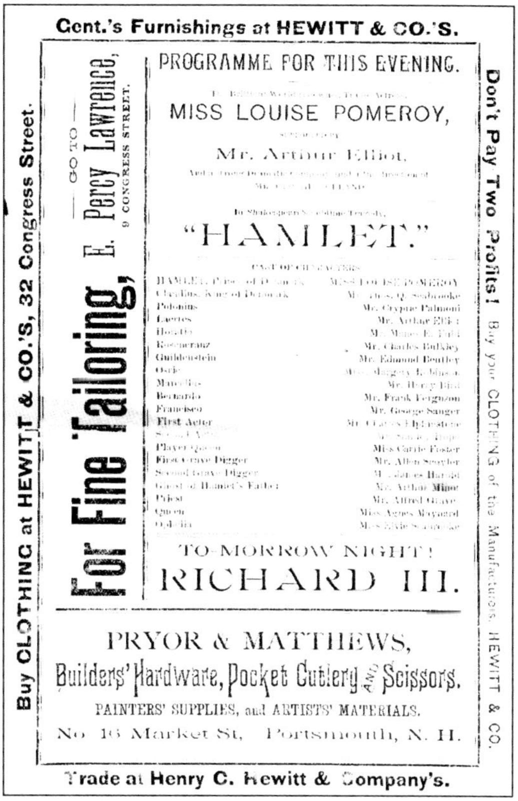

Gent.'s Furnishings at HEWITT & CO.'S.

Buy CLOTHING at HEWITT & CO.'S, 32 Congress Street.

For Fine Tailoring, — GO TO — E. Percy Lawrence, 9 CONGRESS STREET.

PROGRAMME FOR THIS EVENING.

MISS LOUISE POMEROY,

Mr. Arthur Elliot,

"HAMLET."

HAMLET, Prince of Denmark	MISS LOUISE POMEROY
Claudius, King of Denmark	Mr. Thos. Q. Seabrooke
Polonius	[illegible]
Laertes	Mr. Arthur Elliot
Horatio	[illegible]
Rosencranz	Mr. Charles Bulkley
Guildenstein	Mr. Edmund Bentley
Osric	[illegible]
Marcellus	Mr. Henry Bird
Bernardo	Mr. Frank Ferguson
Francisco	Mr. George Sanger
First Actor	[illegible]
[illegible]	[illegible]
Player Queen	Miss Carrie Foster
First Grave Digger	Mr. Allen Seaylor
Second Grave Digger	Mr. James Harold
Ghost of Hamlet's Father	Mr. Arthur Minor
Priest	Mr. Alfred [illegible]
Queen	Miss Agnes Maynard
Ophelia	[illegible]

TO-MORROW NIGHT!

RICHARD III.

PRYOR & MATTHEWS,

Builders' Hardware, Pocket Cutlery and Scissors.

PAINTERS' SUPPLIES, and ARTISTS' MATERIALS.

No. 16 Market St, Portsmouth, N. H.

Don't Pay Two Profits! Buy your CLOTHING of the Manufacturers, HEWITT & CO.

Trade at Henry C. Hewitt & Company's.

Fame can be fleeting in an age in which photographs were limited and film was yet to be secured as a method of documentation of the arts. Louise Pomeroy is listed as "The Brilliant World-Renowned Tragic Actress," and yet very little documentation of her performances could be found. She was another actress who made her way by playing male roles. She toured the world extensively and had a great influence on young women everywhere she went.

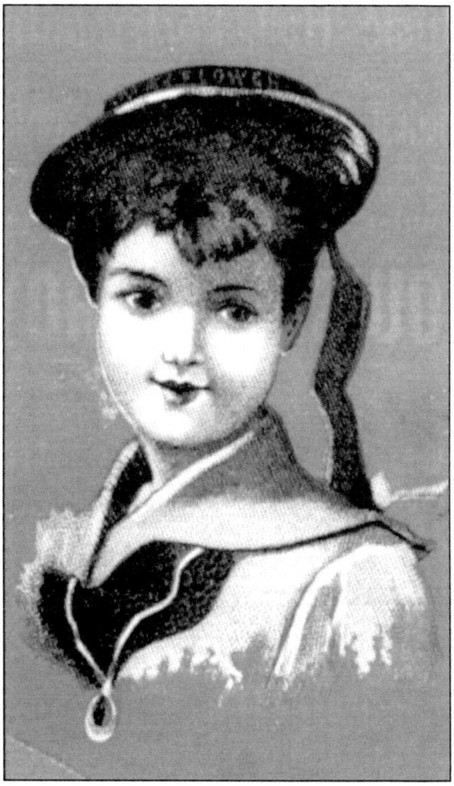

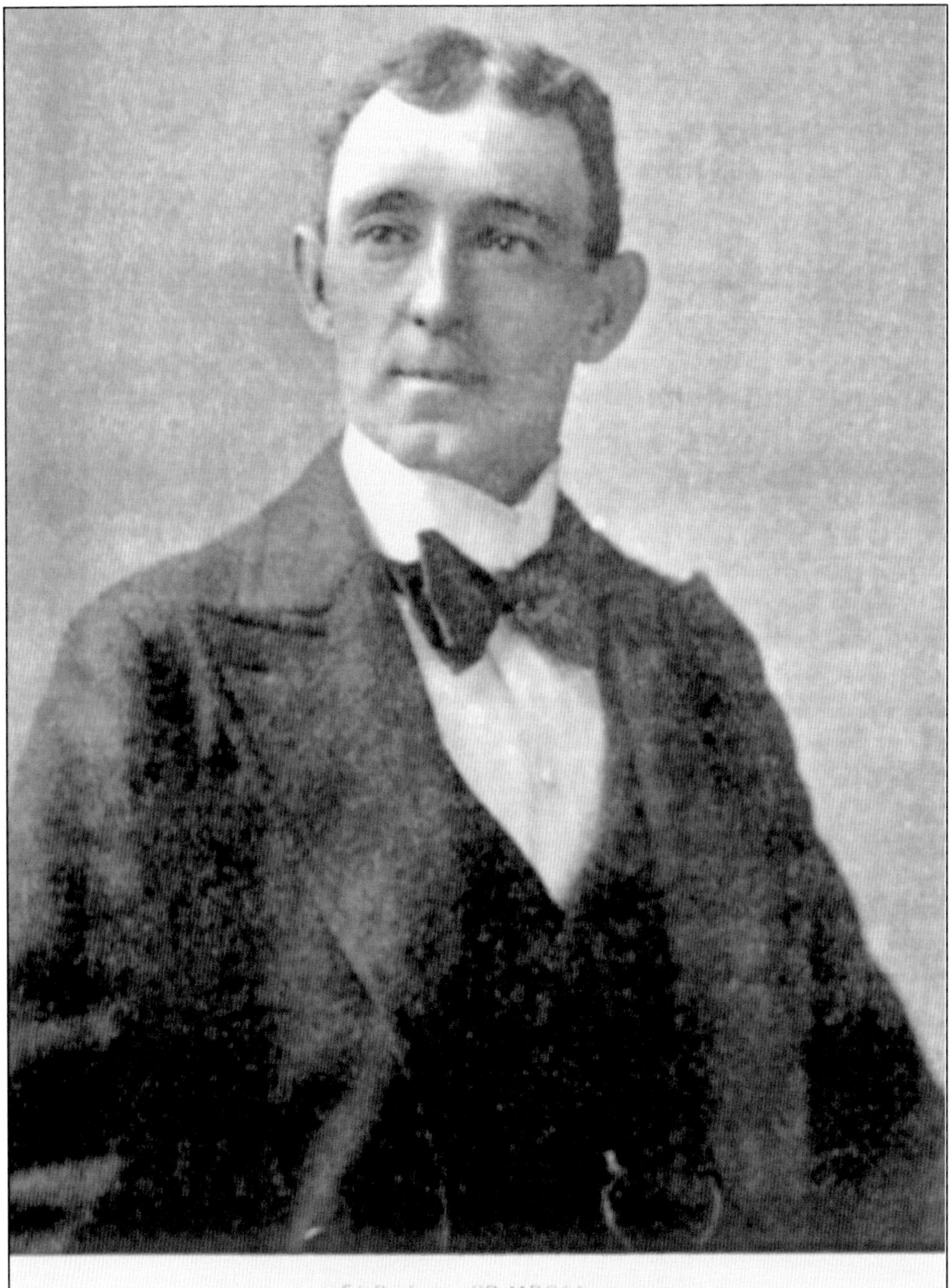

By far the most controversial element of vaudeville was the relationship between blacks and whites. Although the Civil War and the Emancipation Proclamation were 40-plus years in the past, black performers were rarely permitted on the same stage as their white counterparts. Minstrelsy (white performers wearing black makeup), however, was rampant. Primrose and West's Minstrel Company was one of the best known companies and performed in Portsmouth numerous times. It has been said that many people did not recognize George Primrose without his makeup, as shown on this 1886 playbill, so well known was his blackface character. Primrose often worked with other notable performers such as Lew Dockstader and Al Jolson.

Two

FRANK JONES MUSIC HALL 1900–1903

Though Frank Jones only owned the Music Hall for a few years, he is regarded as one of the most influential men in its history. After purchasing the theater, he made a series of renovations that resulted in the image of the building that many people are familiar with today.

Jones bought a parcel of land just to the rear of the Music Hall and expanded the stage by almost 40 feet. With this expansion came a higher ceiling, enlarging the rigging system and creating more dressing rooms to the left of the stage. The most recognizable renovation, however, was made at the front of the stage. Frank Jones can be thanked for the proscenium archway now so closely tied to the Music Hall. By removing the stage above the original orchestra pit, Jones's designers were able to add extra walls, enclosing the area into opera boxes.

Decorative plasterwork, fluted columns with oak leaves, and cherubs flying overhead with musical instruments flank the wide archway. In the center is the figurehead of the Music Hall, a plaster face fondly called "Frank" by the staff.

As far as entertainment is concerned, vaudeville was alive and kicking at the turn of the century. The Music Hall would have seen everything from opera to juggling, often on the same night. The age of the actor-manager, this period was full of touring companies. The companies made a name for themselves by returning year after year to every town in New England that had a theater, as most of them did. Portsmouth newspapers included New York entertainment columns and often dedicated an entire page to the upcoming evening festivities, as well as, more often than not, glowing reviews of the previous night's performances.

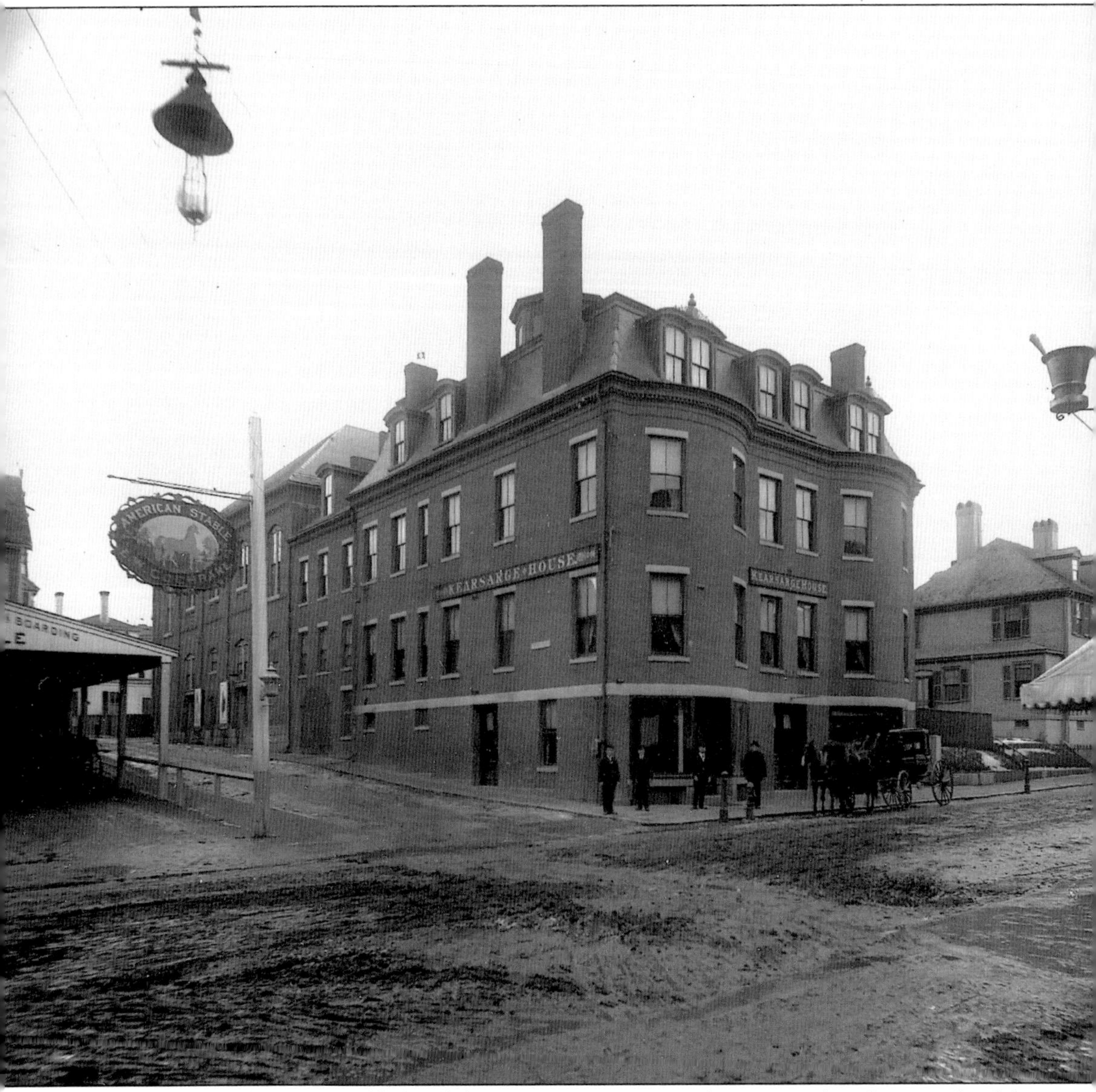

The Music Hall, positioned behind the Kearsage House, can be seen in this photograph of the corner of Chestnut and Congress Streets. Two posters can be seen beside the central door, and with careful inspection, one can glimpse the gas lantern recently upgraded to electricity. Shown in the foreground and mid-ground are the drugstore on the corner of Vaughan Street and the family home of the Peirces, the builders of the Music Hall. (Courtesy of the Patch Collection, Strawbery Banke Museum.)

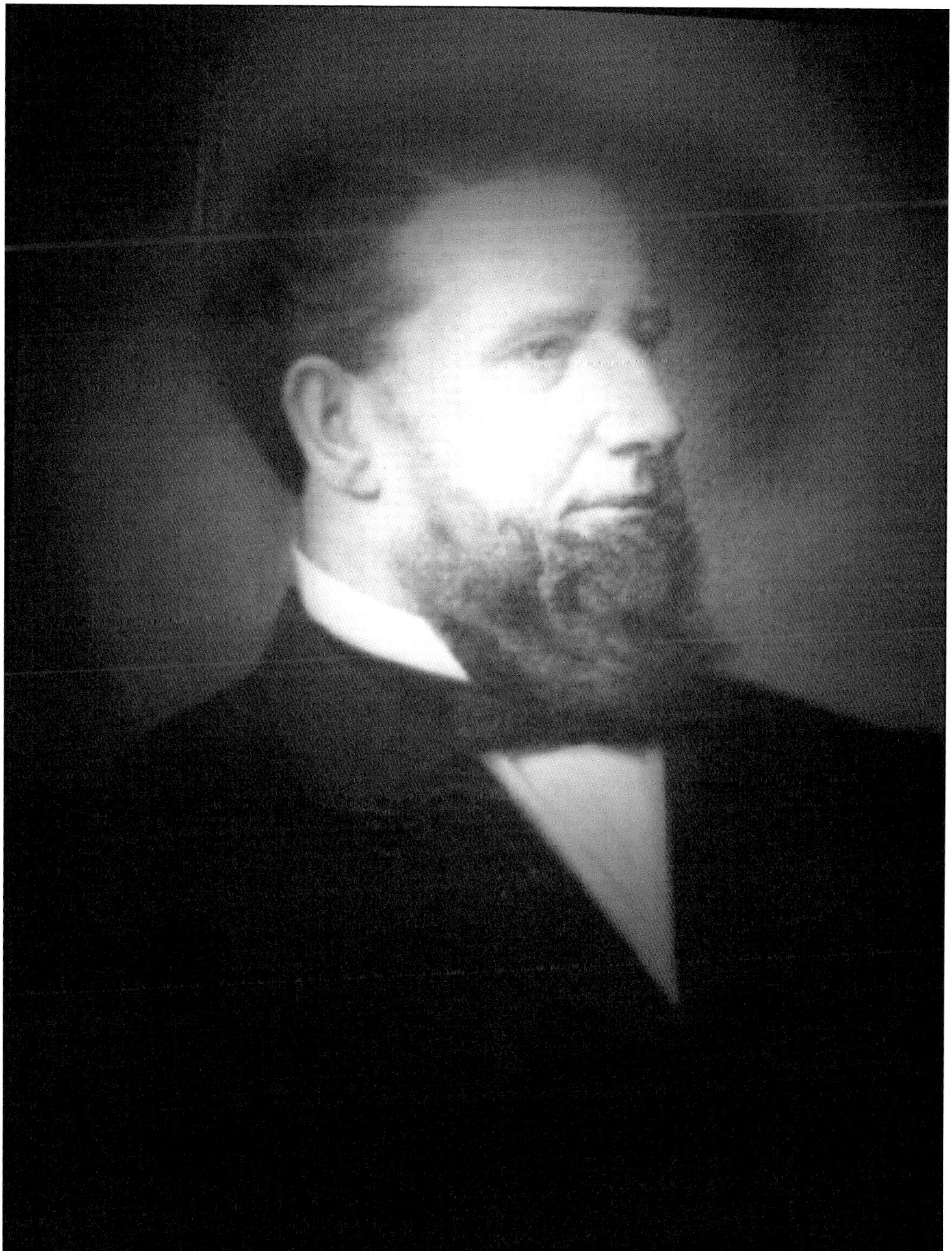

Frank Jones was prominent in the Portsmouth area as a brewer and general businessman. Three years before his death, he purchased the Music Hall for his adopted daughter, Emma Sinclair, who was an amateur opera singer. Although some work had been done on the building prior to Jones's ownership, it was under his direction that the first major renovation to the hall was completed. Jones purchased a parcel of land behind the theater, enlarged the stage by almost 40 feet, and built what is now familiar to local stagehands as the fly rail and grid: the 60-foot-high rigging system above the stage. (Courtesy of the Portsmouth Athenaeum.)

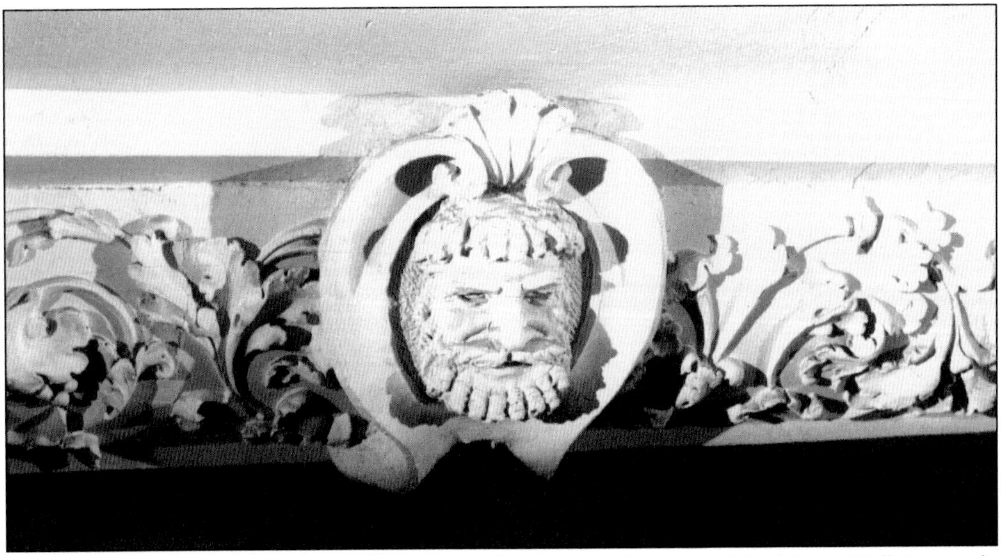

In the center of the proscenium archway hangs the unofficial mascot of the Music Hall. Lovingly named "Frank" by the staff, this plaster face is more likely Bacchus (Roman), or Dionysus (Greek), the god of theater. Frank is not the only named item in the building; the technical crew has given nicknames to much of the equipment as well: an electric control unit is named Frankenstein, the projectors are Felicia and Bernadette, and the ever-faithful house light control box is Bob.

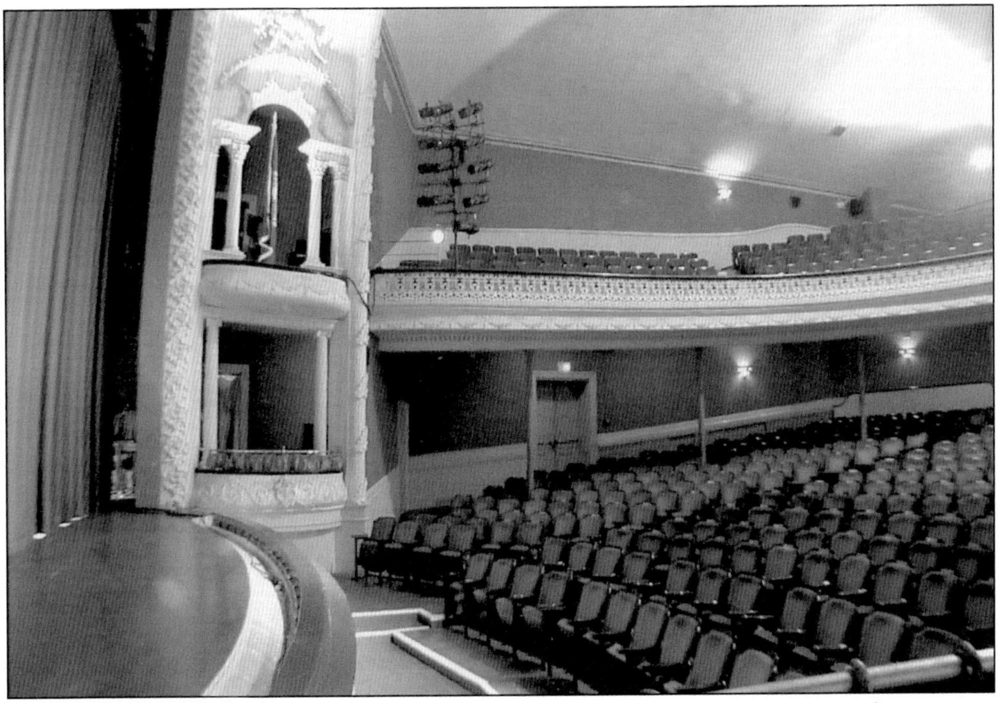

One of the cherished additions to the theater is the proscenium archway, shown here as it is today. It was first believed that Frank Jones extended the archway into the audience chamber to make room for the beloved opera boxes and decorative plaster columns; however, recent discoveries have proven that the stage was actually cut back to allow the extra space.

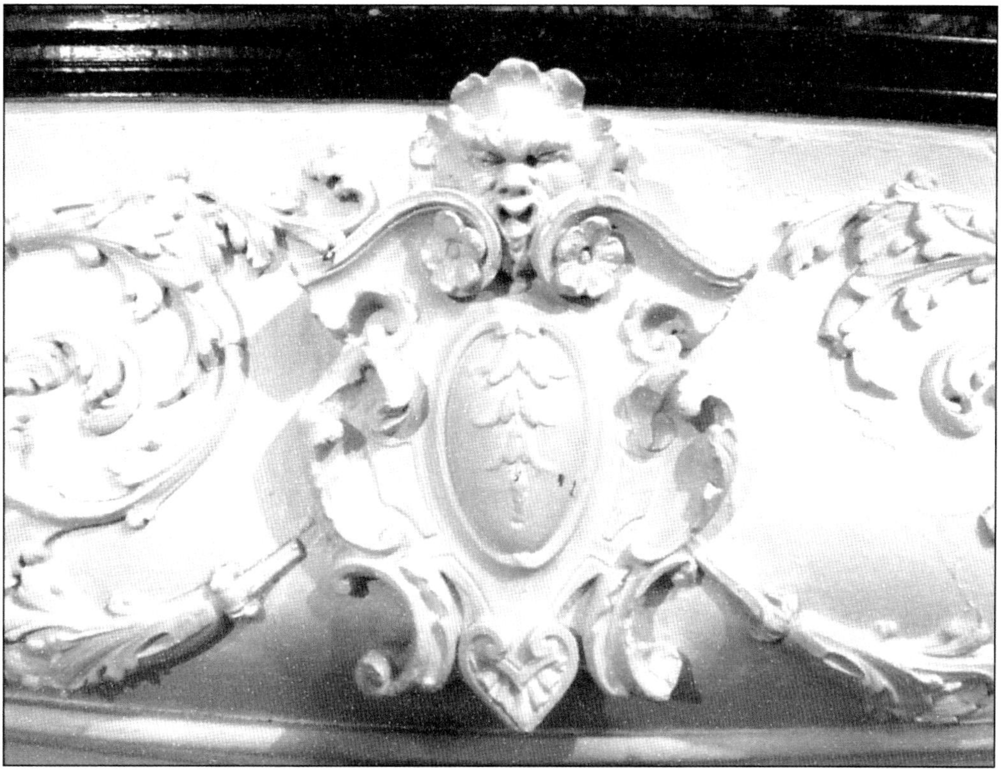

This lion's head decorates the face of the opera boxes.

This six-inch-high piece of plasterwork was found in the basement in 1998. Upon close inspection, one can see that the vertical element in the center is actually an arm holding onto a branch. The colors do not match any description, nor does the pattern. It is possibly part of a sample brought in when the plasterwork was being designed for Frank Jones but never actually used in the hall.

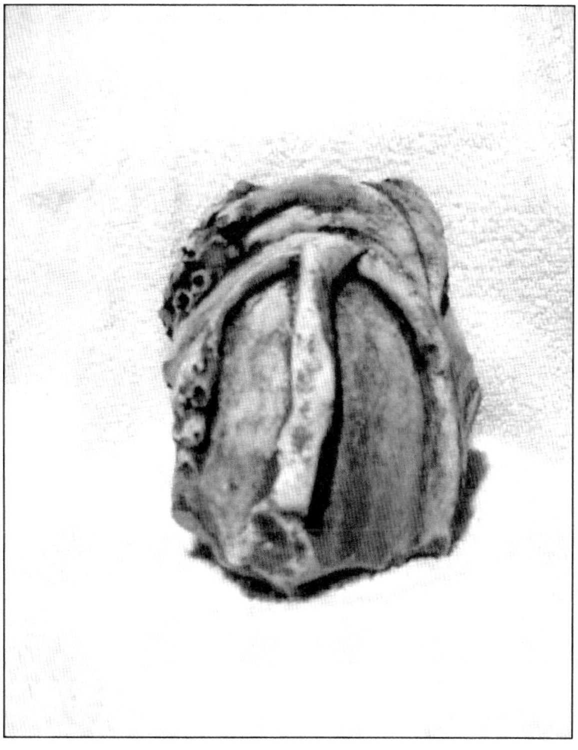

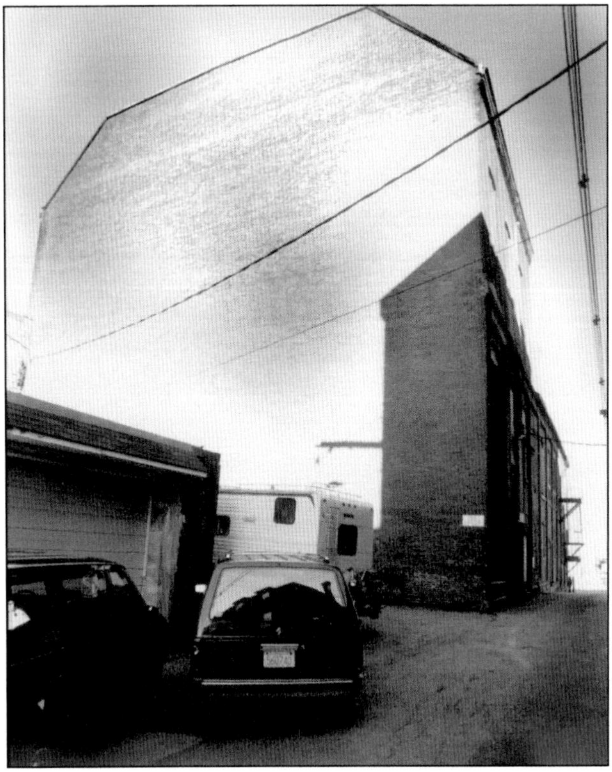

Probably the largest untouched brick wall in Portsmouth, the rear face of the Music Hall was part of Jones's reconstruction in 1901. The newspapers reported that the new stage house could be seen clearly from Christian Shores, a half-mile away. With the highest flat roof in the city, the building can still be seen from blocks away in almost any direction. From the roof, on a clear day, one can view the Isles of Shoals and, on a Fourth of July night, the fireworks of Portsmouth and of Hampton, in the south, and of York, in the north.

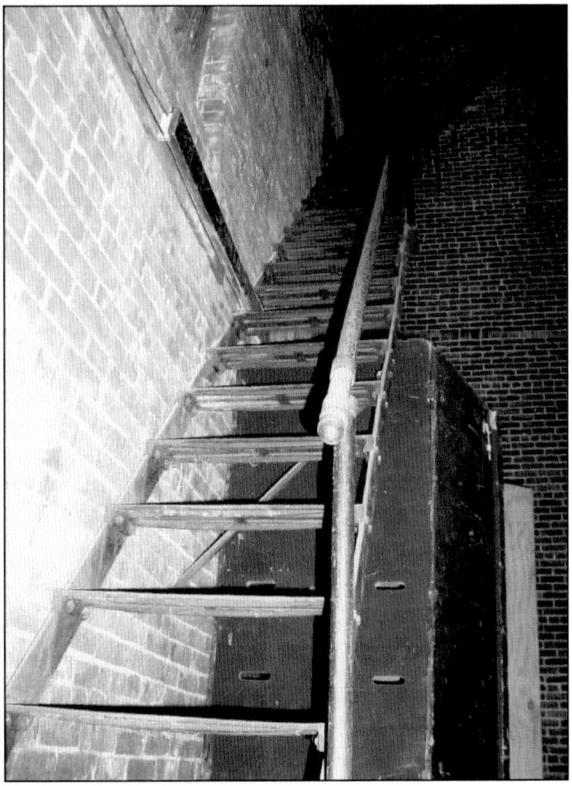

Looking at the grid from the stage can be daunting—a floor made out of two-by-fours on edge, with nothing on top of them and four-inch spaces in between them. Yet, it is this set of stairs leading up to the grid that causes many people to discover a fear of heights they never knew they had. Iron stairs wind their way up to a height of 60 feet above the stage floor and to a view like none other in Portsmouth. This is the highest flat roof in the city, only a few feet lower than the North Church steeple, and the view is quite a reward if you can actually make it up to the top. (Courtesy of Chris Smith.)

Much of Portsmouth transferred to electric lighting in the 1880s and 1890s, but it is most likely that the Music Hall wired up during the Frank Jones renovation in 1901. These wires, long since disconnected, still run through the fly rail and attic. (Courtesy of Chris Smith.)

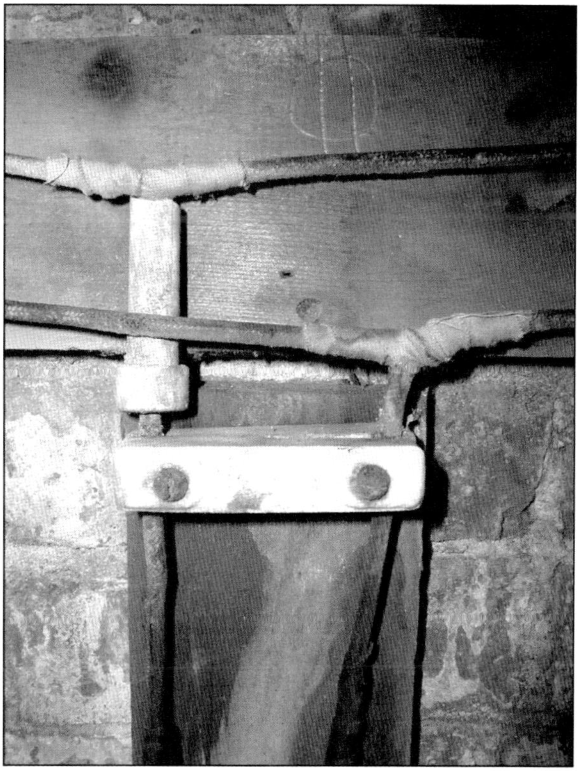

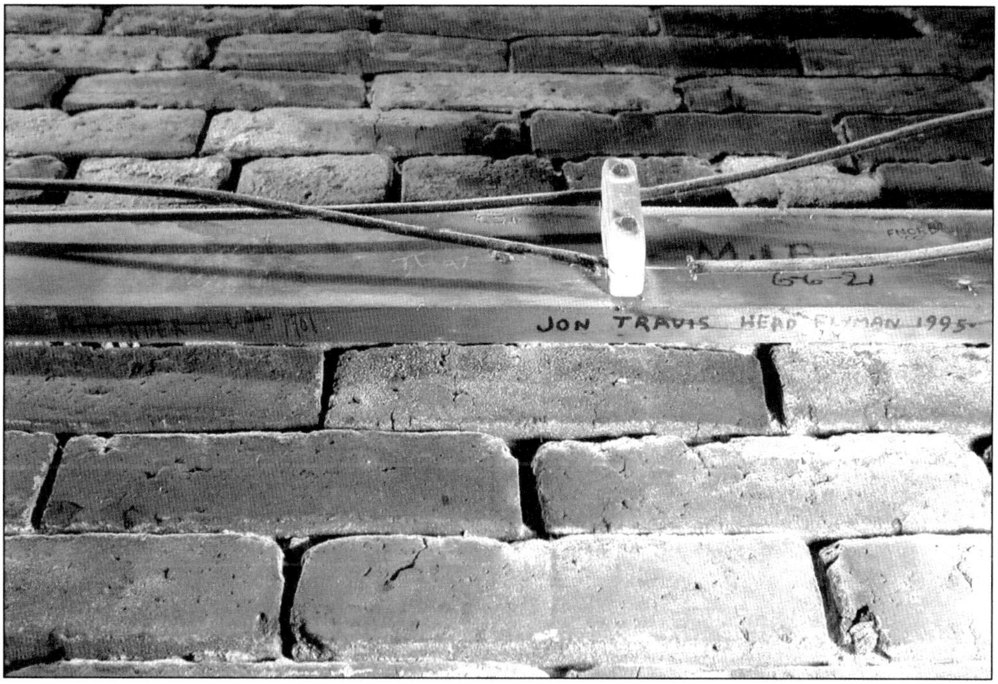

The wooden planks used to support the electric wiring are full of signatures of staff members. This section spans a century, with W.F. Pinder in lead pencil from 1901 and John Travis in magic marker from 1995. (Courtesy of Chris Smith.)

PROGRAMME.

A Picturesque New England Play by Alice E. Ives and Jerome H. Eddy, entitled

The Village Postmaster

Produced under the Stage Direction of BEN TEAL, and the management of J. WESLEY ROSENQUEST. Also Mrnager of "The Great Ruby" and 14th Street Theatre, New York.

CAST OF CHARACTERS.

SETH HUGGINS, MR. ARCHIE BOYD
The village postmaster and boss in the village, with political aspirations

JOHN HARPER. MR. ASA LEE WILLARD
The Methodist minister's son, in love with the postmaster's daughter

BEN DEANE, MR. AL. PHILLIPS
The village lawyer and political heeler for Huggins

EBENEZER TODD, sexton of the Baptist church, MR. WM. S. GILL

THOMAS JEFFERSON HUGGINS, MR. TOM MAGUIRE
A very bad boy, and a heavy responsibility to Samantha

CALEB SPRINGER, father of Mrs. Gibbs, MR. RICHARD NESMITH

REV. CHARLES GIBBS, the Baptist minister, MR. GEORGE MARTIN

SILAS TONER, a young farmer, MR. GEORGE S. PELZER

JIM PENNEL, of the church choir, MR. JOSEPH R. SPRAGUE

LUTHER SCHENCK, the mail carrier, MR. WM. R. SINCLAIR

MIRANDA HUGGINS, MISS ANGELA RUSSELL
The educated and lovable daughter of Seth

MARY BARDEN, MISS JOSEPHINE STOFFER
A seamstress, whom nobody knows

HATTIE BURLEY, MISS JANE MARBURY
A coquette, "but knows her own mind"

SAMANTHA HUGGINS, sister of Seth, MISS GRACE GRISWOLD
She carries a "stiddy" hand, but will quote poetry

Alice Emma Ives was one of the more prolific women playwrights of the Victorian era. This production of *The Village Postmaster* is actually a revival of the 1896 play produced at the 14th Street Theater in New York. A man named Jerome Eddy is credited as cowriter; it is possible that it is the same man thought to be one of the first press agents in the industry.

PROGRAMME.

Jere McAuliffe Big Stock Co.

Managrment of Mr. Harry Katzes Presenting

MR. GEORGE HEATH and MISS HAZEL PUGHSLEY
and a First-class Company of Dramatic Players in

Tom Edson, the Electrician.

CAST OF CHARACTERS.

TOM EDSON, the electrician, GEORGE HEATH

KENNETH SAVAGE, W. RANDALL
vice president Denver National bank

ROBERT L. SESSIONS, BURT McCANN
president Denver National bank

BILL TURNER, FREDERICK MALCOLM
foreman Edson Electric plant

JOHN R. EDSON, the inventor, A. W. WILSON

CHARLES YORKE, JERE McAULIFFE
representative Pref. Accident Insurance Co.

JUDGE MERRITT, not on the bench, HARRY BROOKS

BARNEY MARTIN, helper at the plant, THOS. RUSSELL

EDWARD FOSTER, paying teller at D. N. bank, FRED SAUNDERS

SAMUEL PARSONS, ALBERT LEES
receiving teller at the D. N. bank

JAMES HOULTON, private officer D. N. bank, ALF THOMAS

HORACE CRUMPTON, HARRY ALLEN
of Crumpton & Co., attorneys

EDITH SESSIONS, MISS HAZEL PUGHSLEY
the president's daughter

PROGRAMME CONTINUED ON PAGE 4.

Many actors moved on to form their own companies in the boom of theater in the early 20th century. Jere McAuliffe only had a few acting credits to his name when he formed the Big Stock Company that performed this obvious tribute to, or parody of, the great inventor Thomas Edison. The playwright Charles Blaney lived on Long Island and is reported to have purchased 68 acres along the coast to build winter housing for his circus.

Three

The Portsmouth Theatre 1904–1945

By 1903, Frank Jones had passed away and the Music Hall was sold to F.W. Hartford and his partners. Hartford had been involved with the Music Hall since the early days as manager under both the Peirce administration and his good friend Frank Jones. As far as we know, the owner of the *Portsmouth Herald* and future seven-time mayor had the longest direct association with the hall in its 125 years. For more than 35 years, he maintained a relationship as either manager or owner until the hall was sold to John Bartlett and eventually shut down to touring entertainments. Hartford's first term as mayor began in 1920; it can be presumed that he gave up the theater to focus on his political career.

During Hartford's reign as owner, between 1903 and 1916, the Music Hall flourished. Shows with upwards of 100 people on stage were common, and the early signs of moving pictures flashed on the screen. It was under his direction that the Music Hall began its battle with other theaters. The Arcadia and Olympia opened shortly after 1910 and the Colonial in 1915. To compete with the modern appeal of these other theaters, Hartford attempted to bring a touch of class to his establishment, introducing regulations regarding audience conduct and providing personal services the larger theaters might not be able to afford.

After 1916, however, the Music Hall began to take a back seat to these other theaters. Without Hartford's leadership, the Music Hall became the playhouse for the community. It seems as though films disappeared completely, and touring companies rarely came through the doors. The hall was used primarily as a place for graduations and local productions and was finally shut down in the late 1930s to await another hero to open its doors and discover the magnificence. Fortunately, the wait was not long.

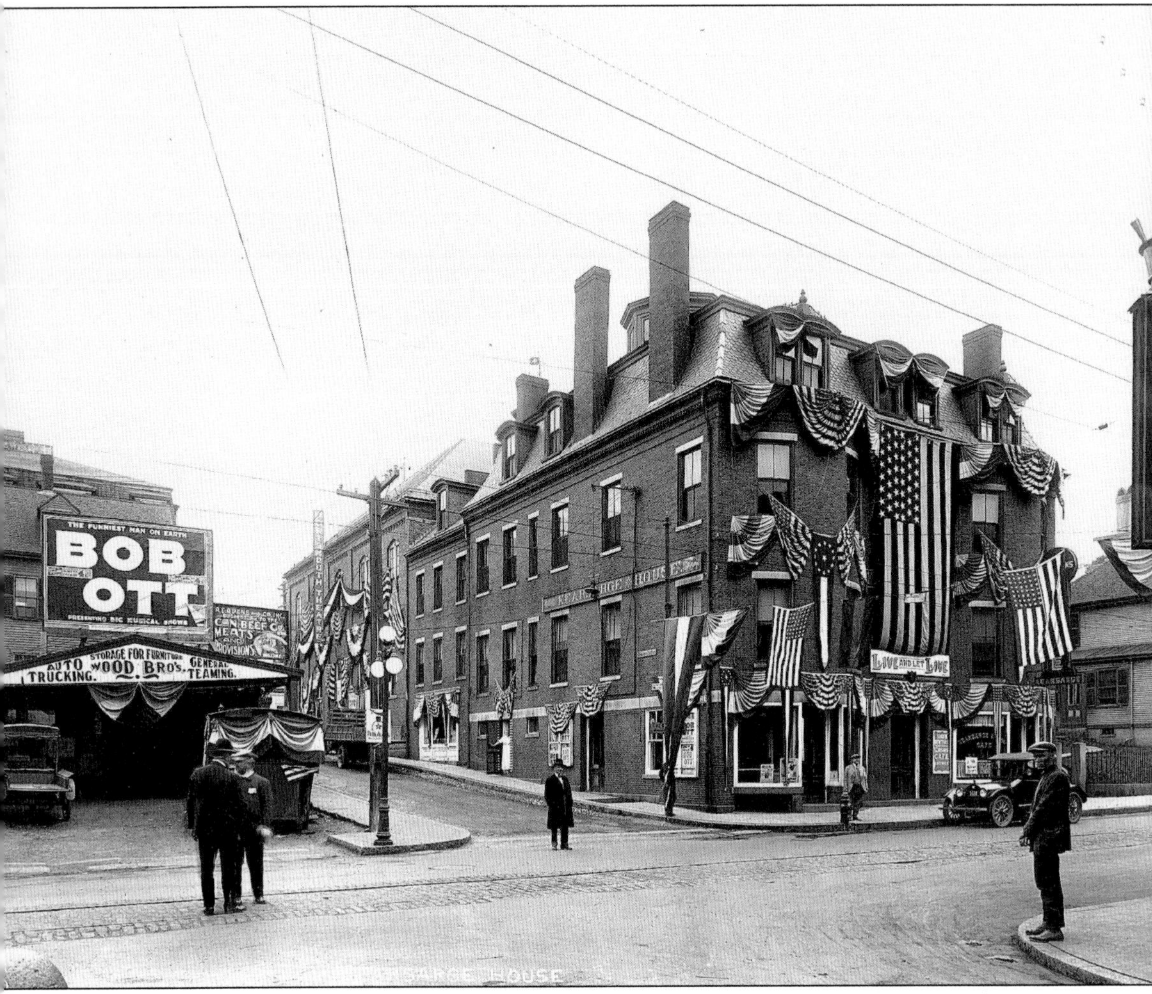

Another rare shot of the Music Hall front as viewed from Congress Street illustrates the attempt by the owners (Allied Theater Company, 1920) to bring the marquee out onto the main thoroughfare. Electricity was now running throughout the city, and the stable on the corner was now enlarged to allow room for automobiles. A vertical marquee was placed on the front of Portsmouth Theatre—the Music Hall was renamed when F.W. Hartford took over in 1903. (Courtesy of Strawbery Banke Museum.)

Maude Fealy, the leading lady of Gillette's production of *Sherlock Holmes*, is shown here on a card similar to those that young boys would start collecting on baseball players in years to come. Fealy, who lived well into her 80s, was known as an actress, playwright, and drama coach to such stars as Douglas Fairbanks Sr. Rumored to have had at least a small role in every Cecil B. DeMille film made after the advent of talkies, she was buried in the Hollywood Memorial Park Cemetery with funds provided by the estate of her longtime friend DeMille, who had died much earlier. (Courtesy of the Portsmouth Public Library.)

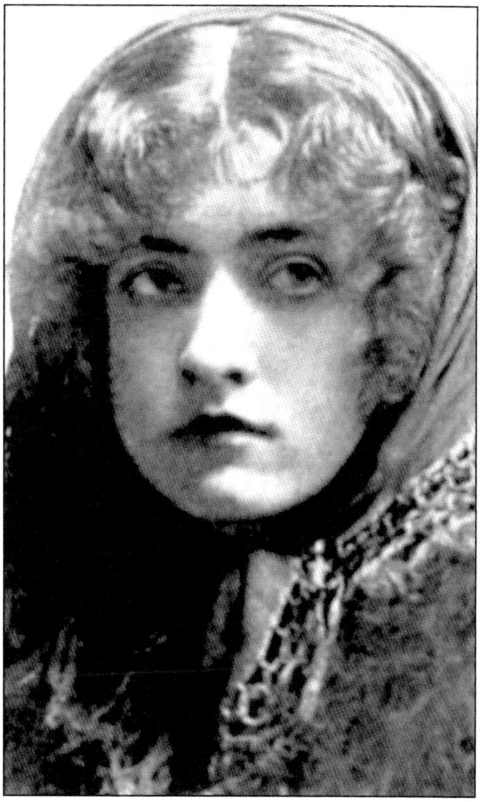

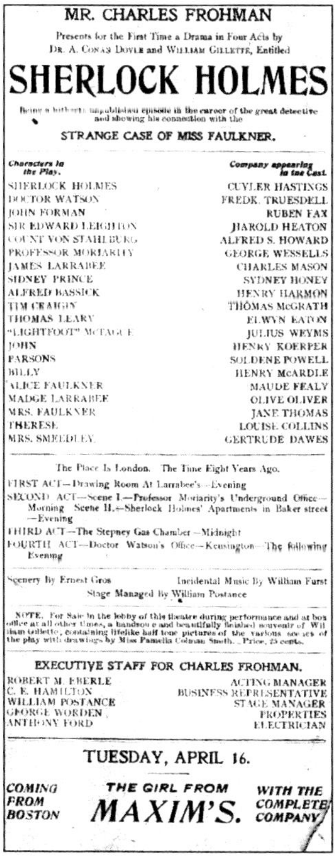

MR. CHARLES FROHMAN

Presents for the First Time a Drama in Four Acts by DR. A. CONAN DOYLE and WILLIAM GILLETTE, Entitled

SHERLOCK HOLMES

Being a hitherto unpublished episode in the career of the great detective and showing his connection with the

STRANGE CASE OF MISS FAULKNER.

Characters in the Play.	Company appearing in the Cast.
SHERLOCK HOLMES	CUYLER HASTINGS
DOCTOR WATSON	FREDK. TRUESDELL
JOHN FORMAN	RUBEN FAX
SIR EDWARD LEIGHTON	HAROLD HEATON
COUNT VON STAHLBURG	ALFRED S. HOWARD
PROFESSOR MORIARTY	GEORGE WESSELLS
JAMES LARRABEE	CHARLES MASON
SIDNEY PRINCE	SYDNEY HONEY
ALFRED BASSICK	HENRY HARMON
TIM CRAIGIN	THOMAS McGRATH
THOMAS LEARY	ELWYN EATON
"LIGHTFOOT" McTAGUE	JULIUS WEYMS
JOHN	HENRY KOERPER
PARSONS	SOLDENE POWELL
BILLY	HENRY McARDLE
ALICE FAULKNER	MAUDE FEALY
MADGE LARRABEE	OLIVE OLIVER
MRS. FAULKNER	JANE THOMAS
THERESE	LOUISE COLLINS
MRS. SMEEDLEY	GERTRUDE DAWES

The Place Is London. The Time Eight Years Ago.

FIRST ACT—Drawing Room At Larrabee's—Evening

SECOND ACT—Scene I.—Professor Moriarity's Underground Office—Morning Scene II.—Sherlock Holmes' Apartments in Baker street—Evening

THIRD ACT—The Stepney Gas Chamber—Midnight

FOURTH ACT—Doctor Watson's Office—Kensington—The following Evening

Scenery By Ernest Gros — Incidental Music By William Furst

Stage Managed By William Postance

NOTE. For Sale in the lobby of this theatre during performance and at box office at all other times, a handsome and beautifully finished souvenir of William Gillette, containing lifelike half tone pictures of the various scenes of the play with drawings by Miss Pamelia Colman Smith. Price, 25 cents.

EXECUTIVE STAFF FOR CHARLES FROHMAN.

ROBERT M. EBERLE	ACTING MANAGER
C. E. HAMILTON	BUSINESS REPRESENTATIVE
WILLIAM POSTANCE	STAGE MANAGER
GEORGE WORDEN	PROPERTIES
ANTHONY FORD	ELECTRICIAN

TUESDAY, APRIL 16.

COMING FROM BOSTON — THE GIRL FROM MAXIM'S. — WITH THE COMPLETE COMPANY

This 1901 production of *Sherlock Holmes, Strange Case of Miss Faulkner* brought to the Music Hall a variety of famous names. Originally written by Sir Arthur Conan Doyle, the play was rewritten (with Doyle's approval) by William Gillette, who would make the role and the character famous. Although it appears from the cast list that Gillette took this particular tour off, most of the cast had considerable stage credits to their names. George Wessells, who played the role of Professor Moriarty, is an example of the power of family connections ever present in the theater. Wessells's niece and protégé was Antoinette Perry, who, among her many credits, directed the original production of *Harvey* and was honored posthumously with an award named after her: the Tony Award. (Courtesy of the Portsmouth Public Library.)

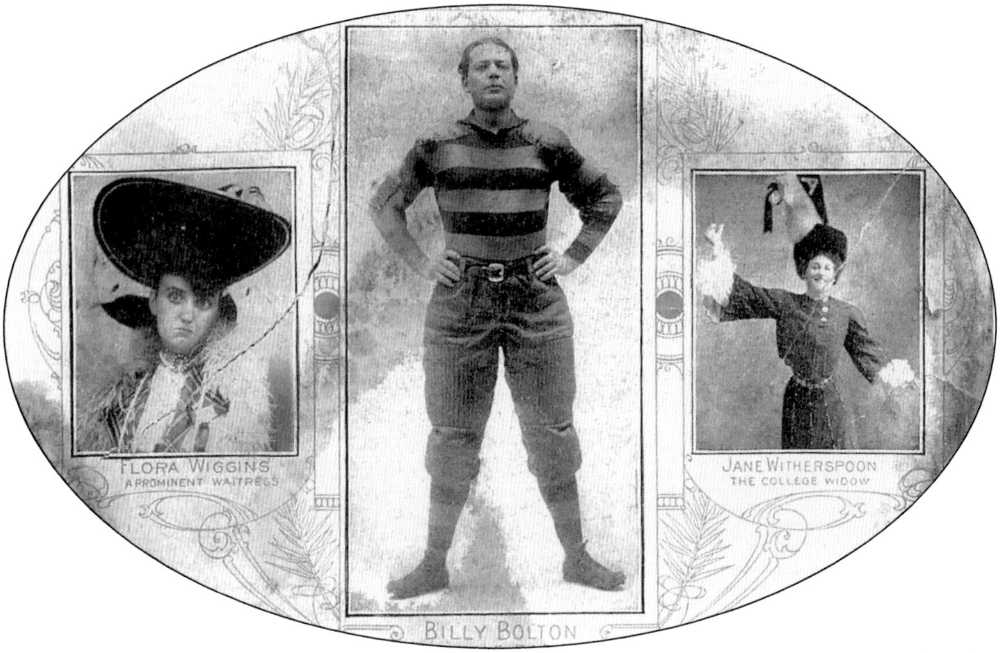

This football-shaped postcard shows characters from the very popular George Ade play *The College Widow* in 1905. The play, which defined the term "college widow" to mean an older woman who hangs around college campuses, earned more than $2 million in its first Broadway run and was the impetus for at least two films and three other plays.

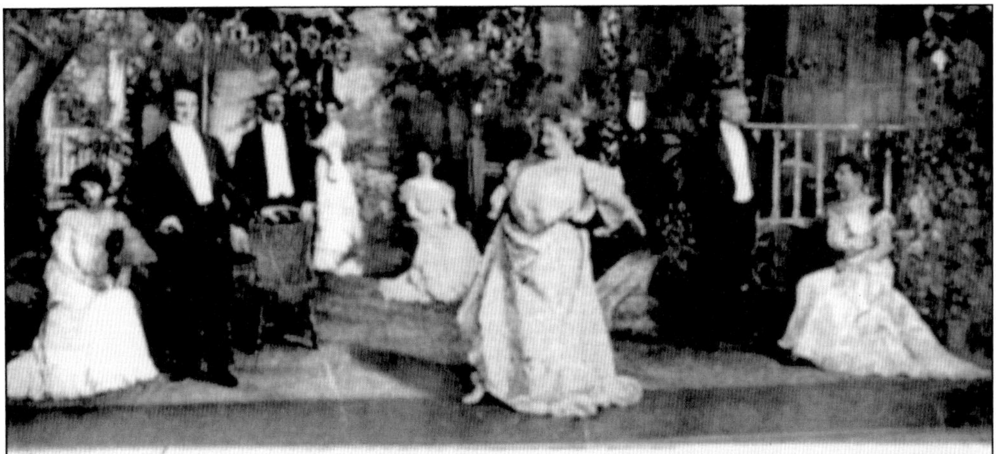

It is unclear whether this postcard of May Irwin in *Mrs. Black is Back* is from the stage show she made famous in 1904 or the film version in 1914. A daughter of Scottish immigrants, Irwin managed to be a part of a number of entertainment firsts. While performing in a Broadway hit titled *The Widow Jones*, she was asked by Thomas Edison if he could film her and her leading man, John Rice, reenacting a scene from the play for the camera. The short film, possibly the very first movie shown in Canada and certainly one of Edison's firsts, became known as *The Kiss*, as it was simply one minute of May Irwin and John Rice doing just that. (Courtesy of the Harbor Arts Museum and the Richard Smith Collection.)

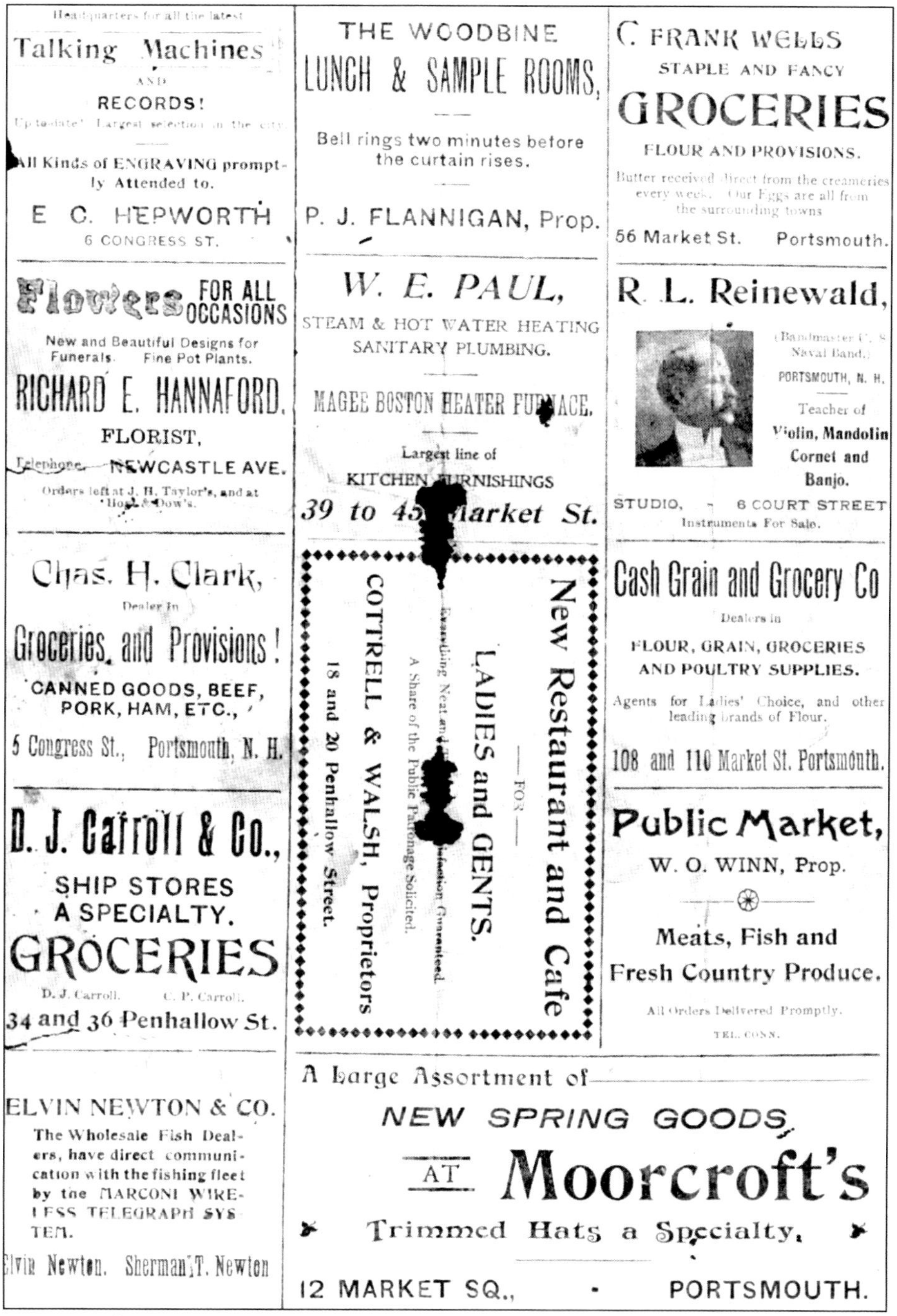
Headquarters for all the latest

Talking Machines

AND

RECORDS!

Up-to-date! Largest selection in the city

All Kinds of ENGRAVING promptly Attended to.

E. C. HEPWORTH

6 CONGRESS ST.

THE WOODBINE

LUNCH & SAMPLE ROOMS,

Bell rings two minutes before the curtain rises.

P. J. FLANNIGAN, Prop.

C. FRANK WELLS

STAPLE AND FANCY

GROCERIES

FLOUR AND PROVISIONS.

Butter received direct from the creameries every week. Our Eggs are all from the surrounding towns

56 Market St. Portsmouth.

Flowers FOR ALL OCCASIONS

New and Beautiful Designs for Funerals. Fine Pot Plants.

RICHARD E. HANNAFORD,

FLORIST,

Telephone. NEWCASTLE AVE.

Orders left at J. H. Taylor's, and at Hoyt & Dow's.

W. E. PAUL,

STEAM & HOT WATER HEATING

SANITARY PLUMBING.

MAGEE BOSTON HEATER FURNACE.

Largest line of

KITCHEN FURNISHINGS

39 to 45 Market St.

R. L. Reinewald,

(Bandmaster U. S. Naval Band.)

PORTSMOUTH, N. H.

Teacher of

Violin, Mandolin

Cornet and

Banjo.

STUDIO, - 6 COURT STREET

Instruments For Sale.

Chas. H. Clark,

Dealer In

Groceries, and Provisions!

CANNED GOODS, BEEF, PORK, HAM, ETC.,

5 Congress St., Portsmouth, N. H.

New Restaurant and Cafe

— FOR —

LADIES and GENTS.

Everything Neat and Satisfaction Guaranteed.

A Share of the Public Patronage Solicited.

COTTRELL & WALSH, Proprietors

18 and 20 Penhallow Street.

Cash Grain and Grocery Co

Dealers in

FLOUR, GRAIN, GROCERIES AND POULTRY SUPPLIES.

Agents for Ladies' Choice, and other leading brands of Flour.

108 and 110 Market St. Portsmouth.

D. J. Carroll & Co.,

SHIP STORES

A SPECIALTY.

GROCERIES

D. J. Carroll. C. P. Carroll.

34 and 36 Penhallow St.

Public Market,

W. O. WINN, Prop.

Meats, Fish and

Fresh Country Produce.

All Orders Delivered Promptly.

TEL. CONN.

ELVIN NEWTON & CO.

The Wholesale Fish Dealers, have direct communication with the fishing fleet by the MARCONI WIRELESS TELEGRAPH SYSTEM.

Elvin Newton. Sherman T. Newton

A Large Assortment of

NEW SPRING GOODS

AT Moorcroft's

Trimmed Hats a Specialty.

12 MARKET SQ., · PORTSMOUTH.

This interior of a 1903 playbill is a perfect example of the advertising style at the beginning of the 20th century. Note the Elvin Newton & Company advertisement in the lower left corner announcing direct contact with the fishing fleets through "Marconi Wireless Telegraph System" and the "talking machines and records" listed for sale at E.C. Hepworth's in the upper right corner. The advertisement for the Woodbine Lunch and Sample Room claims that a bell will ring there two minutes prior to the curtain rising at the Music Hall so that patrons can get to their seats in time.

IMPORTANT NOTICE.

Whistling, shouting or other disorder will not be permitted. The management has provided the cleanest and most comfortable gallery in New England, and trusts that its patrons will contribute to each other's enjoyment by observance of the respect due to those on the stage.

Notices such as this one were necessary in an age when talking back to the actors, throwing fruit, and spitting were not uncommon. One has to wonder if these instructions in small print on the back page of a playbill had any more effect that they would have today.

IMPORTANT NOTICE.

Physicians who have patients to whom they may be called suddenly, and who have heretofore remained away from the Theatre for fear of being out of call in such cases, can now leave their seat numbers in the box office, and be called as quickly as in their office. Ushers will deliver messages to them promptly upon receipt of same over the telephone.

Parties finding lost articles in any portion of the Theatre will please leave them at the Ticket Office. The Manager will not be responsible for articles placed under the seats.

This complicated message was printed on the back of the 1900 *Village Postmaster* playbill. One would think that a simple message such as "Physicians may leave their seat number with the box office if they are expecting word from a patient" would have been sufficient.

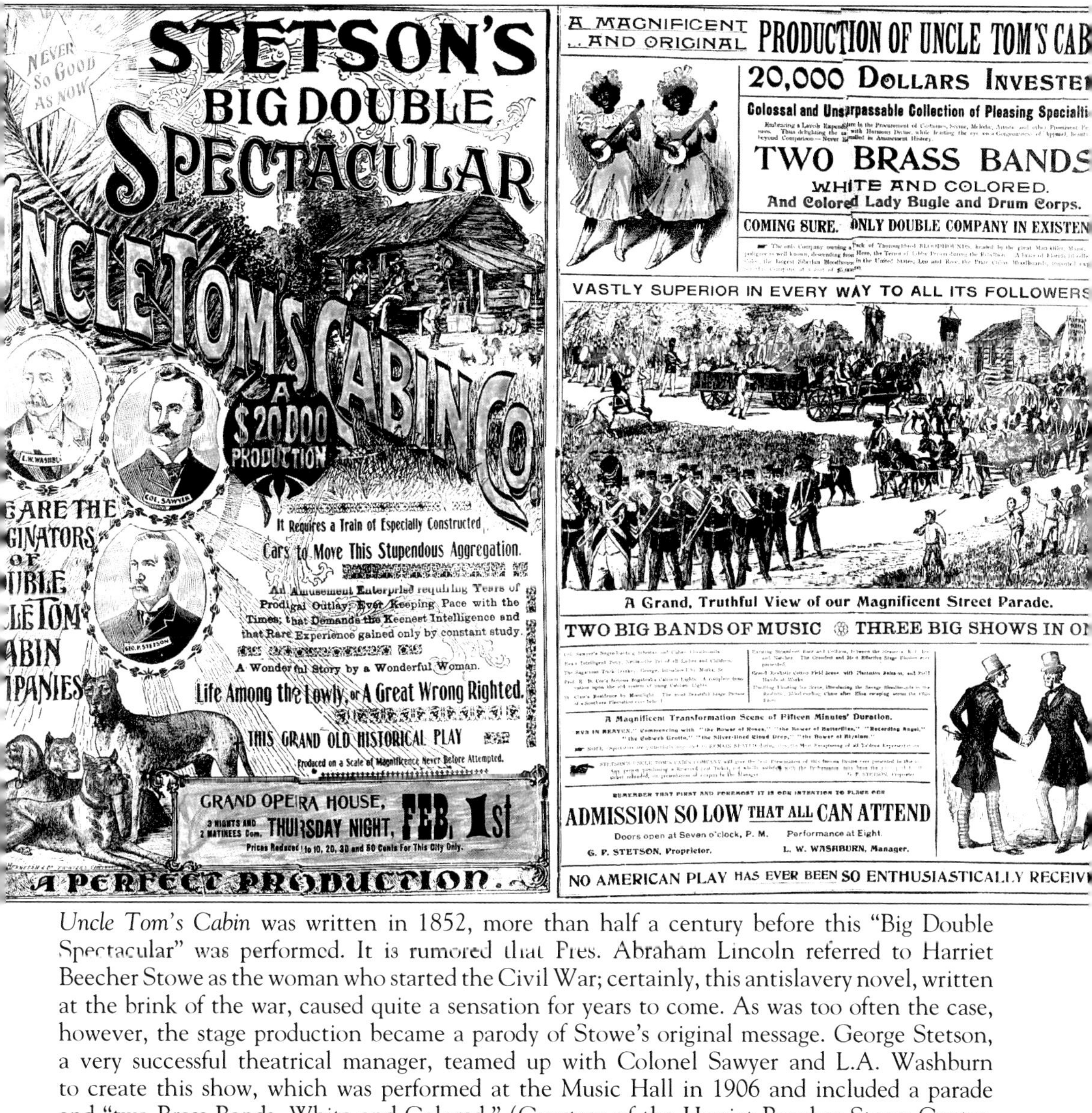

Uncle Tom's Cabin was written in 1852, more than half a century before this "Big Double Spectacular" was performed. It is rumored that Pres. Abraham Lincoln referred to Harriet Beecher Stowe as the woman who started the Civil War; certainly, this antislavery novel, written at the brink of the war, caused quite a sensation for years to come. As was too often the case, however, the stage production became a parody of Stowe's original message. George Stetson, a very successful theatrical manager, teamed up with Colonel Sawyer and L.A. Washburn to create this show, which was performed at the Music Hall in 1906 and included a parade and "two Brass Bands, White and Colored." (Courtesy of the Harriet Beecher Stowe Center, Hartford, Connecticut.)

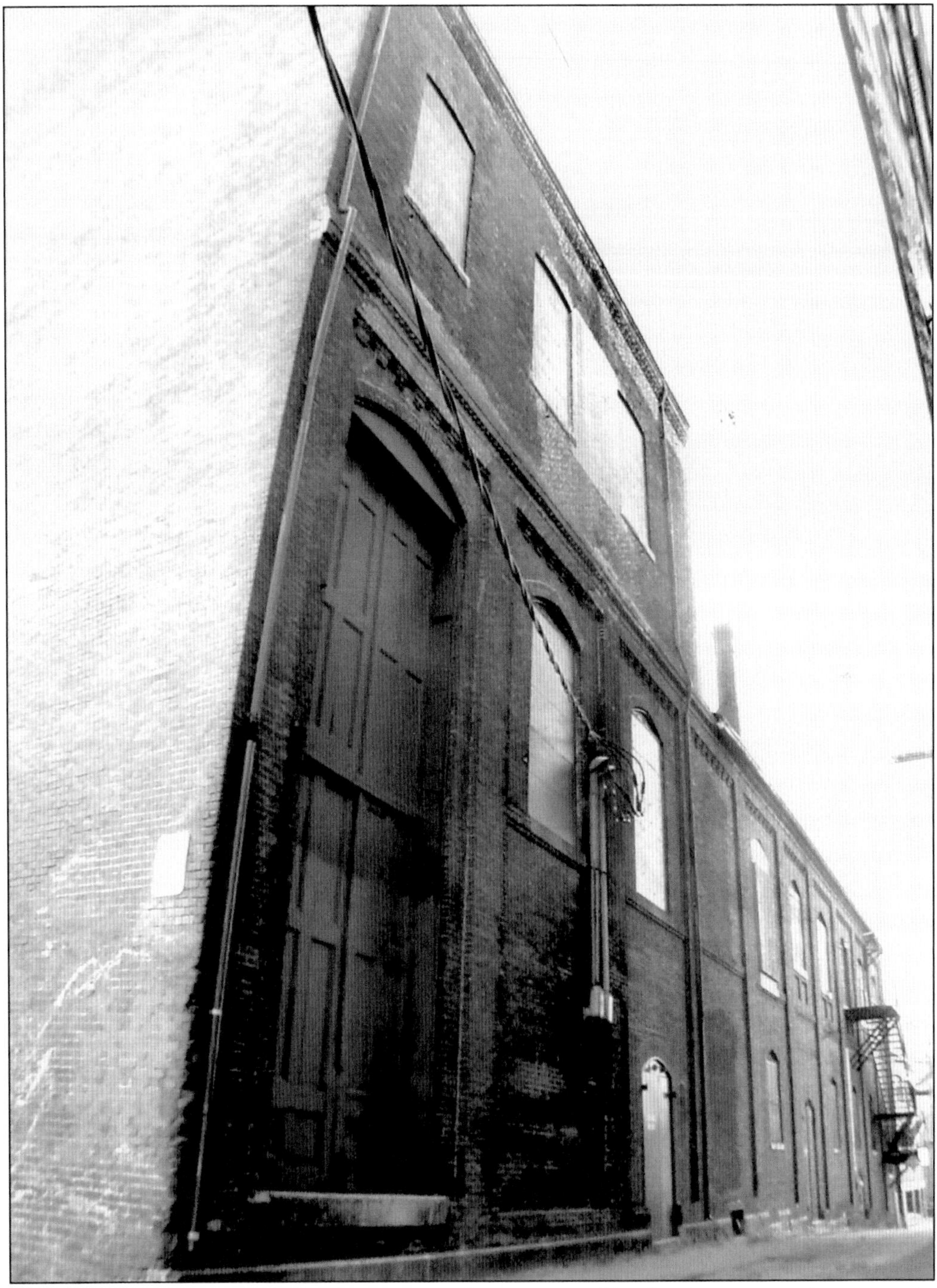

This enormous stage entrance, containing what are possibly the largest wooden doors in Portsmouth, would have been necessary to load in the materials for a performance such as George Stetson's "Big Double Spectacular" *Uncle Tom's Cabin*. Several newspapers reported the doors as being large enough to admit several adult elephants.

The Portsmouth Athletic Club, first organized in 1885, held annual minstrel shows at the Music Hall. Undoubtedly an all-white cast, local performers appeared in blackface in songs such as "Dis Bird am Mine" and "Dat's de Way to Spell Chicken." Now considered a dark spot in the memories of Portsmouth residents, there are still those who can recall performing in blackface on the Music Hall stage as children.

THE PROGRAMME.

Portsmouth Athletic Club
MINSTRELS

FIRST EDITION

INTERLOCUTOR
Mr. F. W. Hartford

CORNER MEN

Percy Lawrence — Charlie Test

RIGHT ENDS	LEFT ENDS
Perry Conner	"Wally" Lear
Al. Frost	"Lew" Jones
Fred Turner	"Gus" Dondero
Fred Hayes	"Buzz" Trefethen

PROGRAMME

CHORUS TITLES

Opening Chorus, — P. A. C. Minstrels
1 Curtain Song, "Miame," Indian Serenade
2 "Clidee, Oh!"
3 "When Reuben Comes to Town,"
Reuben—R. H. Spinney
4 "I'm From Missouri"
5 "Zephyrs of the Sea," Spanish Serenade
6 "Dis Bird am Mine"
Parson—W. R. Dearborn
7 "Dat's de Way to Spell Chicken"
8 "Pie, Pie, Pie,"
Russell L. Test and Lennox Hopkins, Waitresses

Portsmouth Theatre

Friday Evening, February 25 -1915

OSCAR F. HODGE PRESENTS

NEIL O'BRIEN

AND HIS

Great American Minstrels

On Their Fourth Annual Tour.

(Continued on next page)

As shown by the long-lasting run of minstrelsy, this form of entertainment was carried over into the 20th century and performed in theaters all over the world. Neil O'Brien was one of the better-known managers, often sharing performers with other famed minstrel shows, such as Dockstader and Primrose and West.

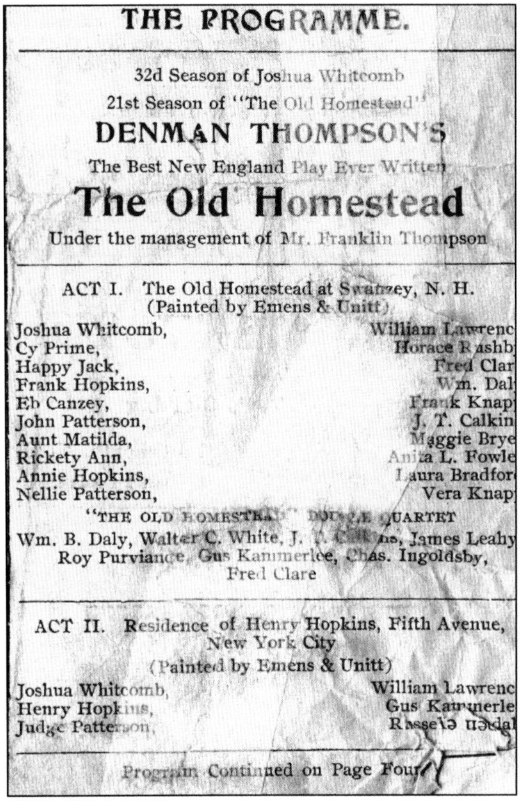

THE PROGRAMME.

32d Season of Joshua Whitcomb
21st Season of "The Old Homestead"
DENMAN THOMPSON'S
The Best New England Play Ever Written
The Old Homestead
Under the management of Mr. Franklin Thompson

ACT I. The Old Homestead at Swanzey, N. H.
(Painted by Emens & Unitt)

Joshua Whitcomb,	William Lawrenc
Cy Prime,	Horace Rashb
Happy Jack,	Fred Clar
Frank Hopkins,	Wm. Dal
Eb Canzey,	Frank Knap
John Patterson,	J. T. Calkin
Aunt Matilda,	Maggie Brye
Rickety Ann,	Anita L. Fowle
Annie Hopkins,	Laura Bradfor
Nellie Patterson,	Vera Knap

"THE OLD HOMESTEAD DOUBLE QUARTET
Wm. B. Daly, Walter C. White, J. [illegible], James Leahy
Roy Purviance, Gus Kammerlee, Chas. Ingoldsby,
Fred Clare

ACT II. Residence of Henry Hopkins, Fifth Avenue,
New York City
(Painted by Emens & Unitt)

Joshua Whitcomb,	William Lawrenc
Henry Hopkins,	Gus Kammerle
Judge Patterson,	[illegible]

Program Continued on Page Four

In 1906, F.W. Hartford brought home one of New Hampshire's own. Denman Thompson reportedly performed the role of Joshua Whitcomb in *The Old Homestead* 15,000 times in the 40 years following the character's debut in a vaudeville skit in the mid-1880s. Although originally from Pennsylvania, Thompson made his home in Swanzey, New Hampshire, where the residents still produce a revival of this play every summer. (Courtesy of the Portsmouth Public Library.)

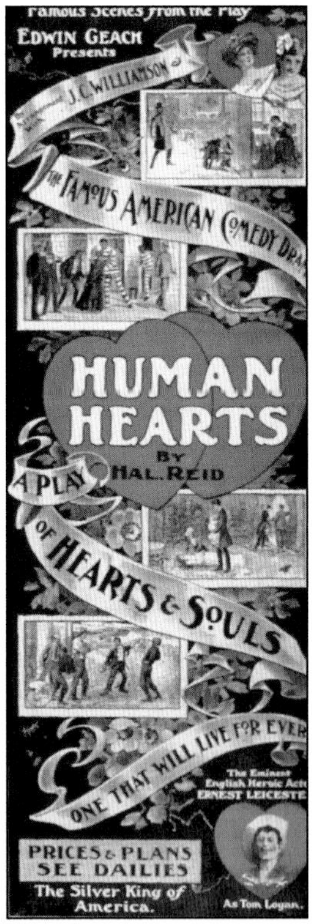

Hal Reid was a prolific playwright and director at the beginning of the 20th century, although he was overshadowed by his son Wallace Reid's silent film acting career. His play *Human Hearts* was presented at the Music Hall in January 1906. (Courtesy of the State Library of Tasmania.)

The new moving pictures, while fascinating, did not appease the community's need for entertainment, and large vaudeville shows such as *The Girl from Rectors* were still quite popular when this performance came through in 1910. While little is known about the play, it appears in a number of editorials denouncing the immorality of theater in the early part of the century. One can only imagine the plot. (Courtesy of the State Library of Tasmania.)

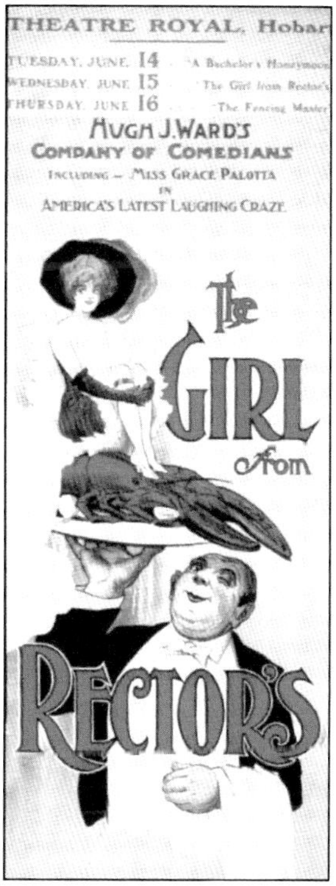

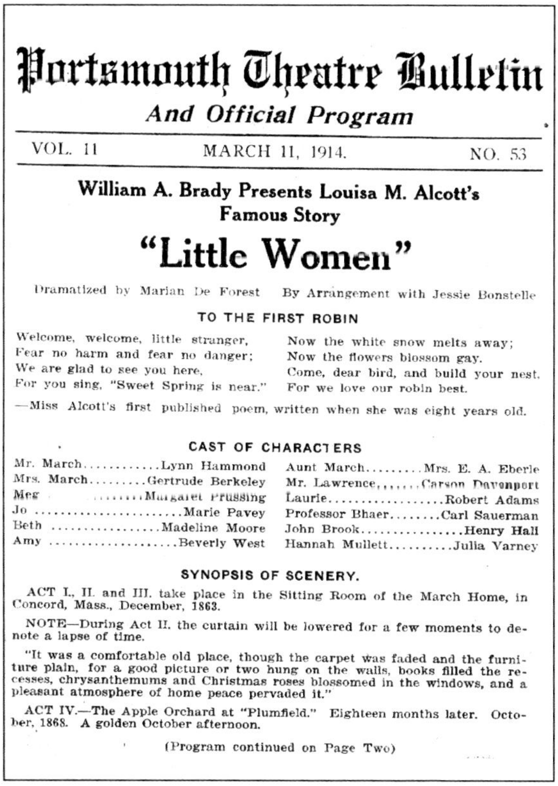

Portsmouth Theatre Bulletin

And Official Program

VOL. 11 MARCH 11, 1914. NO. 53

William A. Brady Presents Louisa M. Alcott's Famous Story

"Little Women"

Dramatized by Marian De Forest By Arrangement with Jessie Bonstelle

TO THE FIRST ROBIN

Welcome, welcome, little stranger,
Fear no harm and fear no danger;
We are glad to see you here,
For you sing, "Sweet Spring is near."
Now the white snow melts away;
Now the flowers blossom gay.
Come, dear bird, and build your nest,
For we love our robin best.

—Miss Alcott's first published poem, written when she was eight years old.

CAST OF CHARACTERS

Mr. March	Lynn Hammond	Aunt March	Mrs. E. A. Eberle
Mrs. March	Gertrude Berkeley	Mr. Lawrence	Carson Davenport
Meg	Margaret Prussing	Laurie	Robert Adams
Jo	Marie Pavey	Professor Bhaer	Carl Sauerman
Beth	Madeline Moore	John Brook	Henry Hall
Amy	Beverly West	Hannah Mullett	Julia Varney

SYNOPSIS OF SCENERY.

ACT I., II. and III. take place in the Sitting Room of the March Home, in Concord, Mass., December, 1863.

NOTE—During Act II. the curtain will be lowered for a few moments to denote a lapse of time.

"It was a comfortable old place, though the carpet was faded and the furniture plain, for a good picture or two hung on the walls, books filled the recesses, chrysanthemums and Christmas roses blossomed in the windows, and a pleasant atmosphere of home peace pervaded it."

ACT IV.—The Apple Orchard at "Plumfield." Eighteen months later. October, 1868. A golden October afternoon.

(Program continued on Page Two)

At first glance, this program for *Little Women*, written from the Alcott book by suffragette Marian DeForest, is nothing spectacular, but interesting facts about the era can be found on the inside pages. The Portsmouth Athletic Club Minstrels are scheduled to perform, also scheduled are a series of moving pictures, including the new Vitagraph flicks. The Music Hall takes the opportunity to share some national entertainment news, including an article about the lawsuit between actress Anna Held and the Kinemacolor Company for unauthorized use of her image. Theater manager F.W. Hartford uses the back page to inform patrons that "No hat [is] to be worn in any seat in the theater" and that schedules are subject to change as "the acts and pictures frequently sent to us . . . do not always, upon rehearsal, come up to the standard of merit which this theater insists upon." (Courtesy of the Portsmouth Public Library.)

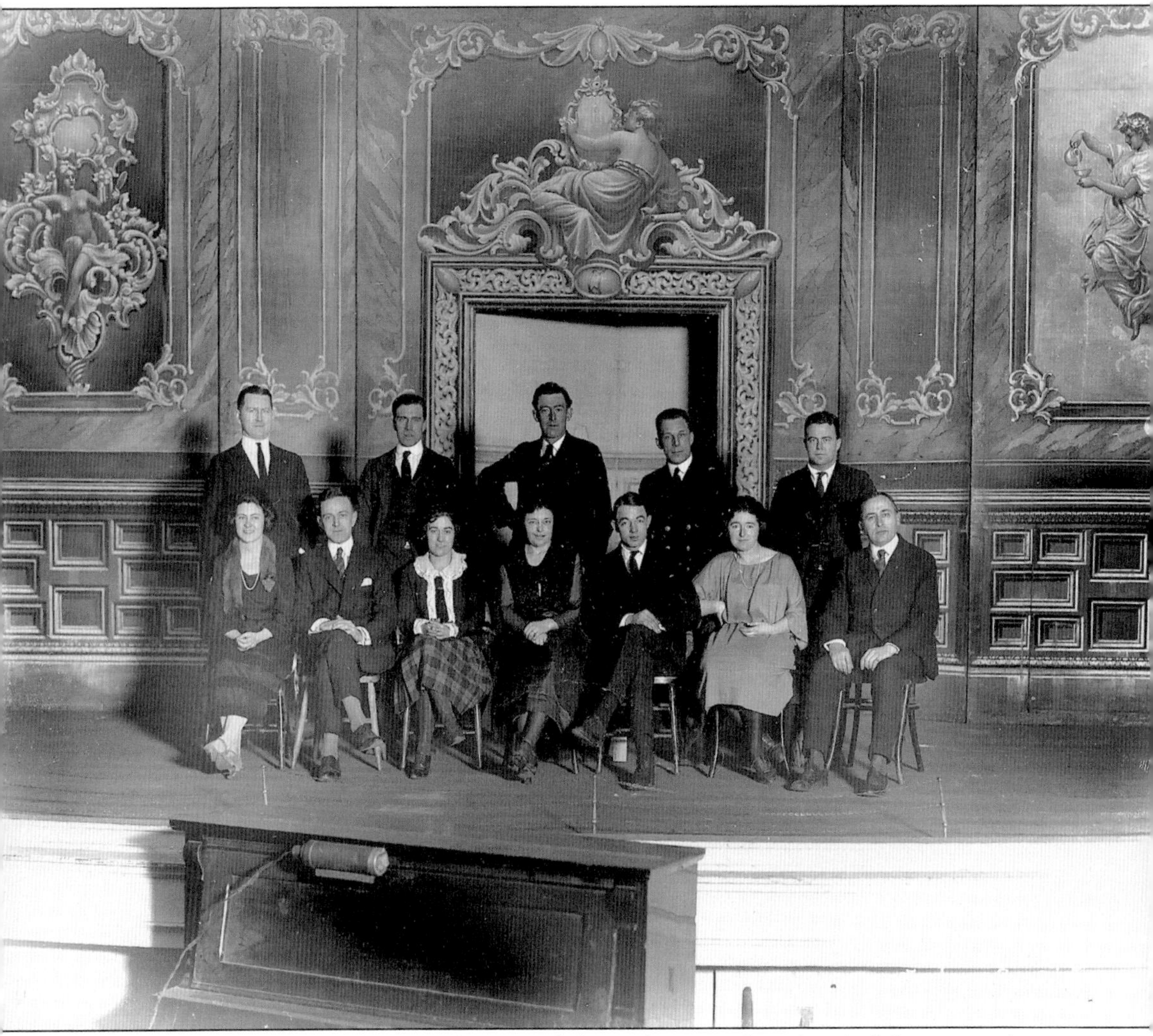

This undated picture of the cast of *Jim's Girl* shows the marvelous detail of the scenic elements on the stage. One can only imagine the beauty of these hand-painted stage flats (which form the back wall) when seen in color. The show is not well known, but the Knights of Columbus, who produced the show, felt that the Seacoast community would enjoy it. (Courtesy of the Strawbery Banke Museum.)

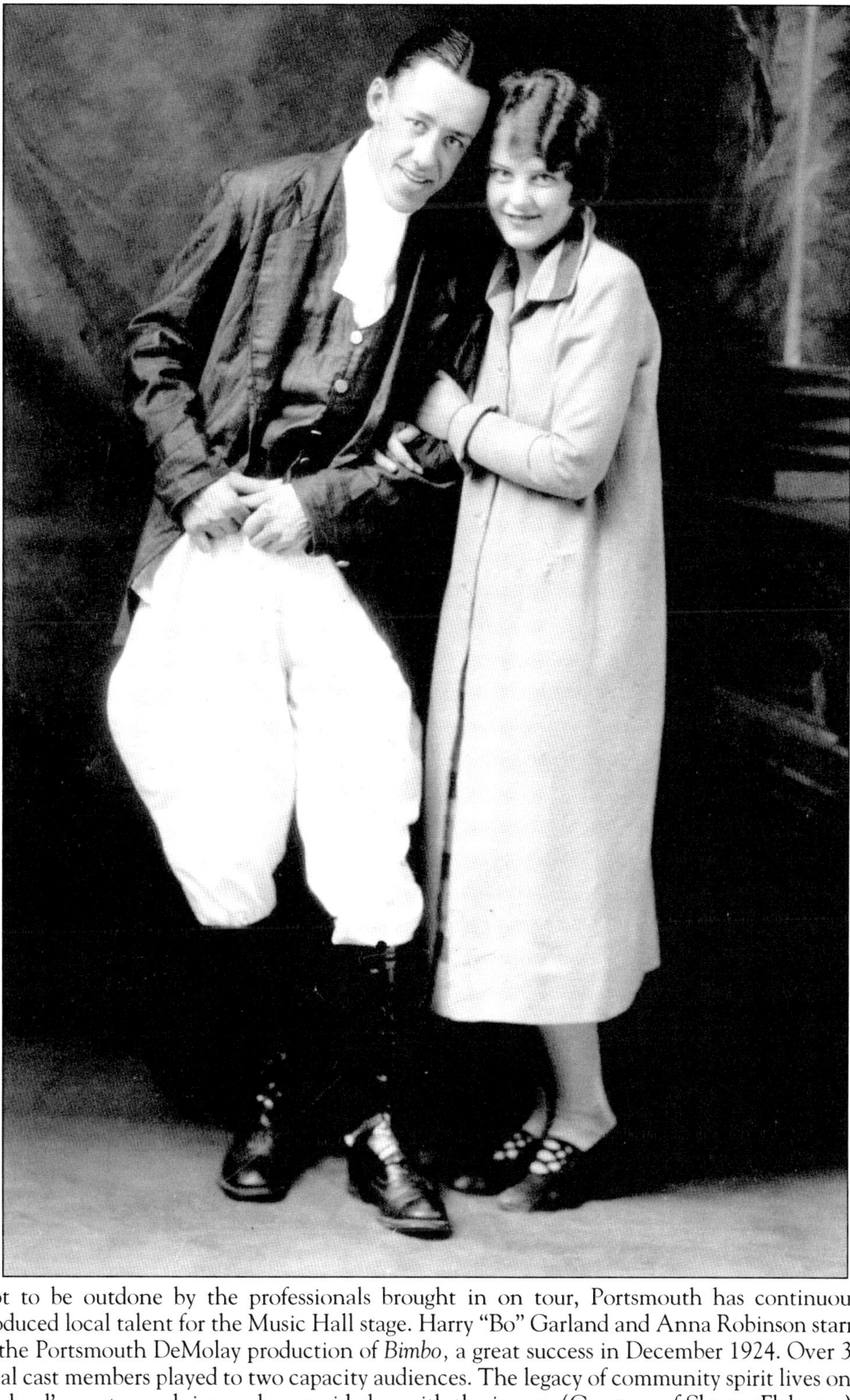

Not to be outdone by the professionals brought in on tour, Portsmouth has continuously produced local talent for the Music Hall stage. Harry "Bo" Garland and Anna Robinson starred in the Portsmouth DeMolay production of *Bimbo*, a great success in December 1924. Over 300 local cast members played to two capacity audiences. The legacy of community spirit lives on in Garland's great-grandniece, who provided us with the image. (Courtesy of Sharon Flaherty.)

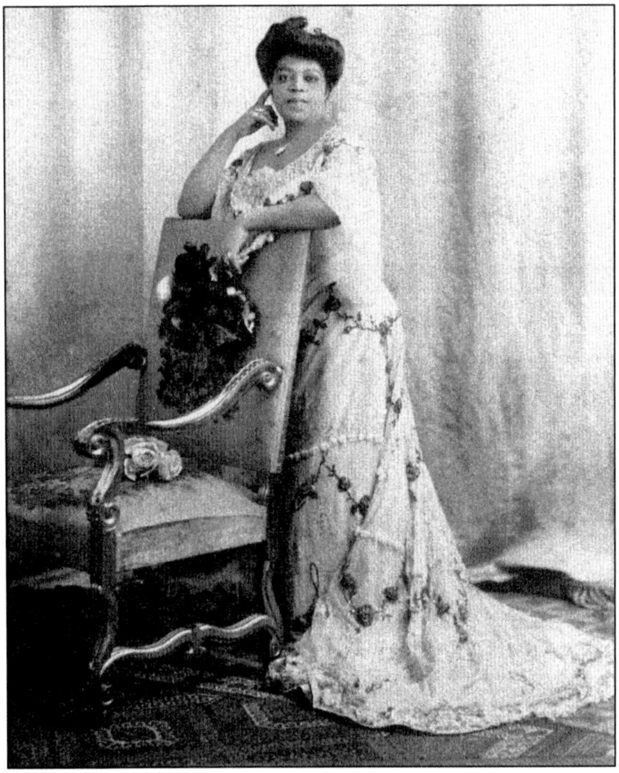

Sometime prior to 1916, when her company disbanded at her retirement, Siseretta Jones brought the Black Patti Troubadours to the Music Hall. Frequently compared to the Italian opera singer Adelina Patti (hence the nomenclature Black Patti), Jones had a voice that carried her to many of the major theaters around the world. Although denied a role at the Metropolitan Opera House due to her color, Jones provided a professional training ground for many black entertainers. (Courtesy of the Portsmouth [Virginia] Public Library and the family of Melvina Beale Colden.)

SHRINERS' FROLIC

AND LADIES' NIGHT

UNDER THE AUSPICES OF THE

Portsmouth Shriners Association

Portsmouth Theatre, Monday Evening, January the twenty-second, 1923

PROGRAM

ORCHESTRA

[D. A. GREEN, Director]

MARCH—Turkish Patrol . . . . *Michaelis*
OVERTURE—Morning, Noon and Night in Vienna . . *Suppe*

VAUDEVILLE

[Booked by the B. F. Keith Agency, Boston and New York]

1 COLUMBIA TRIO Instrumental Artists of International Fame
2 FRED HALL AND RIZA MELTA . . "Just Spoofing"
Comedy Patter and Songs
3 FRANCES ALDRICH . . Dancing—"Her Own Act"
Daintiness Personified
4 JACK SYDNEY . . . . Versatile Monologist
With Up-to-the Minute "Stuff"
5 GRACE AND FLORENCE . . . Singing and Piano
A Pair of High-Class Entertainers
6 SELECTION—Little Nellie Kelley . . . G. Cohen
Orchestra
7 KABARET KLUB . . "By Our Own Girls" (Keith's)
Nice and Snappy
8 FRANK LANE . . . . . The "Talkative Trickster"
Magic and Sleight of Hand
9 COMEDY SKETCH . . . . . . Hal Stack Co.
Three of 'Em—Just Fun
10 BATCHELDER TRIO . . . . . The Team of Color
11 GARDEN CITY TRIO . . Comedy Musical Characters
Three Fun Demonstrators
12 GRAND FINALE . . . . . . By All the Artists
13 MARCH—"Full Broadside" . . . . . H. Lincoln

[Order of program subject to change without notice]

Portsmouth Shriners Association

JOHN H. ROSE, Chairman
CHAUNCEY B. HOYT, Treasurer GEORGE J. KAULA, Secretary
JOHN J. TOTMAN GEORGE E. HOBBS
Dr. S. F. A. PICKERING FRED M. STACEY

ARTHUR HORTON, Stage Manager

This 1923 program for the Portsmouth Shiners' Frolic and Ladies' Night includes descriptions, such as "talkative trickster" and "three fun demonstrators," of the actors brought in by famed vaudeville agent B.F. Keith. Another example of the community spirit associated with the Music Hall, this benefit may have been one of the first the Portsmouth lodge ever held to encourage the philanthropic work for which the association is known. It was not until 1920, some 40 years after the actor William Florence cofounded the organization of high-level Masons, that the Shriners decided to open a hospital and perform charity work. (Courtesy of the Portsmouth Public Library.)

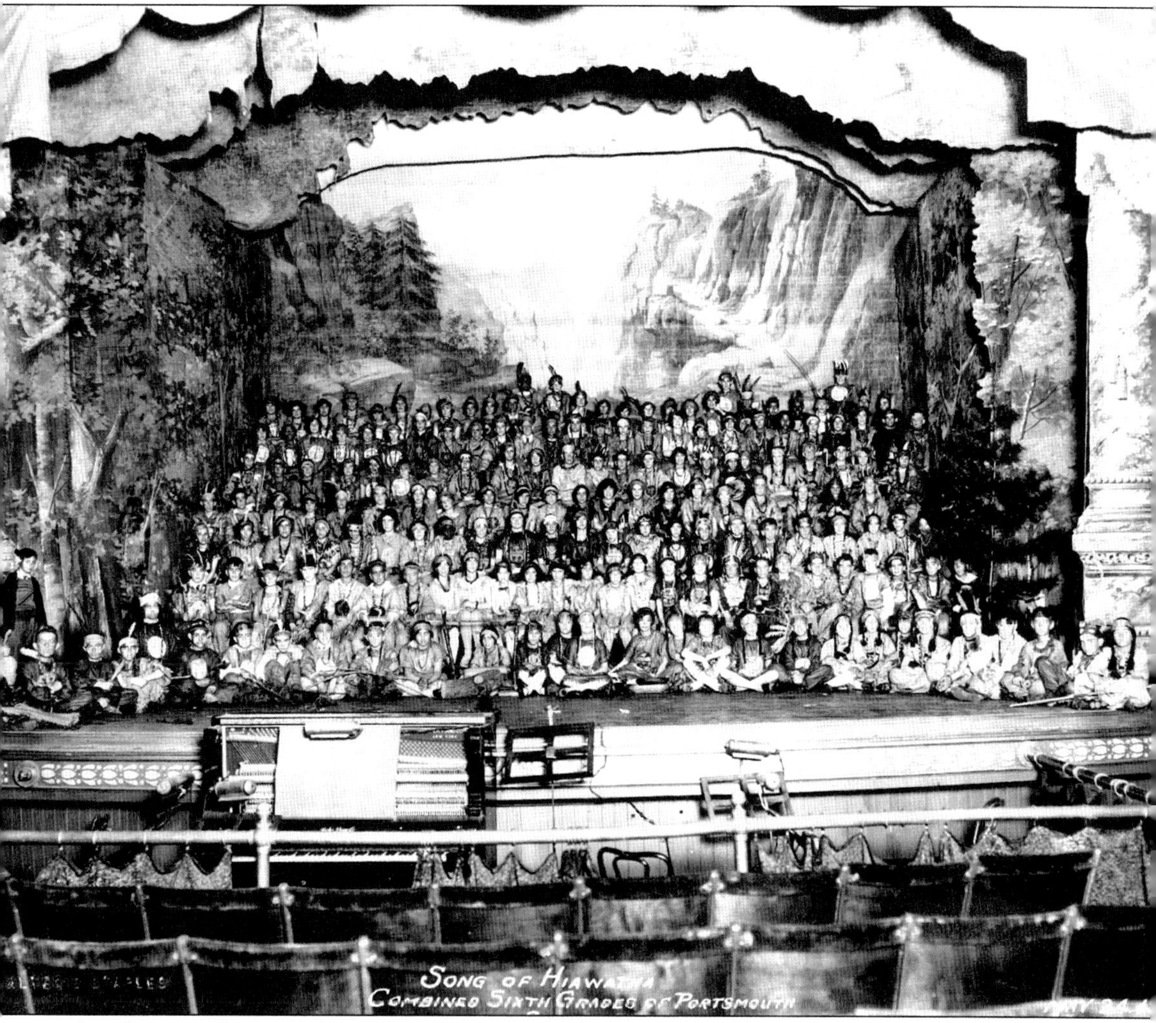

This photograph is a perfect example of the connection to the Portsmouth community that all Music Hall owners have strived for. In 1929, a total of 175 sixth-graders from all of the local schools performed the *Song of Hiawatha*. The beautiful columns in the foreground of the set are actually painted flats similar to the rest of the scenery. School and community performances such as this one had become the mainstay of the Music Hall at this time, though outside touring productions did still appear on occasion. (Courtesy of the Harbor Arts Museum and the Richard Smith Collection.)

PORTSMOUTH THEATRE
Friday, May 7, 1926
DOORS 7:30 PERFORMANCE 8:15

PROGRAMME
H. H. FRAZEE
presents
"NO, NO, NANETTE"
with
JOHN HYAMS and LEILA McINTIRE

A Musical Comedy in Three Acts. Book by Otto Harbach and Frank Mandel. Lyrics by Irving Caesar and Otto Harbach. Music by Vincent Youmans. Staged by E. J. Blunkall. Production under the Direction of Mr. Frazee.

CAST OF CHARACTERS
(In the order of their appearance)

Pauline, cook at the Smith's	Eulalie Young
Sue Smith, Jimmy's wife	Leila McIntyre
Billy Early, a lawyer	Roland Woodruff
Lucille, Billy's wife	Helen Case
Nanette, protege of Sue	Mary Vaughn
Tom Trainor, Lucille's nephew	Floyd English
Jimmy Smith	John Hyams
Betty, from Boston	Mildred Joy
Winnie, from Washington	Myrtle Miller
Flora, from San Francisco	Dorothy Newell
THE MAIDS	
Helen	Ann Hollywood
Ethel	Marjorie Purple
Beatrice	Paula Watkinson
Eva	Emily Satterfield
Beth	Aimee Warren
Margery	Catherine Collins
Hazel	Margaret Purple
Ruth	Nellie Clifton
THE MARRIEDS (Friends of Lucille)	
Mrs. Holmes-Gore	Juliette Louvar
Mrs. Smythe-Smith	Barbara Barbour
Mrs. Townley-Morgan	Irene Evans
Mrs. Brown-Maddox	Lillian Bea
Mrs. Ormesby-Willard	Esther Lawson
Mrs. Webster-Wylie	Oda Kenneth

Until recently, *No, No, Nanette* was considered to be the impetus for the sale of Babe Ruth to the Yankees by Red Sox owner and theater producer H.H. Frazee. Current understanding, however, has it that Frazee sold Ruth simply because the great Bambino caused a lot of trouble with his drinking and womanizing, and not to finance Frazee's latest Broadway show. The now famous sale happened four years prior to the opening of *No, No, Nanette*, and the play went on to make a large sum of money in its own right. This program was from one of more than a dozen national tours of the production. (Courtesy of the Portsmouth Public Library.)

MISS DOT KARROLL
In Songs, Buck and Wing Dancing
MORRIS SMITH
Eccentric Comedian and Dancer
HARRY CODAIRE
In a Little of Everything.
Master GEORGE POWERS
The Pleasing Boy Soprano in New Illustrated Songs.
FOSTER'S
LIFE MOTION PICTURES
Including Corse Payton's exciting and Jangbable Automobile Ride (Posed by Himself), Rube Haskin's and his sister Mandy's trip to the St. Louis Fair, the only authentic Japanese-Russian War Film depicting the bombardment of Port Arthur.
Special Feature, the California Duo
THE SPRAGUELLOS
Comedy Novelty Musical Artists, in Satan's Pastimes concluding with their original creation THE HOULA BOULA DANCE.
Clever Colored Entertainers
JUNIPER & HAYES
in Acrobatic Singing and Dancing.

The back side of this faded ticket shows the introduction of film to the Portsmouth community. No date is attached to the ticket, but Foster's Life Motion Pictures most likely first arrived in Portsmouth just after 1910. The pictures described include "Corse Payton's exciting and Jangbable Automobile Ride" and "Rube Haskin's and his sister Mandy's trip to the St. Louis Fair." The final film clip is listed as the "only authentic Japanese-Russian War Film depicting the bombardment of Port Arthur."

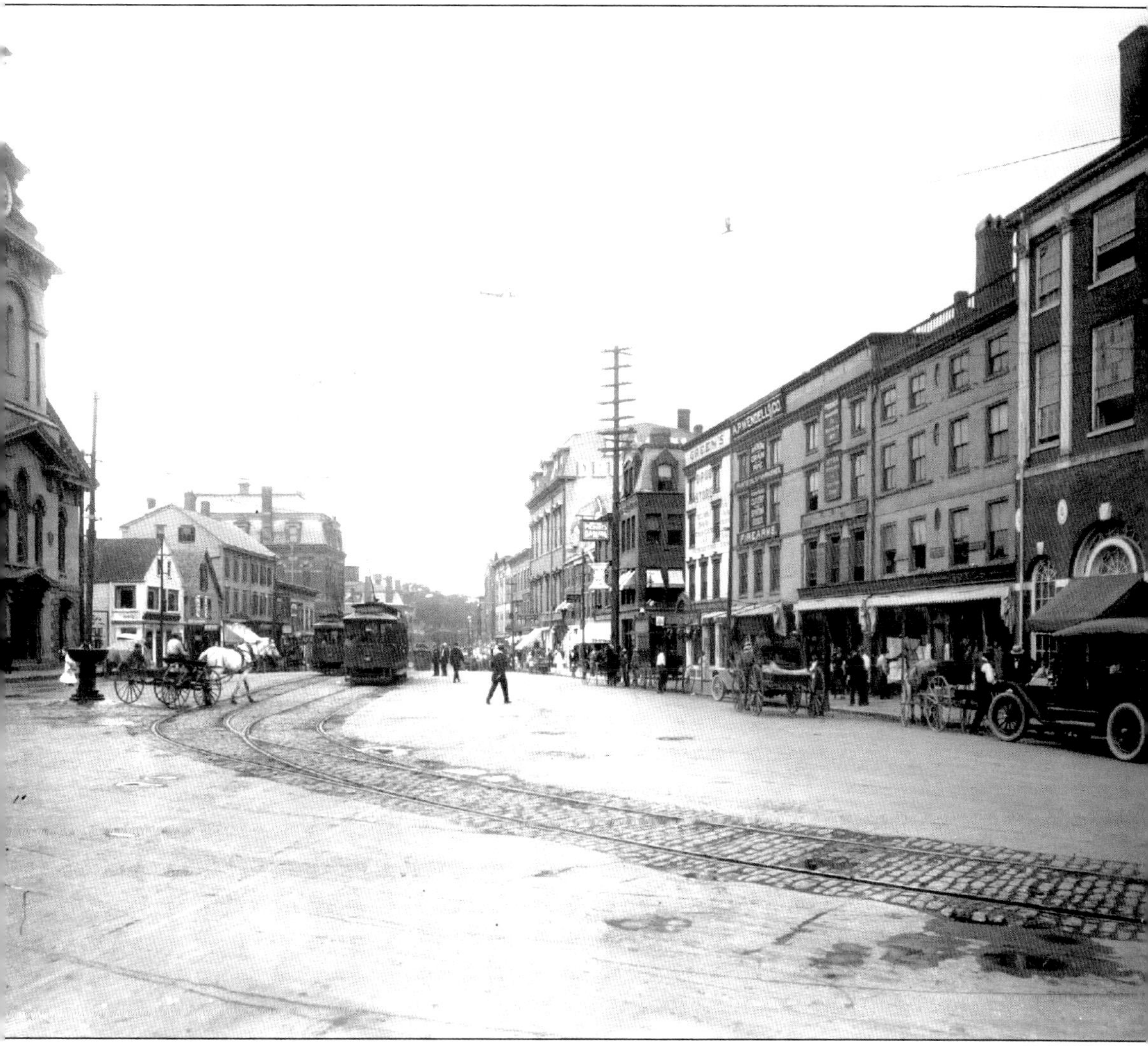

Shortly after 1910, other smaller theaters started to spring up all over the downtown area. Competition for patrons was immediately fierce. Signs, banners, and billboards attracting audiences to the often dark back streets of the Market Square area became increasingly elaborate during the next 30 years. Note the top sign on the telephone pole, which reads, "Moving Pictures, Dancing." (Courtesy of the Portsmouth Athenaeum.)

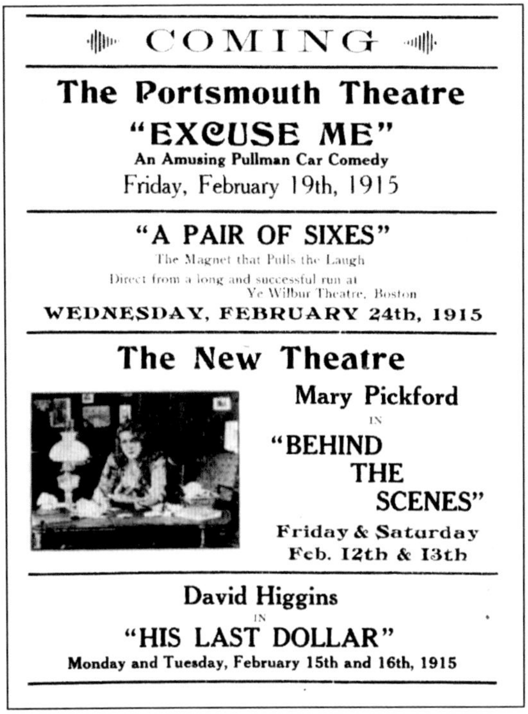

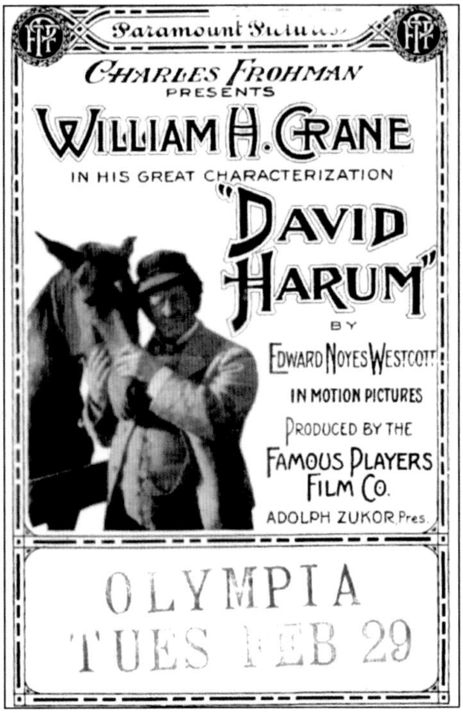

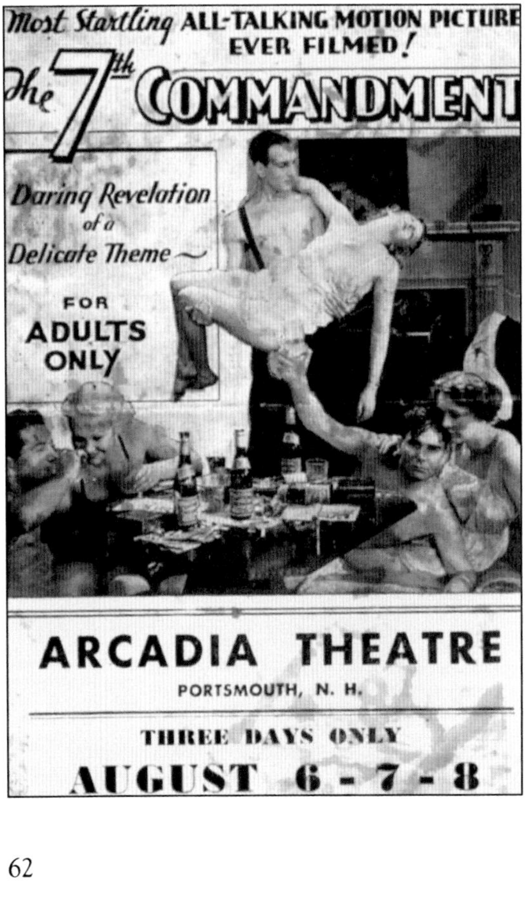

Within the next few years, the Music Hall began to feel the competition from the other theaters in town. John Bartlett owned the New Theatre and leased the Music Hall from F.W. Hartford. The flier for the Portsmouth Theatre (Hartford's name for the Music Hall) shows the declining interest in live events as stars like Mary Pickford began to arrive in film canisters. The advertisement for the film was not even for the Music Hall but for the New Theatre, across the way on Vaughan Street. Within a year the New Theatre (renamed the Olympia) was playing movies such as *David Harum*—a steppingstone for performers May Allison and Harold Lockwood, who would become one of the country's first beloved screen couples. The Arcadia, on Congress Street, catered to visiting sailors with adult films, as seen here in this playbill for *The 7th Commandment* billed as the "most startling all talking motion picture ever filmed." (Courtesy of the Portsmouth Public Library, the Harbor Arts Museum, and the Richard Smith Collection.)

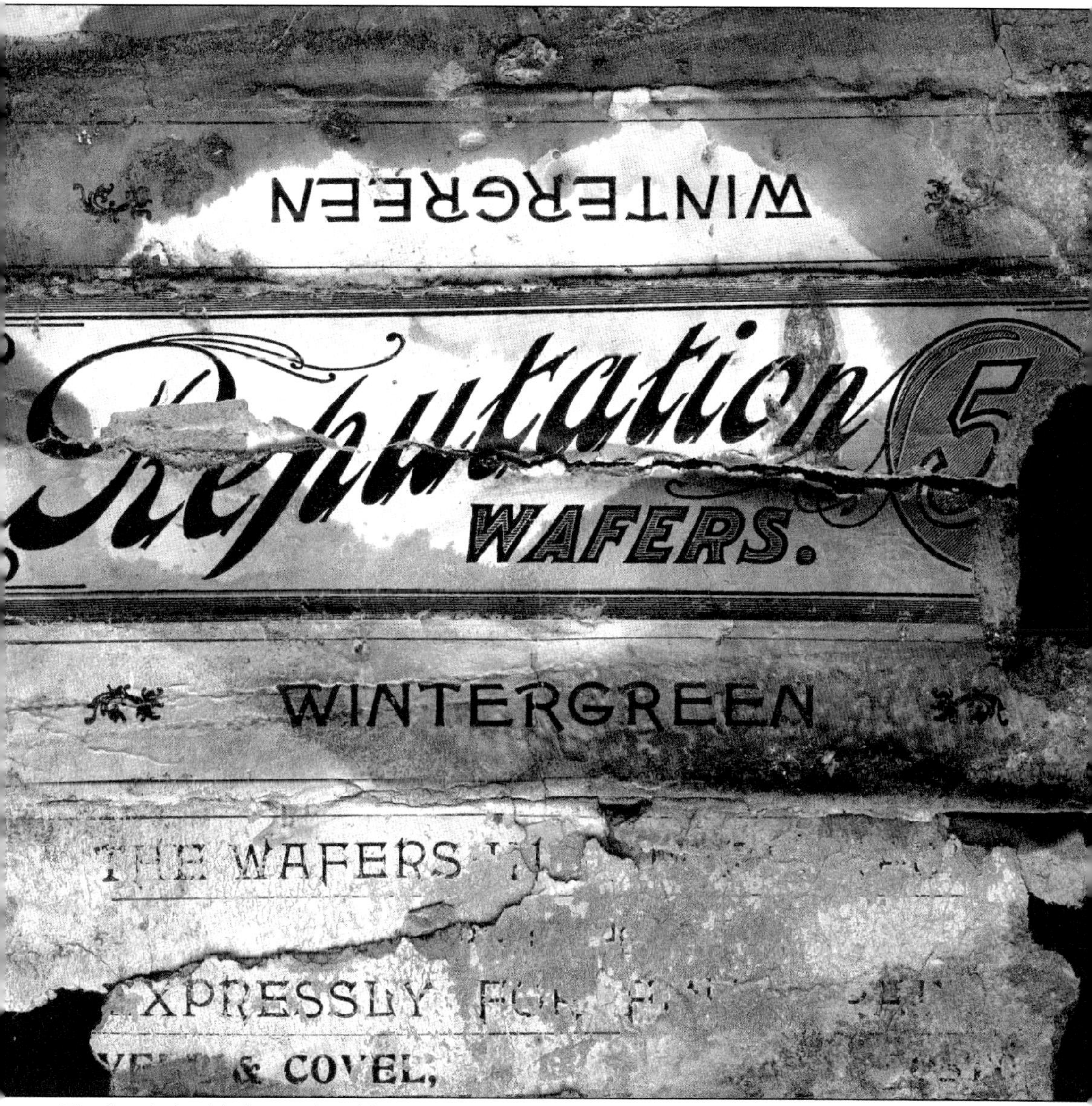

This barely legible box is the oldest piece in what is affectionately called the "candy collection." Found in recent years inside the heating grates, this 5¢ box of wintergreen-flavored Reputation wafers was made by the Lovell & Covel Candy Company. In 1933, the company joined the New England Confectionery Company, better known as Necco, indicating that this box was sold more than 70 years ago.

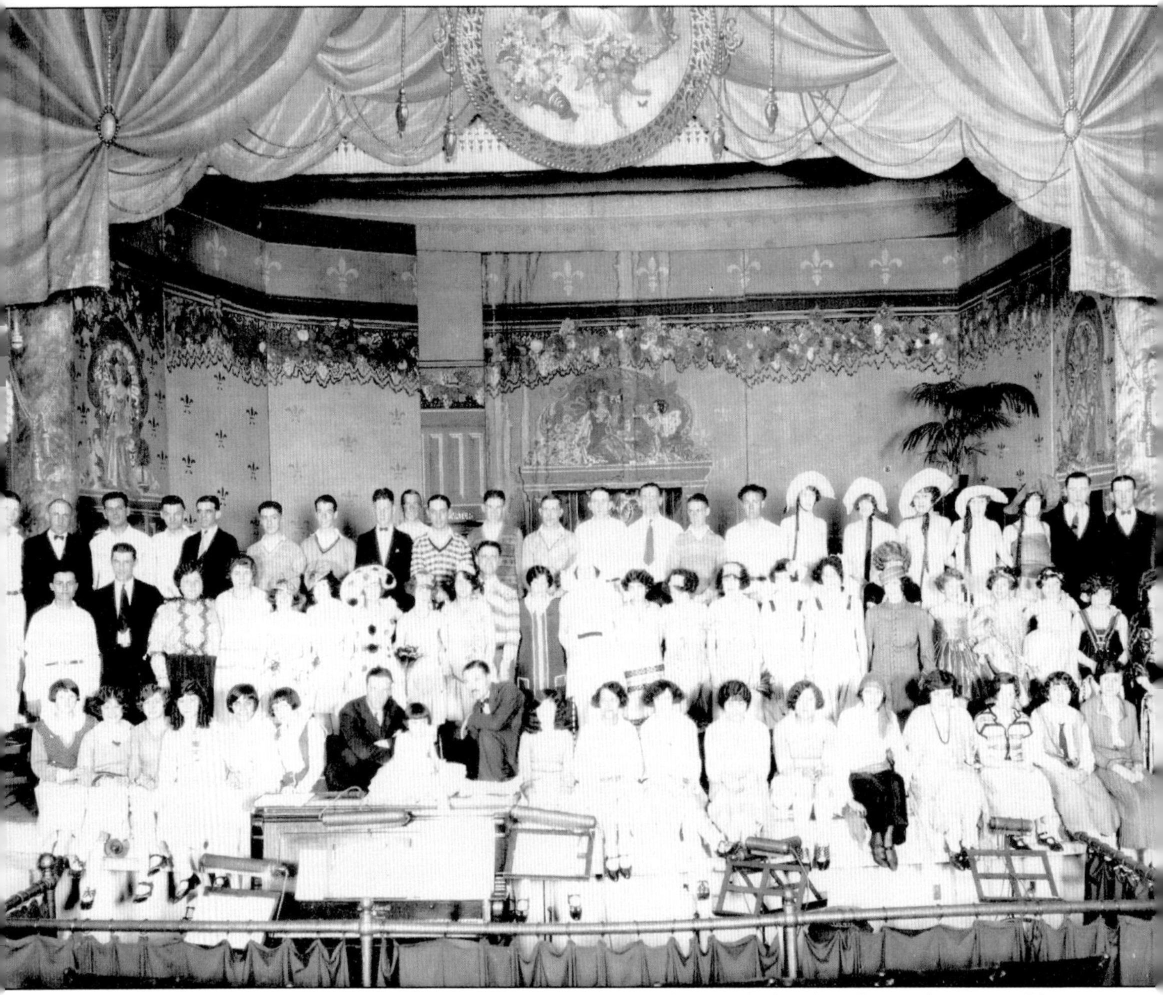

This 1925 photograph of *Out of Step* has been reported to include a local cast, but it could very well be the Broadway production, which opened earlier that year. Included in the Broadway cast were Arthur Hughes, who later starred in the original production of *Mourning Becomes Electra*, and Arthur Willard, star of the original *Our Town*. (Courtesy of the Portsmouth Athenaeum.)

Four

THE CIVIC THEATRE 1945–1982

World War II had brought thousands of sailors, pilots, and laborers to the several neighboring military bases, including the Portsmouth Naval Shipyard, just across the Piscataqua River. Advances in industrial technologies had resulted in hundreds of new factory jobs on the Seacoast. As the resident population grew, so did the demands on the local fishing trade, which responded with more boats and, naturally, more fisherman. Roads were widened and paved, and hundreds of new homes were constructed. Old schools and hospitals were expanded, and new ones were built. With an explosion of historical proportions, Henderson's Point had been blasted out to accommodate larger vessels through the Piscataqua's narrow channel. Bridges were erected to cross the river, creating more water traffic between states. Always a port town first, Portsmouth thrived with the influx of commerce from every point on the compass, and the streets bustled with new residents and visitors from all over the globe. By the mid-1940s, it had evolved into a veritable "Wild West" of the East. The Seacoast labor force had a reputation for enduring harsh conditions and grueling work schedules. The people were known to play as hard as they worked, and Portsmouth's centrally located downtown area was generally the playground of choice. Entertainment had long been a key element of the downtown area's energy and attraction, but the new conditions now demanded it satisfy an increasing volume and range of tastes, attitudes, and appetites.

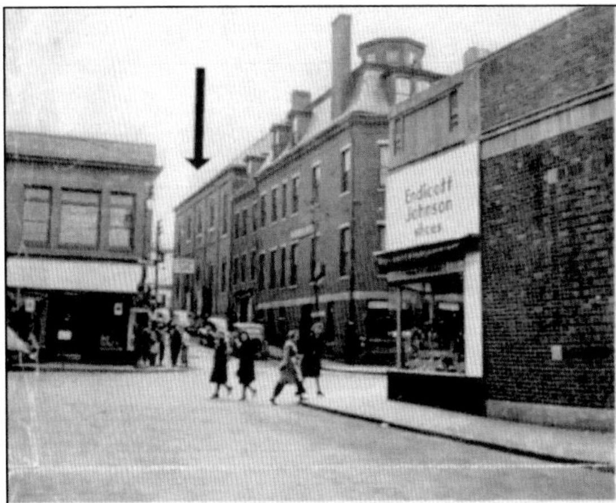

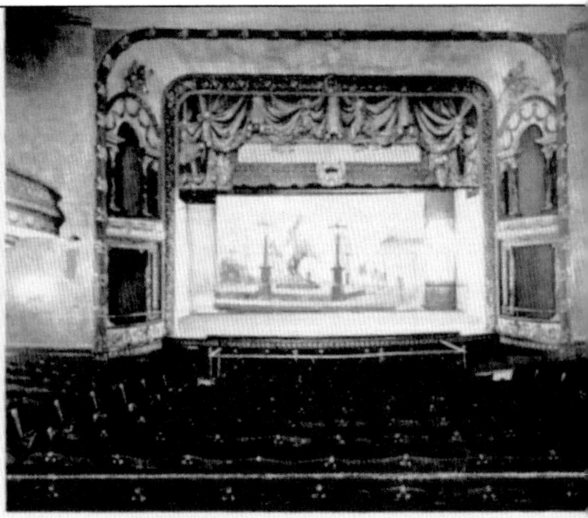

VIEW SHOWING LOCATION IN RELATION TO MAIN BUSINESS STREET

THE PORTSMOUTH THEATRE is located in the thriving business district of the city. The main entrance is on Chestnut Street. The stage door entrance and stage door scenery handling entrance is on Porter Street. There are exits on Porter Street and leading to Congress Street. This well known theatre usually remembered as "The Music Hall" can handle Metropolitan stage productions as well as movies, vaudeville, etc. When it operated as a legitimate theatre it played such attractions as Maude Adams in "Peter Pan," Montgomery and Stone in "The Wizard of Oz," Frank Laylor in "Coming thru the Rye," Douglas Fairbanks in "Hawthorne USA" and many Frohman productions. Many Broadway productions played Portsmouth along with Boston before opening in New York. It was later on the Keith Orpheum circuit and played vaudeville and motion pictures for many years along with stock productions.

THE BUILDING is of solid brick construction with slate roof, having a ground floor area of about 1200 square feet, 75 foot frontage on Chestnut Street and 127 foot frontage on Porter Street.

LOBBY AND ENTRANCE: The entrance to lobby, ticket office, rest rooms, etc., is on ground floor. Entrance to orchestra from both ends of lobby. The lobby is 45 feet x 15 feet.

SEATING CAPACITY: Orchestra 650. Balcony 450. Boxes 40. Or a total of 1140.

TO BE SOLD AT PUBLIC AUCTION ON THE PREM

The Property will be offered in its entirety on

SAMUEL T. FREE

1808-10 CHESTNUT STREET 80 FEDERA

With a statement that continues to ring true, this auction notice reads that "the completely equipped stage is exceptional in that it lends itself to practically every variety of theatrical usage," and continues, "It is believed to be the best property of its kind on the market in Northern New England." The bidding started at 12 o'clock noon on May 3, 1945. Guy Tott, a contractor and developer from Kittery, placed the first bid of $5,000. The auctioneer noted this offer as too low, indicating that no opening bid less than $10,000 would be considered. With no other bids placed, and no apparent competition, he conceded to Tott's second bid of $10,000. The theater was Tott's by 12:20 p.m. After a 19-year sleep, the Music Hall was to be reawakened. Many

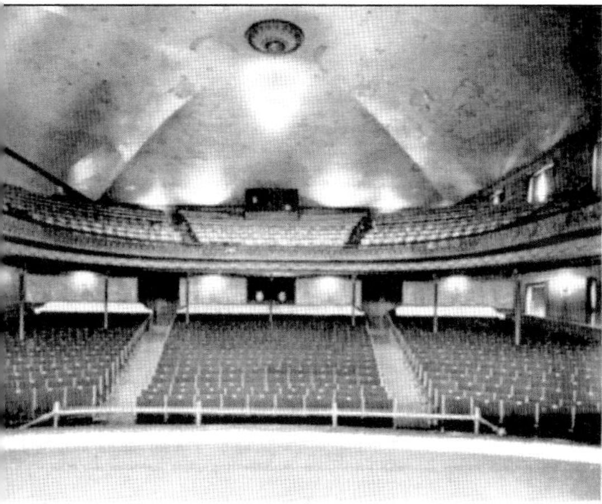

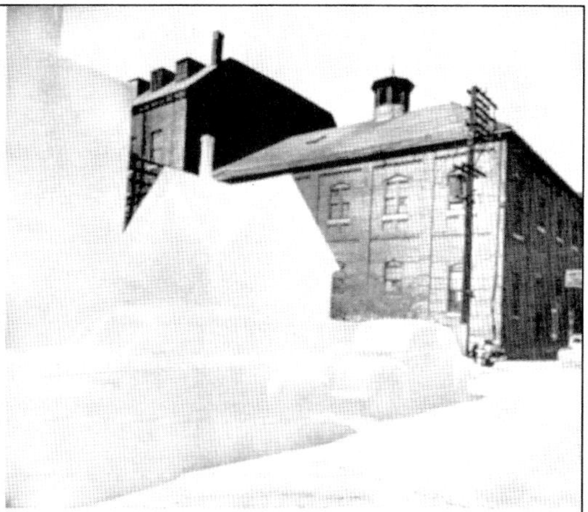

VIEW OF PROPERTY FROM CHESTNUT STREET

STAGE SPECIFICATION: Depth of stage from footlights 49 feet. Depth of stage from curtain 45 feet. Width of stage at proscenium arch 32 feet. Overall width 62 feet. Height of stage from fly gallery 30 feet (fly gallery is completely equipped). Height of grid from stage 64 feet. Four tiers of dressing rooms off stage. Baggage elevator to all dressing rooms. Stage door scenery handling entrance.

Complete high domed orchestra ceiling, considered to have excellent acoustics.

THE PROPERTY WILL BE SOLD free and clear of liens and mortgages of record. Title conveyed by warranty deed. 10% deposit in cash or certified check drawn to the order of the auctioneers will be required at time of sale. Settlement in 30 days from date of sale.

Sale subject to and with the benefit of all rights of way and easements of record.

Complete legal description as contained in the deed is available and may be examined at the office of the auctioneers, Room 618, 80 Federal Street, Boston or at the office of the Herald, Congress Street, Portsmouth, N. H. (See terms of sale on page 4.)

MAY 3 - 1945

Inspection by appointment.

N THURSDAY, MAY 3, 1945 AT 12:00 O'CLOCK NOON

Land, Building and Equipment as one parcel

N & CO.

ESTABLISHED NOV. 12, 1805

AUCTIONEERS

ET, BOSTON

27 WILLIAM STREET

notable details may be found in the photographs included on the auction notice. In the first picture on the left, a sign of the changing times is evident by the number of women present (all the previous pictures from this angle were dominated by men). In the second photograph, the original decorative paint and gold leaf is resplendent on the plasterwork around the stage. The third picture features the only existing image of the Music Hall's original chandelier, though obscured by its own light. A pattern of painted stars and moons is also visible on the dome above. Finally, the fourth photograph shows dormers and a cupola on the roof, which have since been removed from the building's exterior.

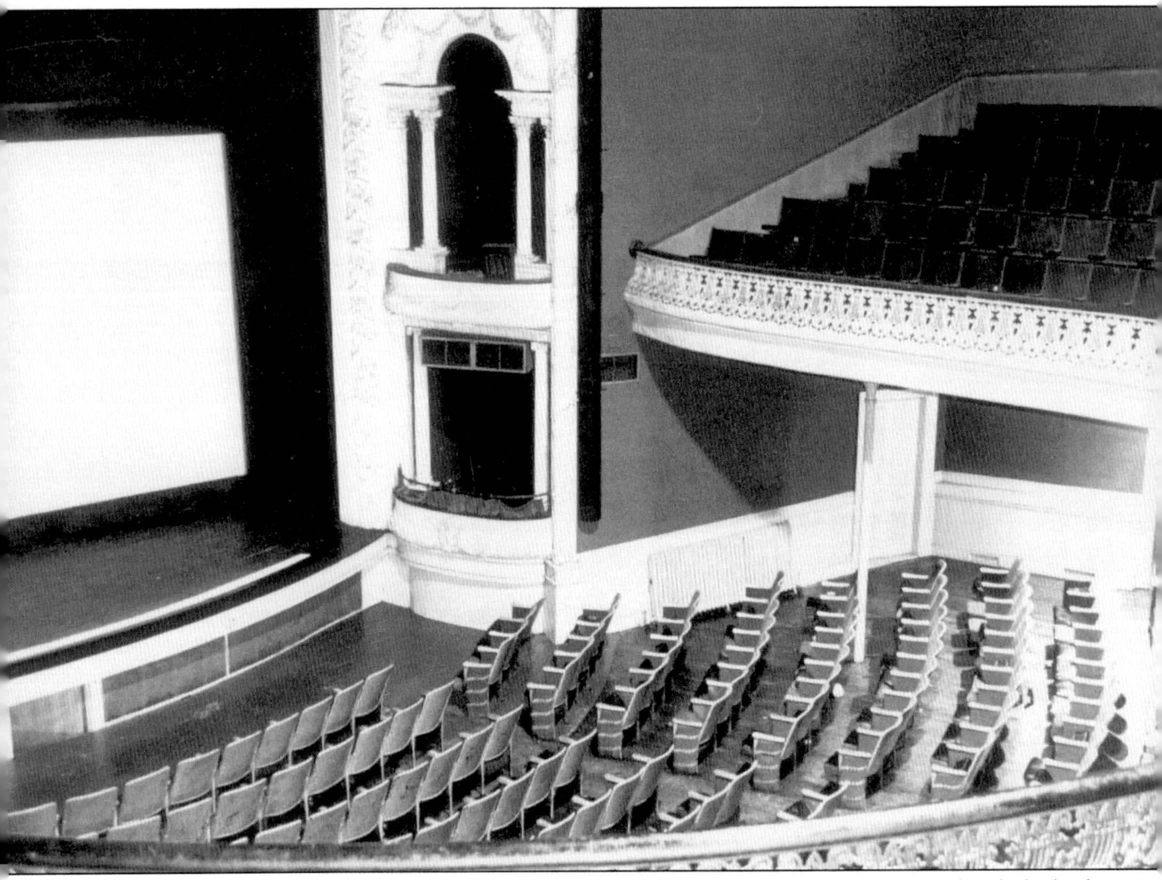

In an ambitious string of renovations, Guy Tott and his management team retooled, refurbished, and reequipped the theater. They painted over the faded reds and flaking gold leaf and replaced the old wooden seats with new ones of modern design. Clearly preparing the building for a competitive future in the movie business, Tott installed the biggest indoor movie screen in town and bought a whole suite of cutting-edge projection equipment.

The Music Hall's original, twin, 35-mm projector heads were built in the 1940s by Brenkert, a company with an enduring reputation for producing quality projection machines. The BX-100 model, shown here, is well known for remaining rock steady after years of play. (Courtesy of Ralph Morang.)

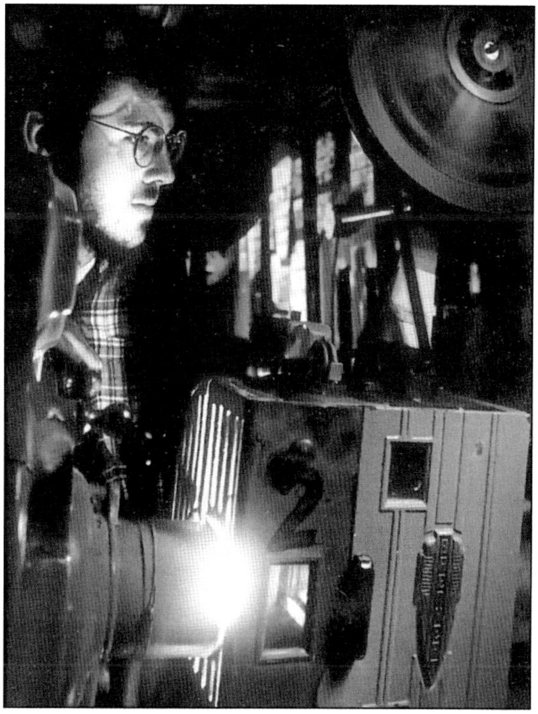

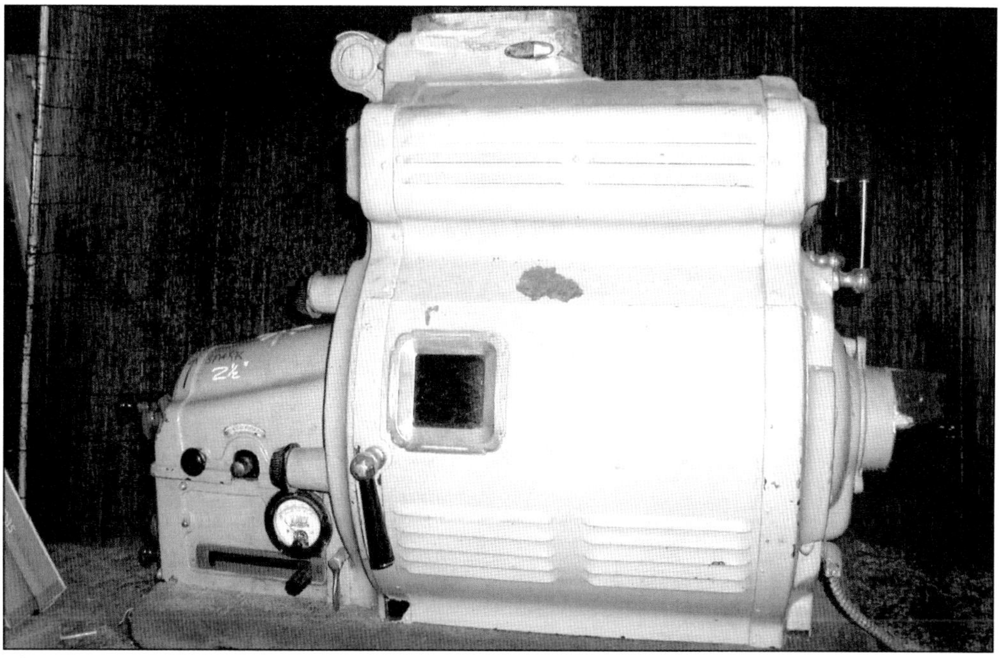

The carbon-arc lamp houses were also built by Brenkert. A chemical reaction between rods burned at very high temperatures resulted in a bright spark of light that was reflected through the projector heads and thrown 60 feet to the big screen. A motor inside the machine was timed to keep the rods just barely touching as they burned down. Designed to contain a potential explosion if the timing failed, these lamp houses were built like battleships. (Courtesy of Chris Smith.)

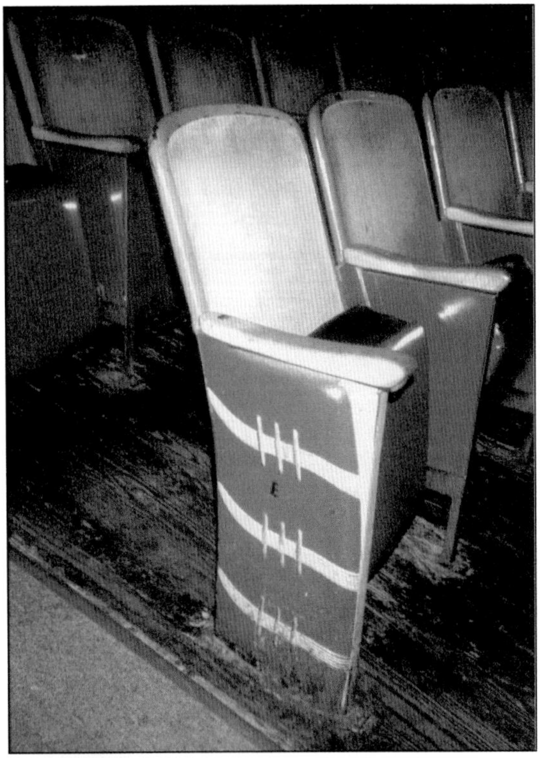

Where 1,200 wooden seats were removed, only 900 new ones were installed. The new seats were far more spacious, cushiony, and generally more comfortable. Their sleek painted metal frames included electric aisle lights.

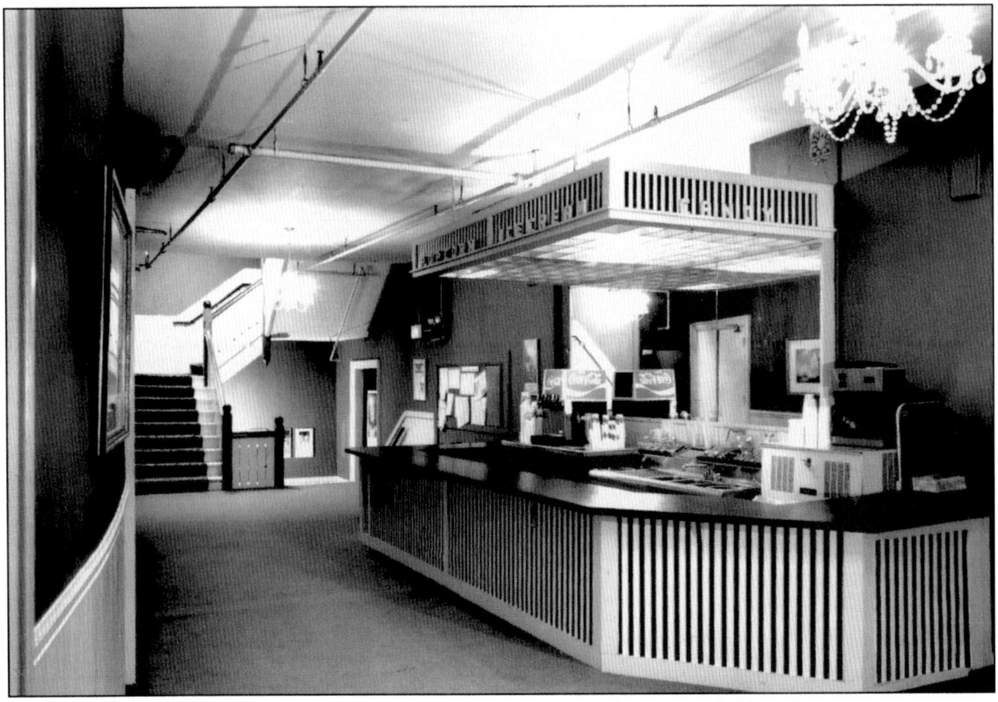

A new, permanent concession stand was constructed in the upper lobby, featuring a popcorn machine and a fully stocked ice-cream freezer. The soda fountain featured separate pumps for a variety of sundae toppings. (Courtesy of George Barker.)

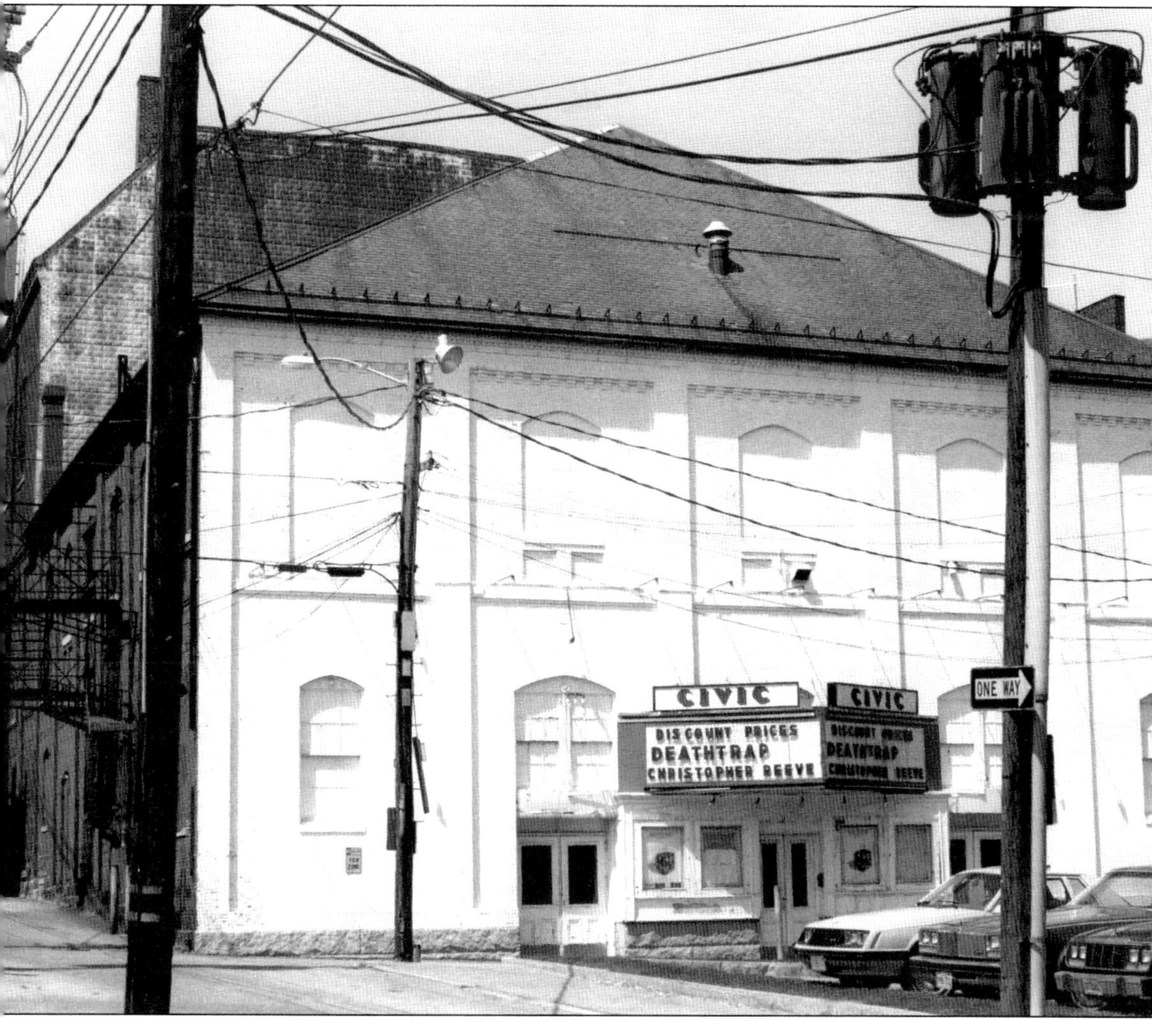

The smaller hanging Portsmouth Theatre sign was replaced by a bank of oversized poster cases and the large, lit, and updatable Civic marquee. Clearly visible at many angles from Portsmouth's main streets, the sign remained a prominent feature of the building's face until the mid-1980s. (Courtesy of the Portsmouth Athenaeum.)

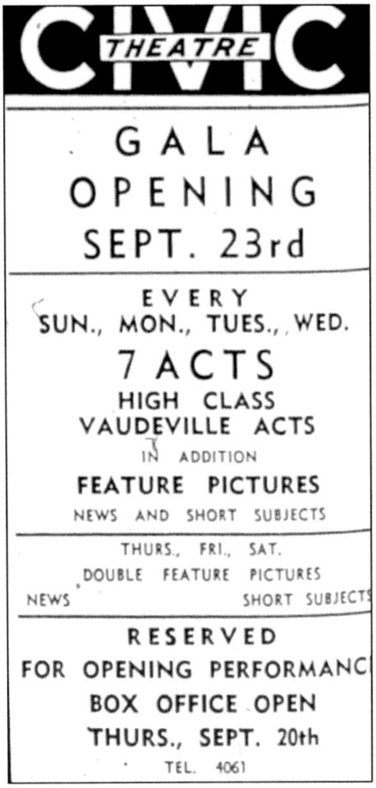

CIVIC THEATRE

GALA
OPENING
SEPT. 23rd

EVERY
SUN., MON., TUES., WED.
7 ACTS
HIGH CLASS
VAUDEVILLE ACTS
IN ADDITION
FEATURE PICTURES
NEWS AND SHORT SUBJECTS

THURS., FRI., SAT.
DOUBLE FEATURE PICTURES
NEWS SHORT SUBJECTS

RESERVED
FOR OPENING PERFORMANC
BOX OFFICE OPEN
THURS., SEPT. 20th
TEL. 4061

The theater reopened on Sunday, September 23, 1945, as the Civic Theatre, with daily performances on the stage and screen and a variety of attractions for all ages. On most days, the shows and screenings would start in the early afternoon and continue in an unbroken cycle until closing time, late at night. Newsreels and short subjects were screened between the live acts and the night's feature film. The decline of vaudeville's popularity started at about the time that movies got top billing in newspaper ads.

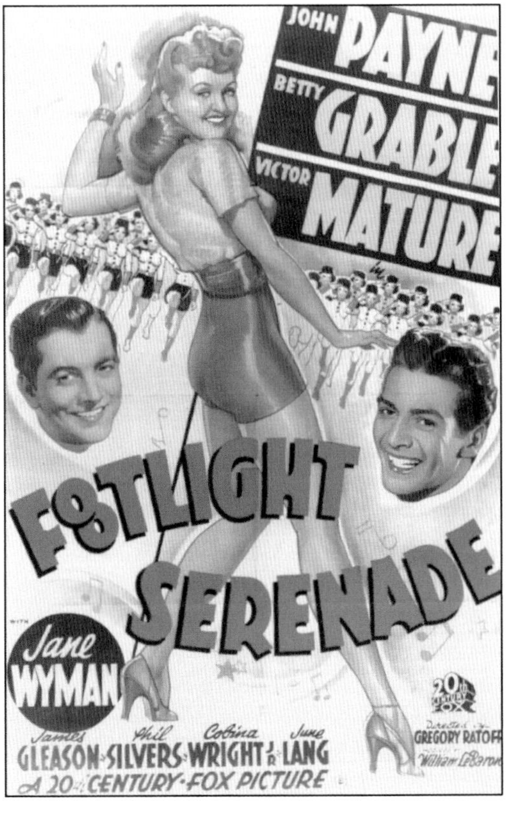

The Civic Theatre's opening feature was a something-for-everyone Hollywood hit. The musical comedy-romance *Footlight Serenade*, starring Betty Grable, one of cinema's hottest performers of the time, marks the theater's Phoenix-like transition from a shuttered old hull to the happening place in town.

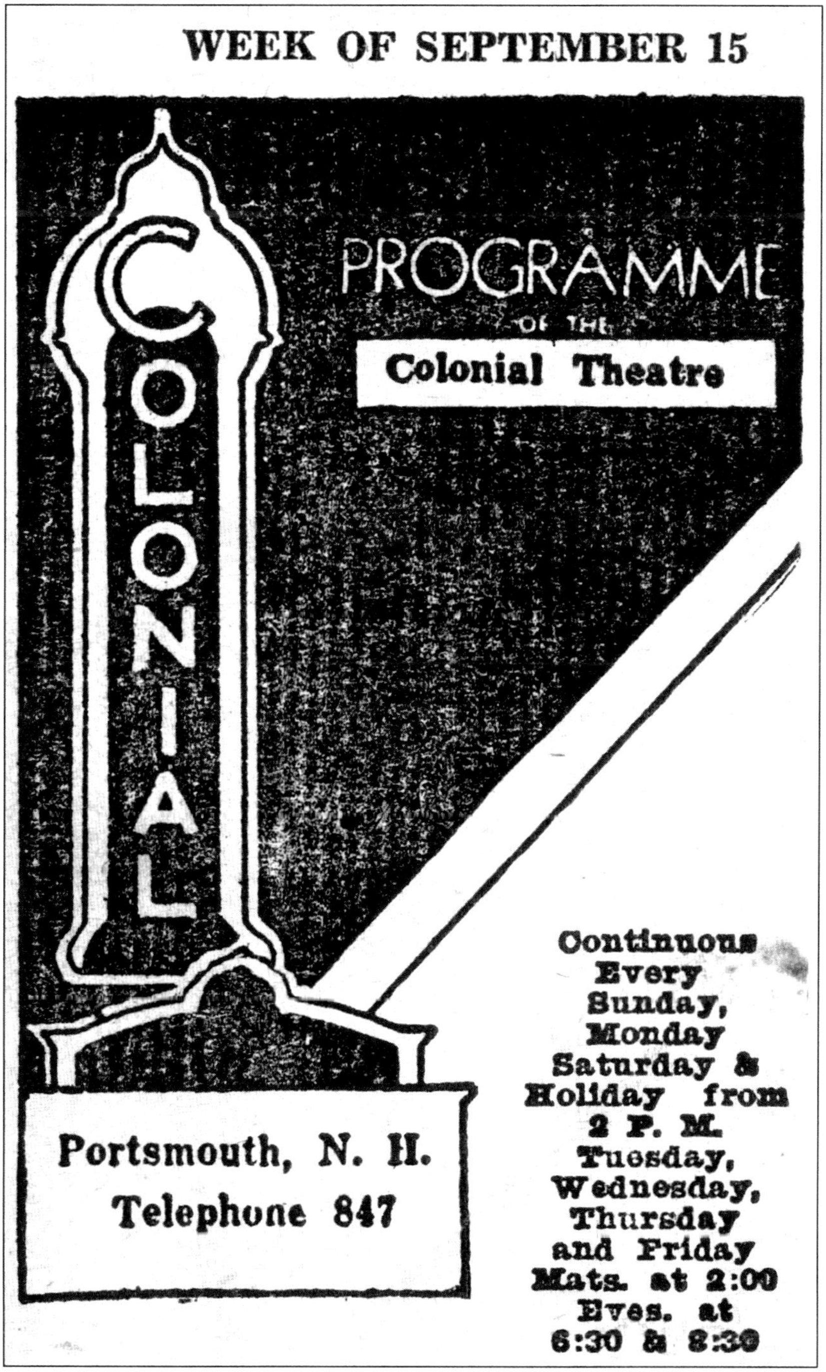

Guy Tott and his manager, Tony Cassal, planned an grand program of first-run features, but found their efforts hampered by Paramount Pictures, which owned both the nearby Arcadia Theatre and the Colonial, in Market Square. This *c.* 1946 promotional program from the Colonial features the popular film noir *Strange Love of Martha Ivers*, starring Barbara Stanwyk and Kirk Douglas, a Paramount first-run release that would only ever play at a Paramount-owned theater. (Courtesy of the Harbor Arts Museum and the Richard Smith Collection.)

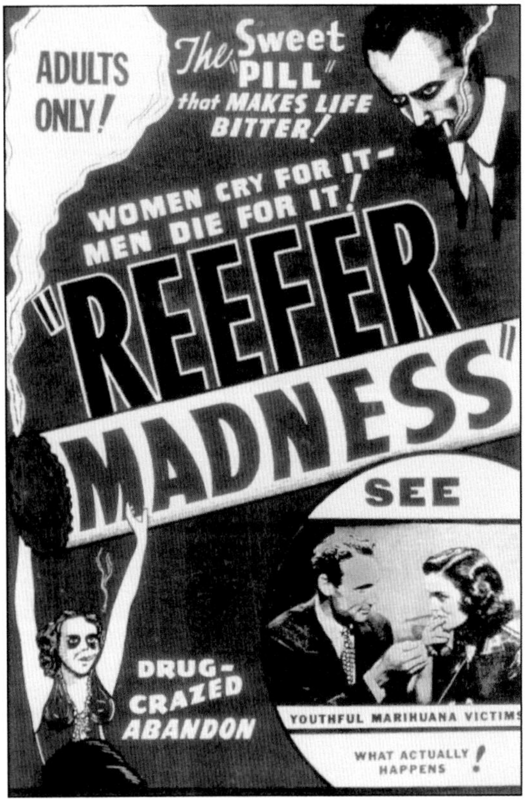

In a fairly obvious attempt to catch the attention of a new audience, the Civic booked the classic (yes, even in 1947) *Reefer Madness*. Originally released in the late 1930s as an educational reel titled *Tell Your Children*, the film rapidly achieved a cult status with the hipper, more artistic, beatnik contingent of the day. The theater was ordered closed for the week by city officials.

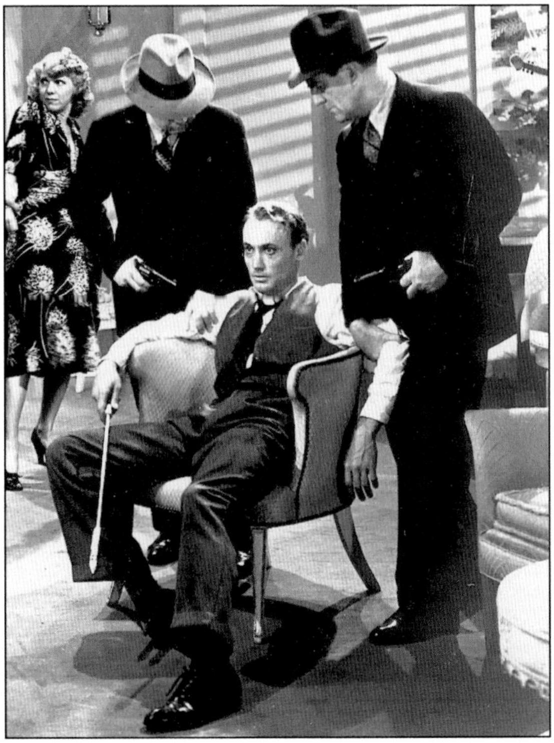

In this terrifically ironic scene from the film, an entertainment seeker is put under the thumb of "the Man." After only two years, Guy Tott became sick of all the stress, gave up, and leased the building to successful New England movie magnate E.M. Loew.

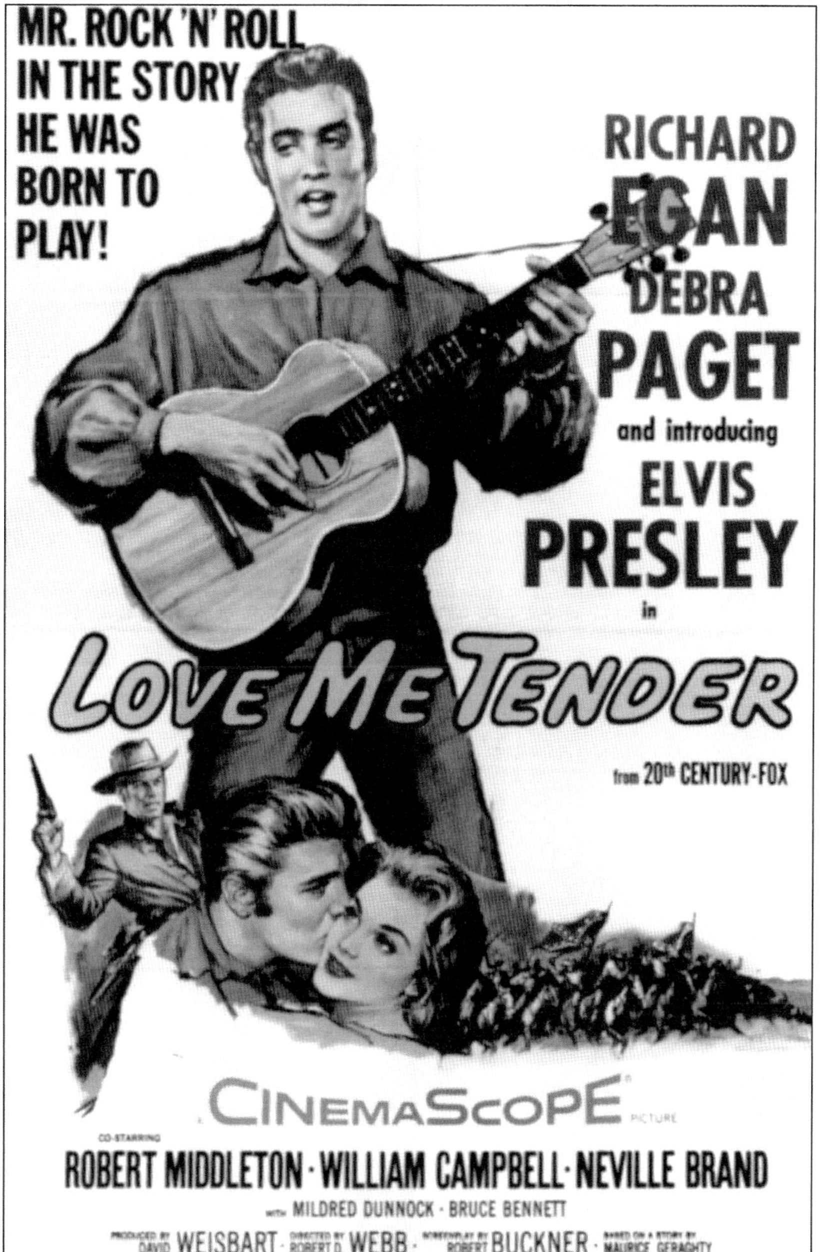

Elias Moishe Loew sailed to the new world as a 13-year-old in 1911. He worked in Boston-area movie theaters in many capacities before founding his own chain of theaters that would eventually span all of New England. Recognizing the potential of the Civic and taking full advantage of the recent upgrades, he used the superior buying power of his chain (and some recent antitrust action against the big producer-distributors such as Paramount) to secure the newest pictures for the bigger and more luxurious house in town. With the latest releases, such as *Love Me Tender*, the comfiest seats, and the biggest screen in town, Loew was able to generate ticket lines that stretched around the block. The transition to a full-time, first-run film program was made.

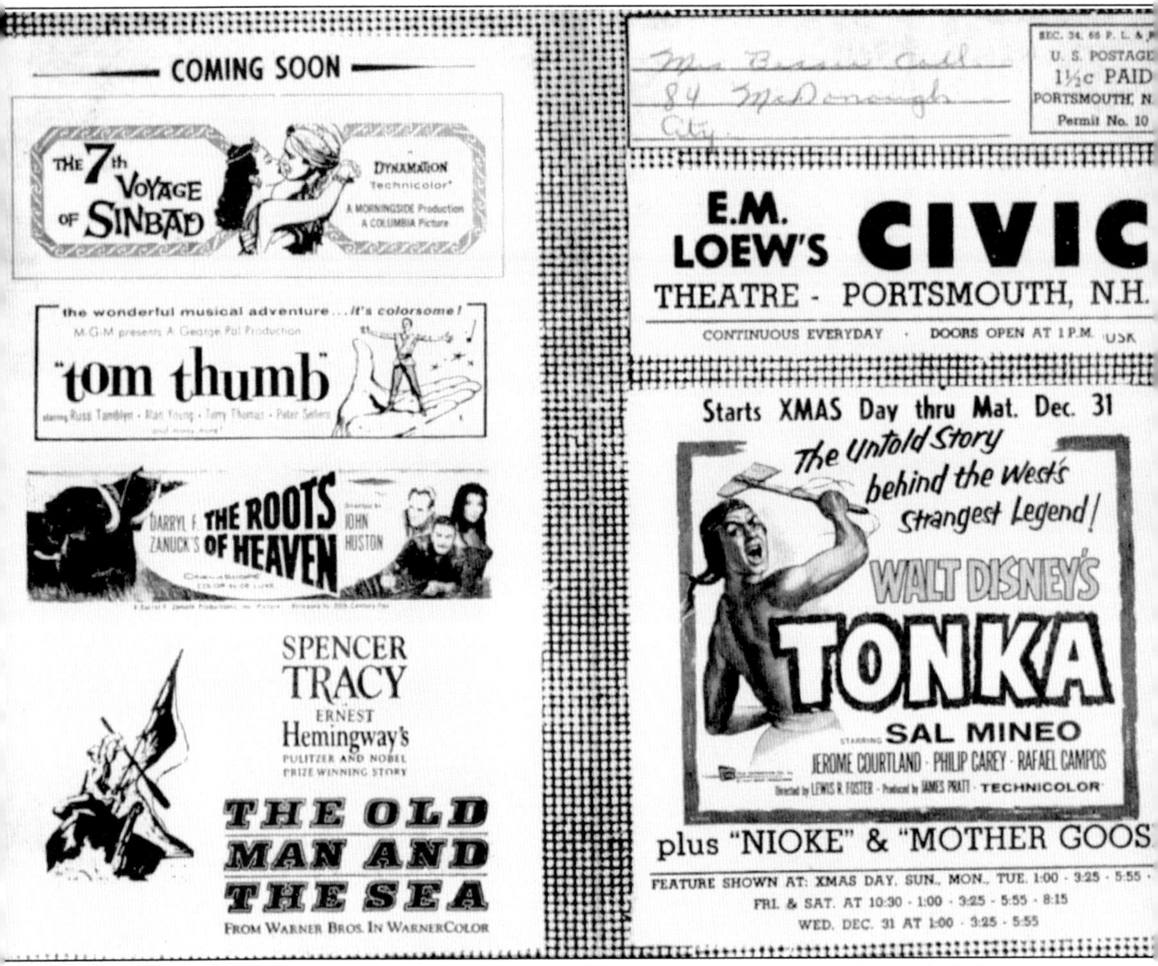

All new releases, these titles advertised in a 1958 promotional movie mailer included romances, adventures, family fare, and intellectual films—representing attractions for almost every audience in town. All the best and latest that Hollywood had to offer was to be seen at E.M. Loew's Civic. The Olympia, in the nearby Franklin Block, having gained some disrepute with its adult programming, closed its doors at this time. In 1963, Paramount gave in to the competition and sold both its Portsmouth theaters. The Arcadia was shuttered and its equipment sold off. Loew purchased the Colonial (only two blocks away from the Civic), in Market Square. (Courtesy of the Harbor Arts Museum and the Richard Smith Collection.)

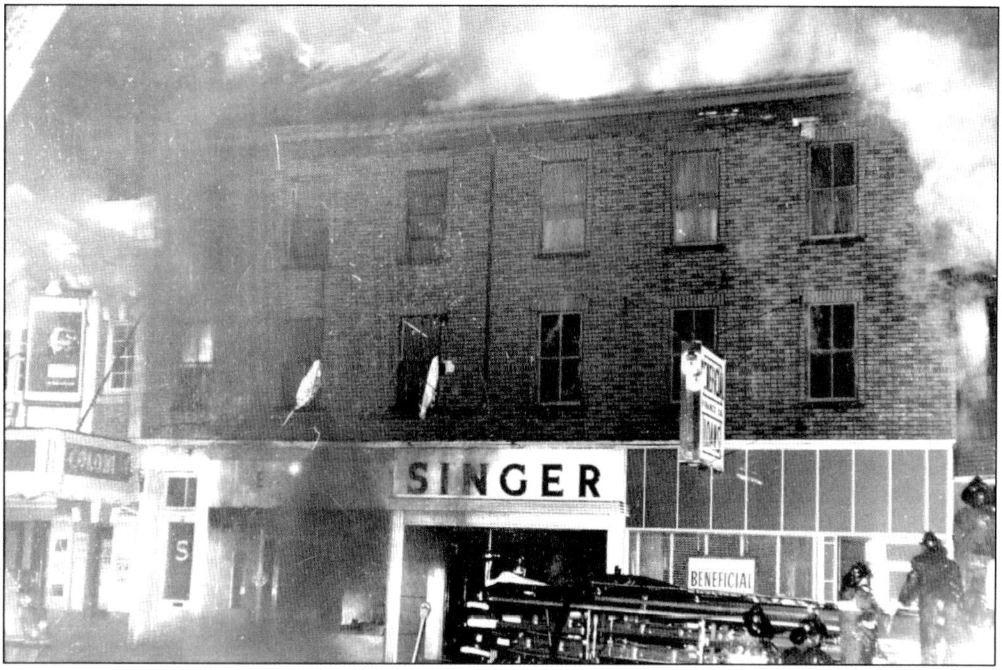

In 1964, an unexplained fire razed the Singer Sewing Machine store and barbershop adjacent to the Colonial, in Market Square. The Colonial marquee can be seen at left. The posters displayed indicate that at this time Loew was still booking the previous year's movies for the Colonial. (Courtesy of the Portsmouth Athenaeum.)

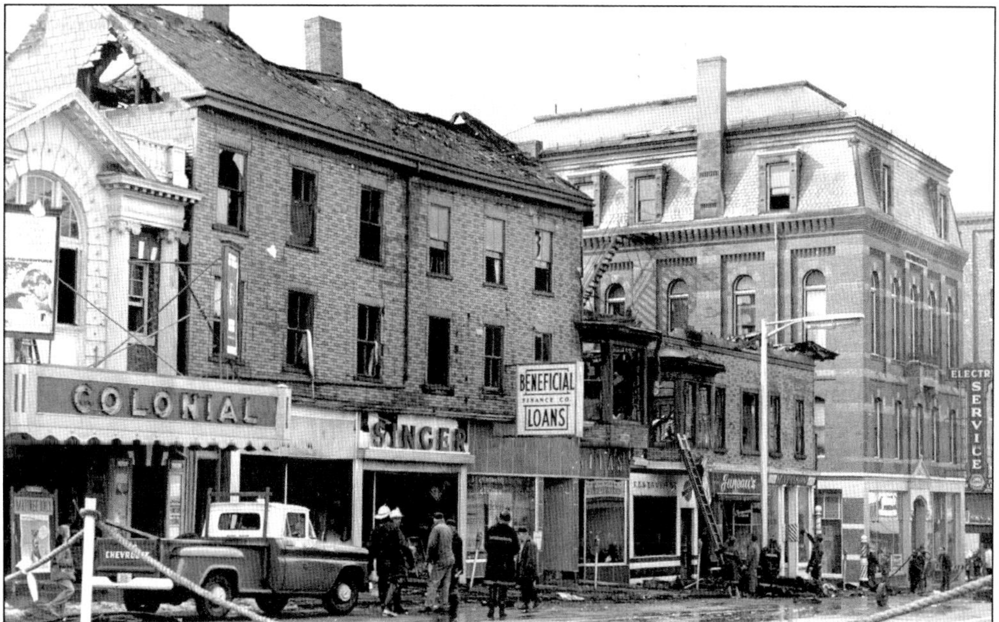

Though the Colonial itself was miraculously untouched by the flames, its seats and drapes smelled terribly of smoke and the screen showed visible smoke damage. Although films continued to be shown for some time, it was clear that some renovation was needed. (Courtesy of the Portsmouth Athenaeum.)

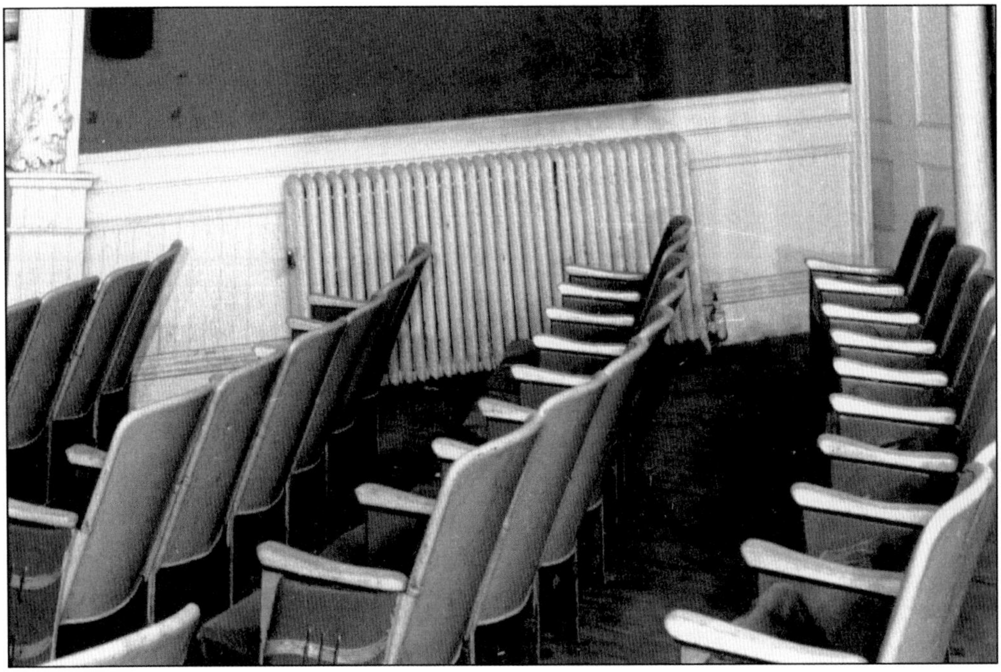

The winter of 1967 was cold. The Civic's auditorium was not just cavernous but also positively drafty. The aging, forced-steam heating system proved not only dreadfully inadequate to provide customer comfort but also expensive beyond the theater's ability to sell tickets. (Courtesy of the Harbor Arts Museum and the Richard Smith Collection.)

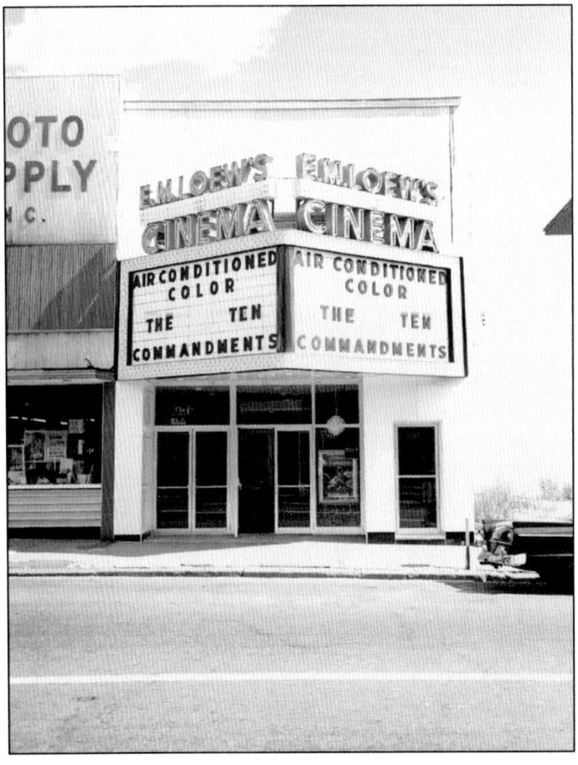

The Colonial, around the corner, was in clear need of restoration but had the advantages of Market Square–front property, as well as a smaller auditorium, which more closely matched the audience numbers of the time. Loew green-lighted a full overhaul of the Colonial, including the addition of a new marquee, which would light Market Square for years to come. (Courtesy of the Portsmouth Athenaeum.)

All of the Colonial's smelly old seats were torn out and transferred to the Civic's balcony. The original benches, which had been there since the Music Hall's opening day, were removed after nearly a century of service. (Courtesy of Larry Lariviere.)

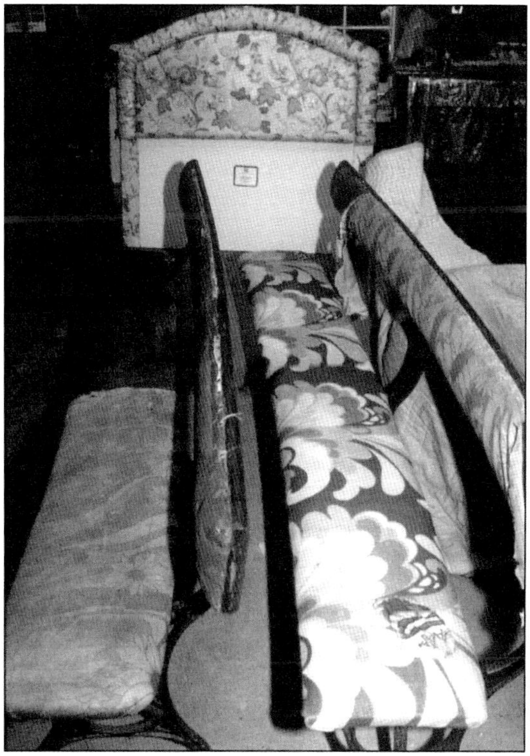

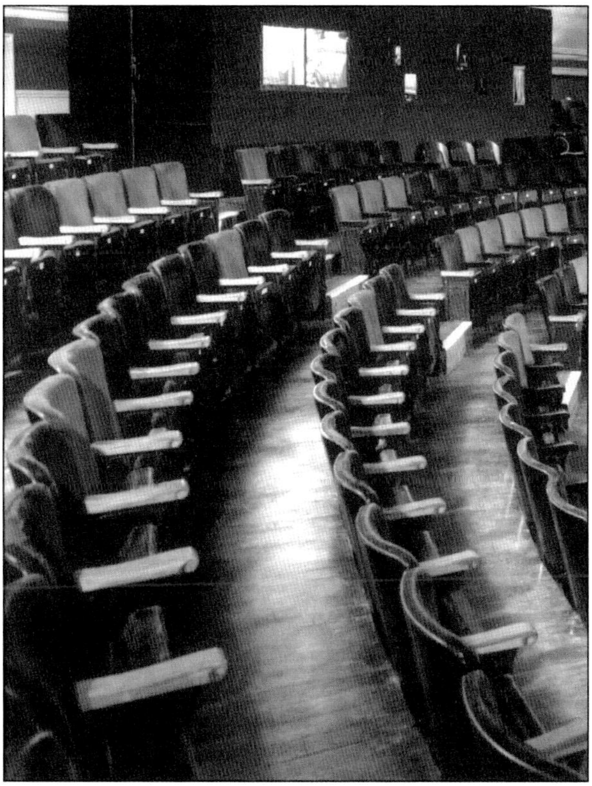

Although the large cast-iron C on the sides of the Colonial's old seats suited the Civic, they posed something of a conundrum to folks later entering the balcony when the name was changed back to the Music Hall. These hand-me-down rows remained in the upstairs sections for more than 30 years. In 1999, all the seating in the house was once again replaced and made uniform for the first time between the balcony and orchestra sections.(Courtesy of George Barker.)

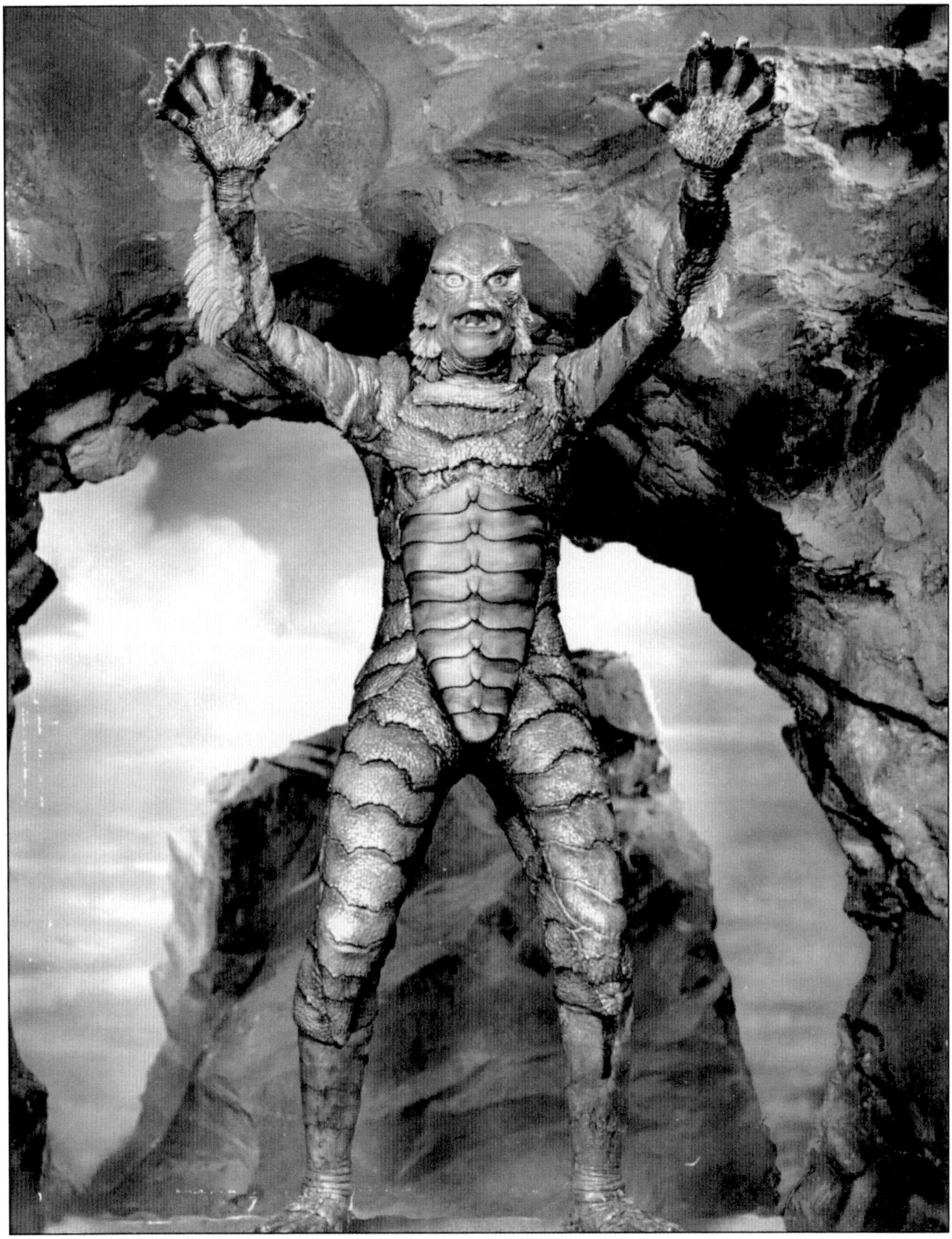

The Civic's unfortunate, new hand-me-down status applied to the movie programming as well. All of Hollywood's latest and biggest hits were played at the newly refurbished Colonial. The Civic got tossed an occasional bone from the table but generally became known as the place to find older B movies and horror films. Parents who wanted to run errands downtown would pay the quarter and leave the kids for the afternoon. In efforts to save money wherever possible, promotional advertisements in the papers were made smaller, and direct mail campaigns were discontinued completely. As the theater's visibility to the community dwindled, so did the audiences, and a tragic downward spiral was established.

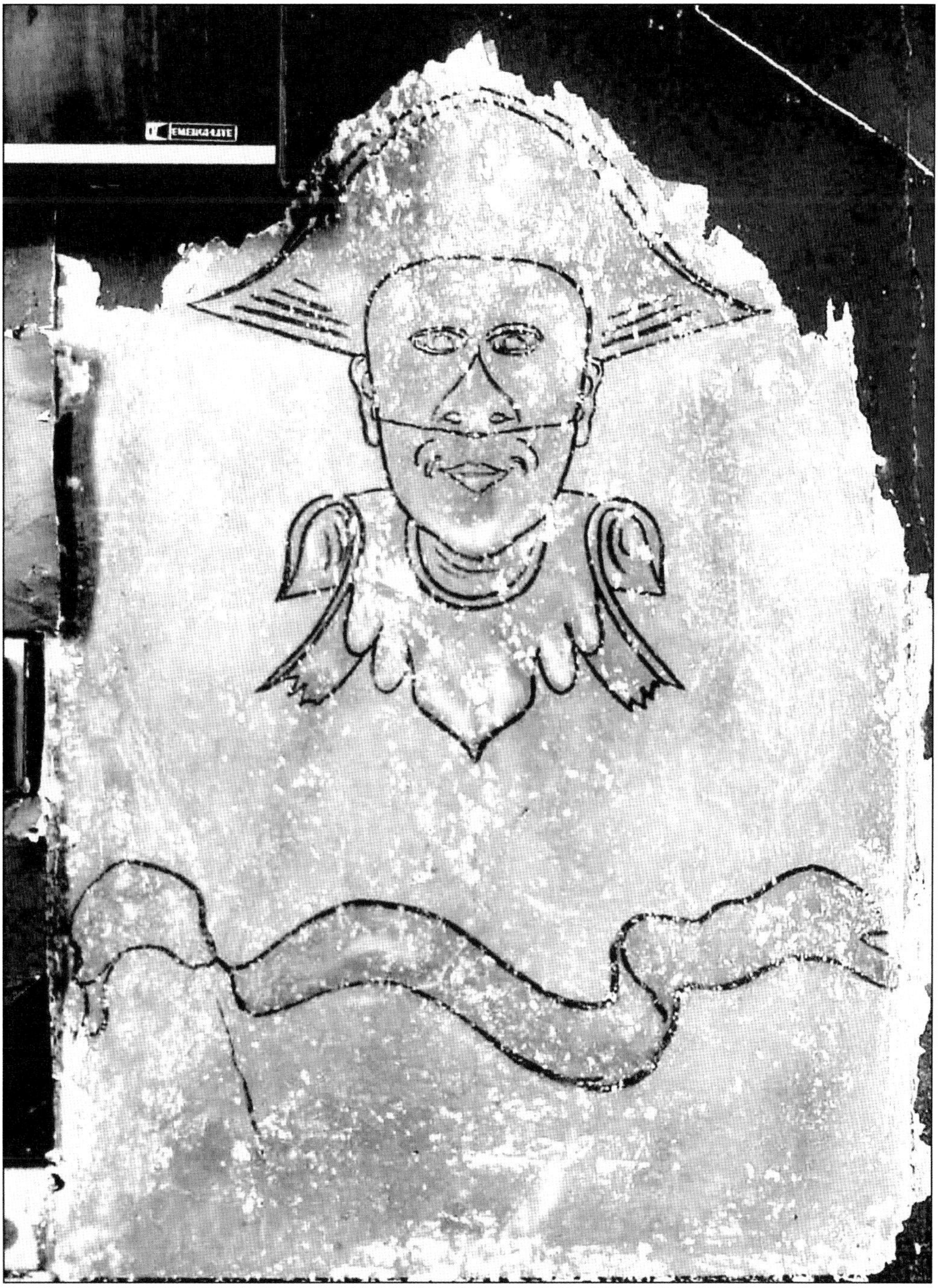

This portrait of a masked man in Colonial garb was painted by an unknown artist on the wall of the lower lobby stairs. Known now only as "the Phantom," it was papered over and remained hidden for 30 years before being discovered by Music Hall employee Dan Hicks as he was preparing the area for repainting. (Courtesy of Rebecca Taylor.)

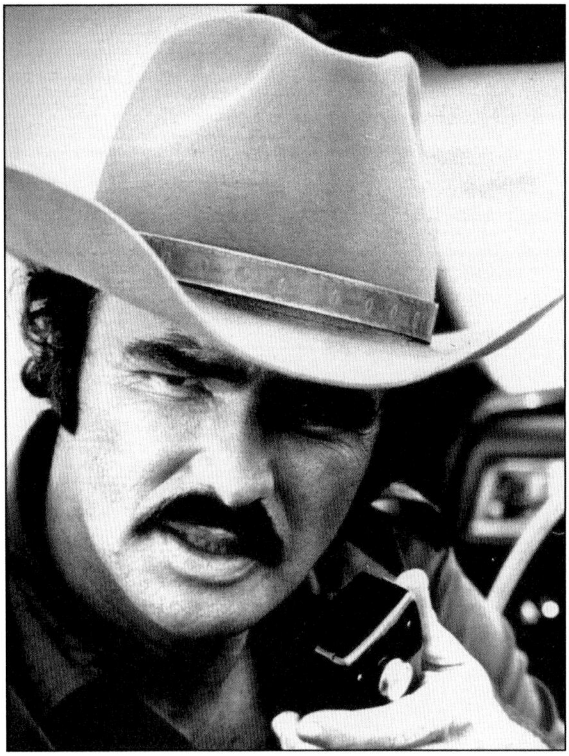

A whole new threat to the downtown film business arrived in the late 1970s with the introduction of multiplex theaters and the summer blockbuster phenomenon. Located a short drive away, but out of the central Market Square area, the Jerry Lewis Cinema, on Lafayette Road, was the first two-screen theater in town. Another cinema with eight screens was opened later at the nearby Newington Mall. With painless parking and fully advanced projection and sound technology, the new cinemas posed simply indomitable competition.

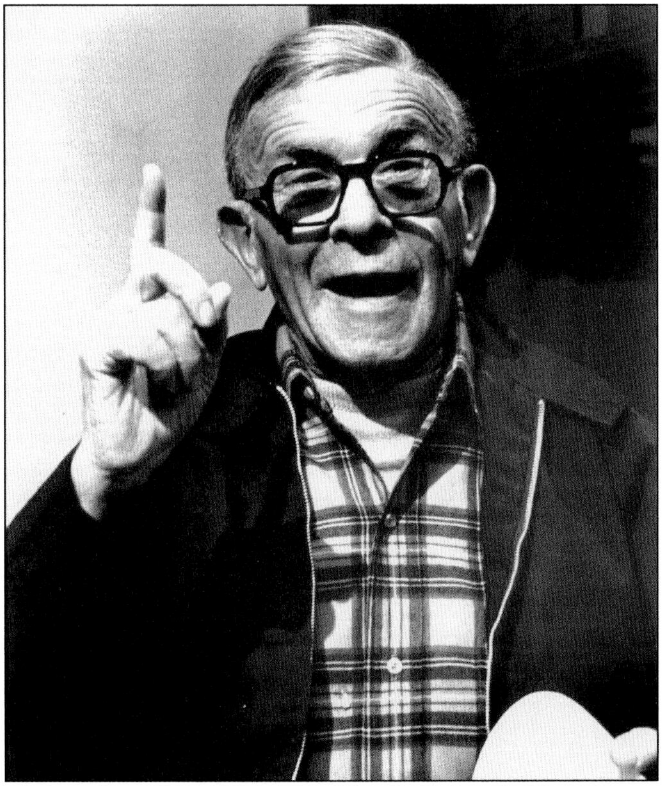

In 1978, the Music Hall's 100th birthday came and went with no apparent fanfare or celebration, only a double feature of two of the previous year's hits: *Smokey and the Bandit* and *Oh, God*. Apparently abandoning any hope of attracting mainstream audiences, but still hoping to hook the discount crowd, Loew's Civic offered double features for 75¢. Even when every other place in town sold tickets for $3 or $4, the scheme still failed to attract audiences large enough to pay the bills.

Losing money rapidly, and with no apparent means to viably compete with the new multiplex theaters, Loew sold both his Seacoast properties in 1982. The Colonial's auditorium, pictured here, was eventually torn down, and the front of the building was remodeled for business space. Loew's marquee, something of a local landmark, remained for dozens of years following the failure of the cinema. (Courtesy of the Portsmouth Athenaeum.)

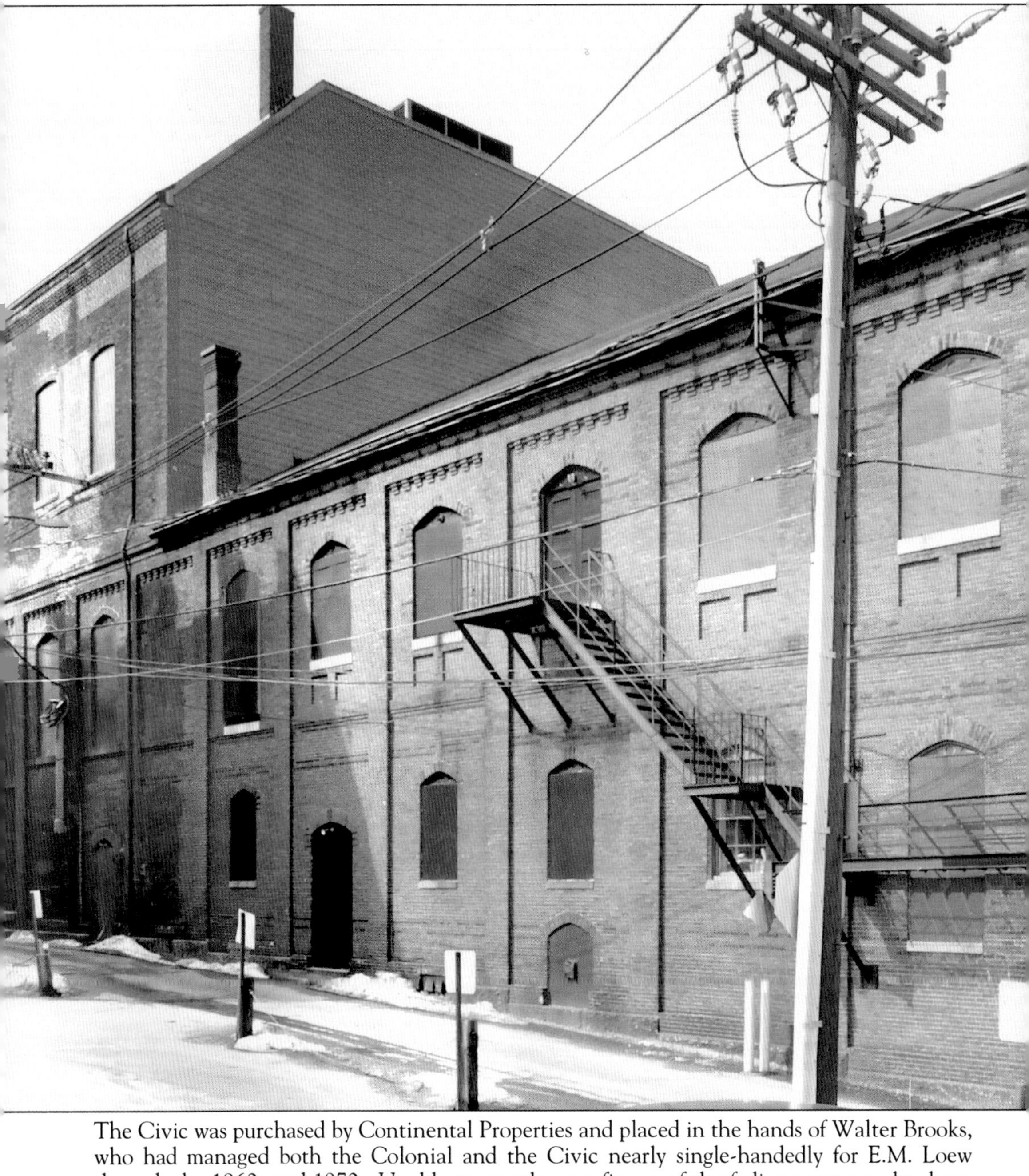

The Civic was purchased by Continental Properties and placed in the hands of Walter Brooks, who had managed both the Colonial and the Civic nearly single-handedly for E.M. Loew through the 1960s and 1970s. Unable to wrestle a profit out of the fading property, the doors closed in 1984, and Brooks left to spend his "retirement" at the Strand Cinema, 10 miles north in Dover. The building stood dormant and untended, its windows boarded over with plywood and its roof leaking unchecked. Sometime during this period, the interior dome's now antique and very valuable crystal chandelier was removed and sold to an unknown party, never to be seen again. (Courtesy of George Barker.)

Five

THE PORTSMOUTH MUSIC HALL 1982–1986

In the late 1970s and early 1980s, Portsmouth's downtown was undergoing a change. The local arts community showed noticeable growth in the number of local musicians, painters, and artisans who performed and exhibited around town. Downtown bars obtained cabaret licenses and presented live performances every night. In attempts to attract more business to and interest in the downtown area, many of the aging buildings received facelifts. New businesses moved in, and new organizations, such as Pro Portsmouth, started holding festivals in Market Square, initially as a showcase for all the local talent and craftspeople. Abandoned to the elements, the Music Hall and its early days of standing ovations and sold-out crowds were all but forgotten. Long years of hot summers, hard rains, and harsh winters had excised a terrible toll on the neglected old structure. Paint peeled from the face of the building. Water seeped through growing cracks into the marquee, rotting it from the inside out. On the building's dark interior, aging plaster cracked and fell. Mice nibbled at the hemp ropes and took up residence between the springs inside the seats. Even through this shabby mask of disrepair and decay, a few local business people could still see the Music Hall's potential, and recognizing the community's increasing demand for centrally located entertainment, they decided to take on the considerable chore of lighting it back up again.

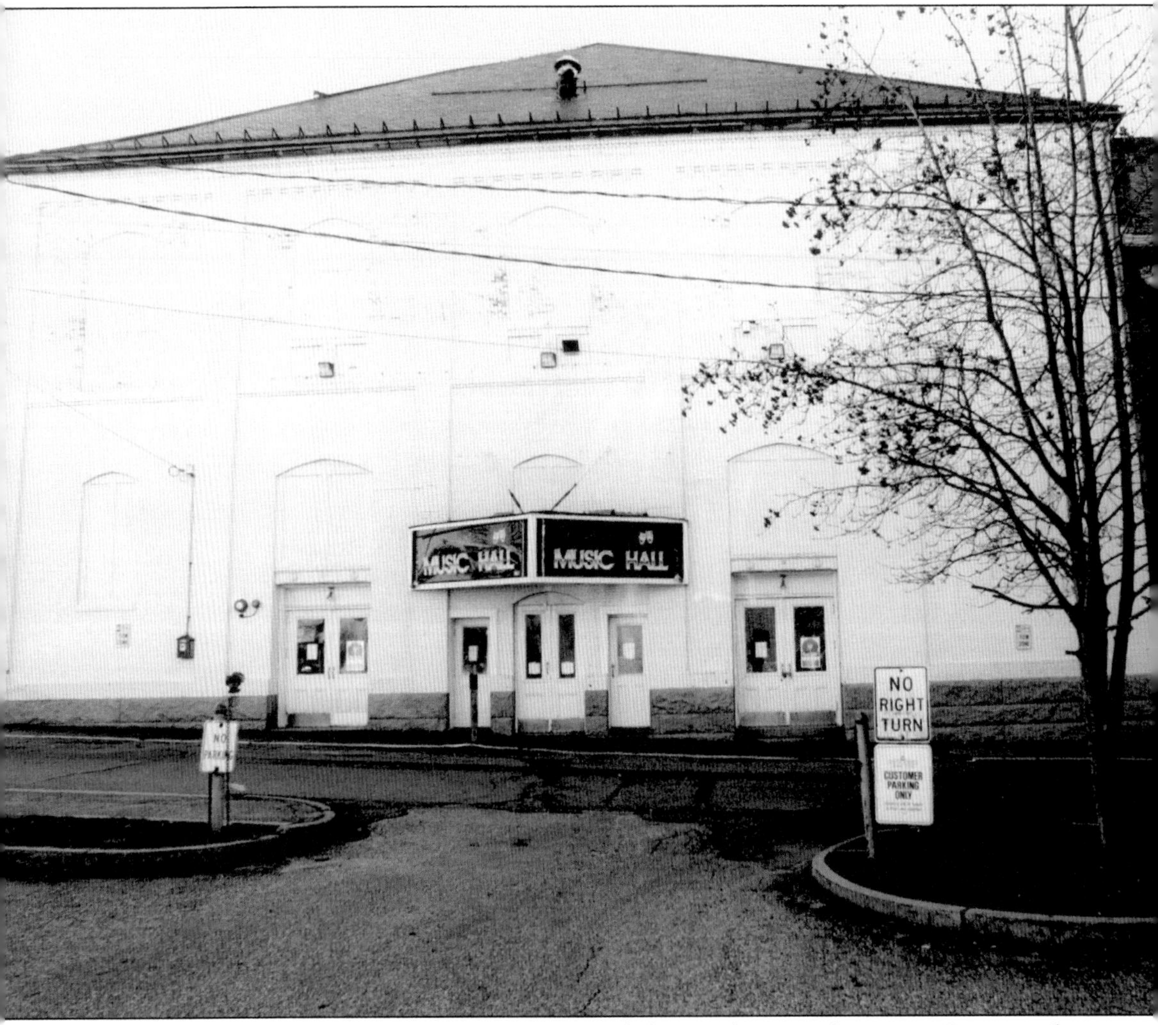

With an intention to reintroduce live music and theater shows to downtown Portsmouth, a small group led by Lewis Shaw bought the building and spent the summer of 1985 renovating it. While taking care to preserve the theater's ability to show films, the main efforts were directed at restoring the facility's capacity for live productions and making it presentable again to the public. The rotted poster cases were torn off the front of the building, and the weathered, long-broken Civic marquee was removed and replaced with a smaller, more discreet wooden one. In addition to restoring the Music Hall's facilities, Shaw's group also restored its original name. (Courtesy of George Barker.)

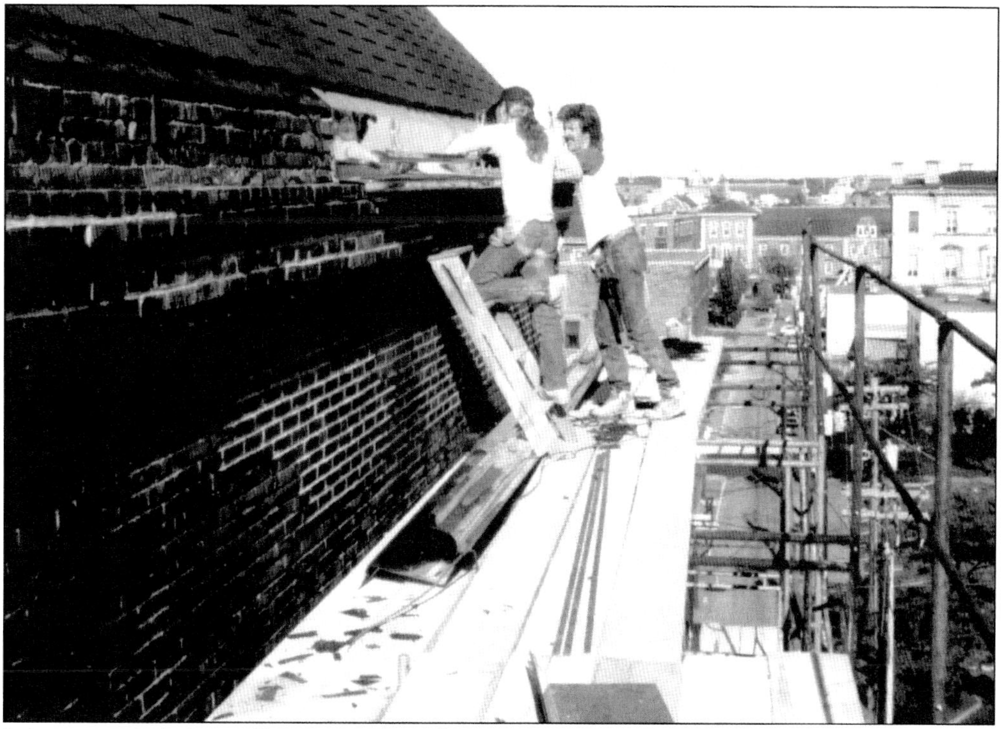
Laborers scaled the walls to complete the extensive work required to fix and replace the crumbling brick around the roofline. (Courtesy of George Barker.)

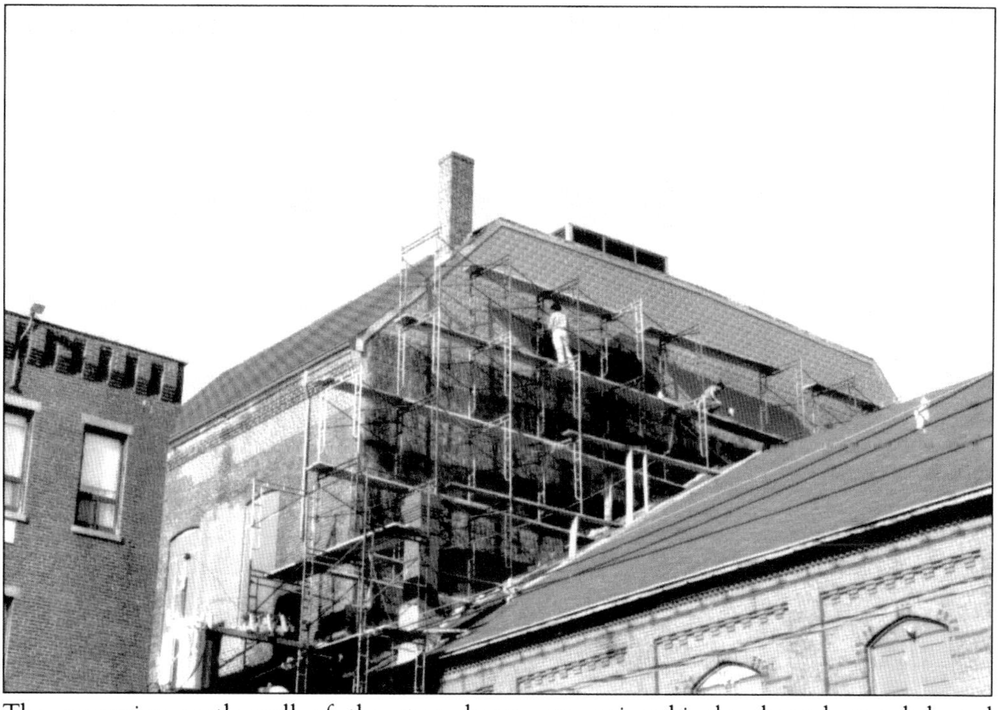
The expansive north wall of the stage house was painstakingly cleaned, mended, and weather-sealed. (Courtesy of George Barker.)

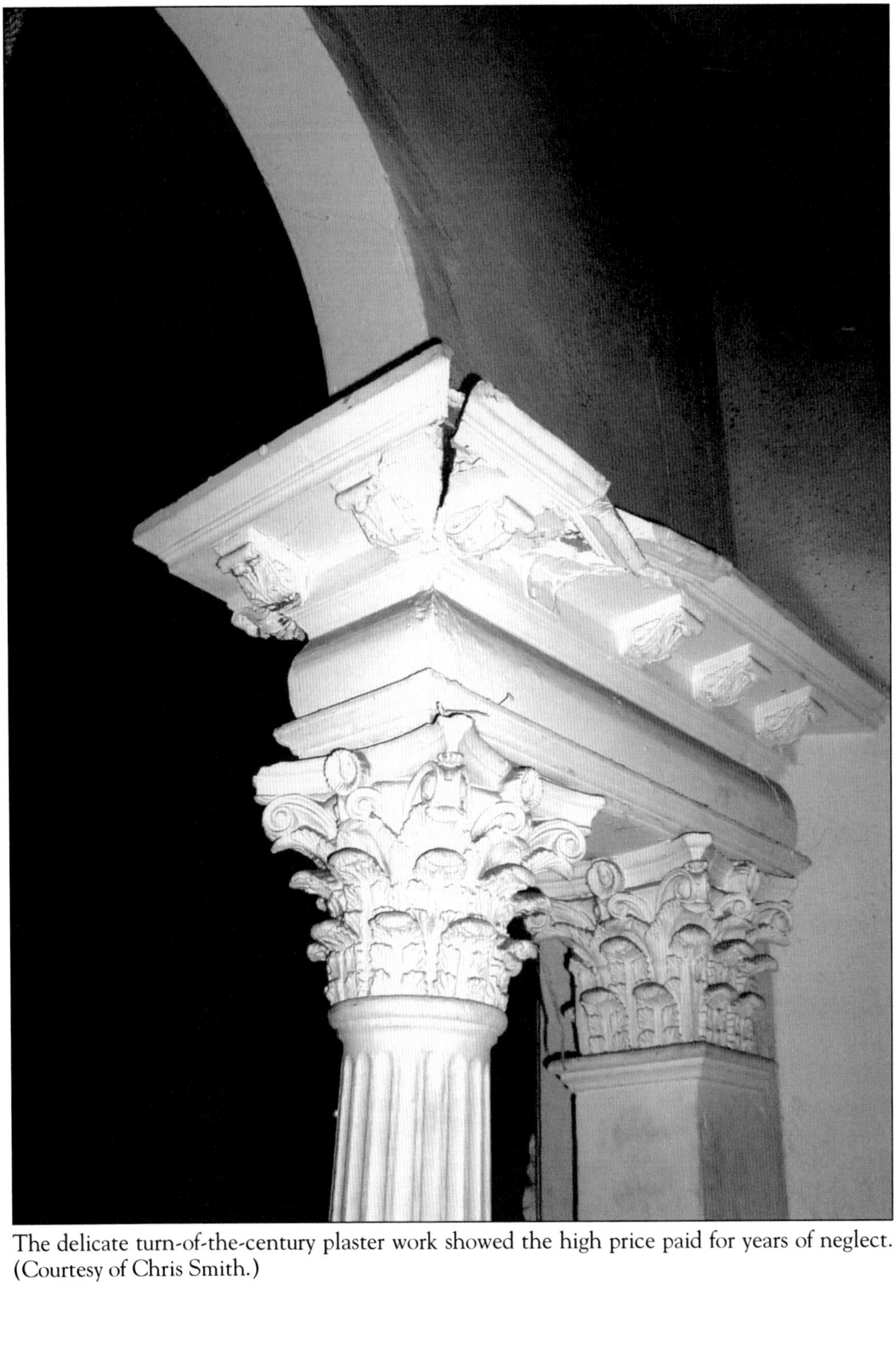

The delicate turn-of-the-century plaster work showed the high price paid for years of neglect. (Courtesy of Chris Smith.)

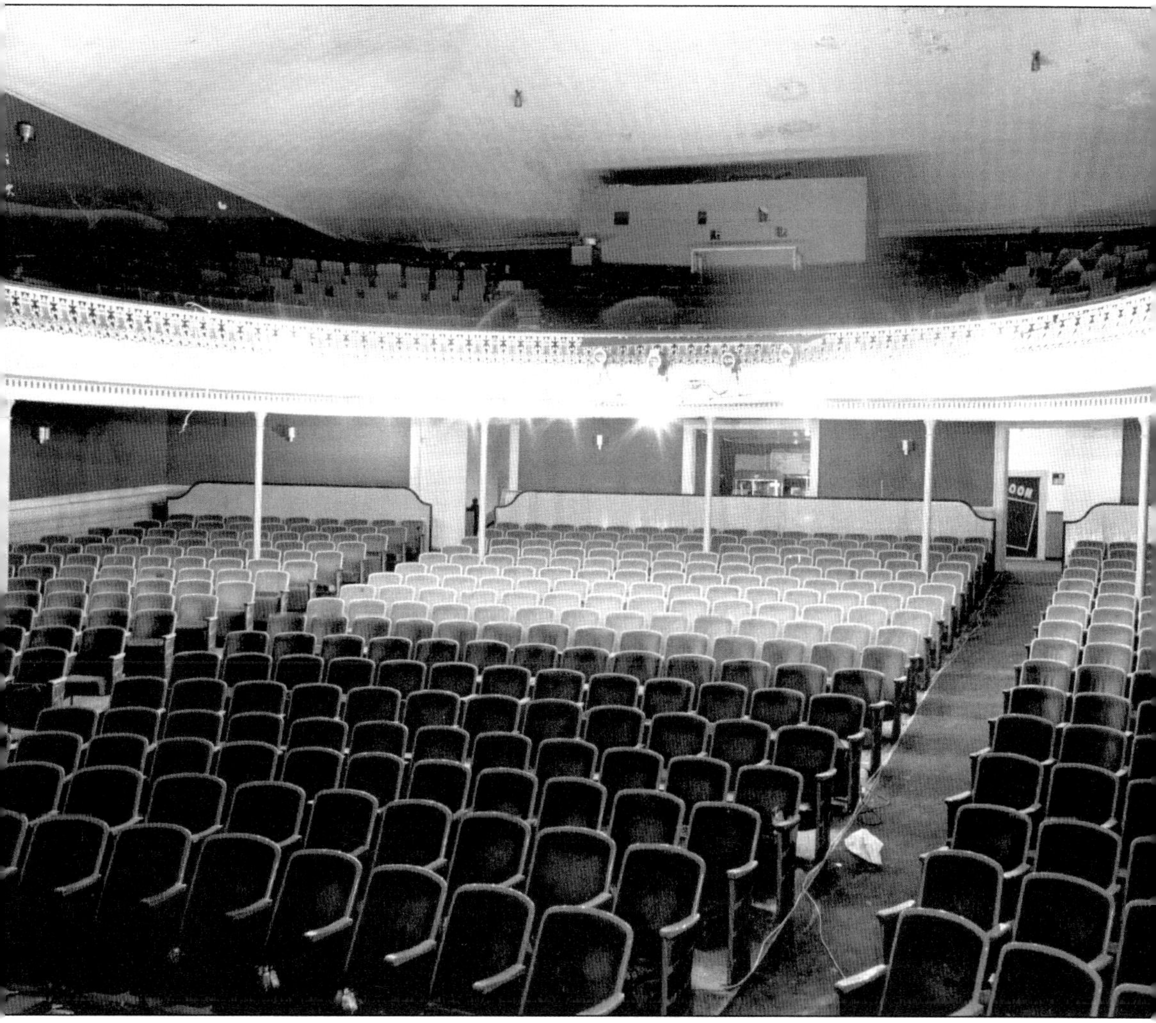

The plaster on the large dome ceiling had been heavily damaged by water and required some significant attention. The leaks had also spread down into the floor of the balcony, necessitating the temporary removal of gallery left seats to refinish the decayed, wooden floorboards. (Courtesy of George Barker.)

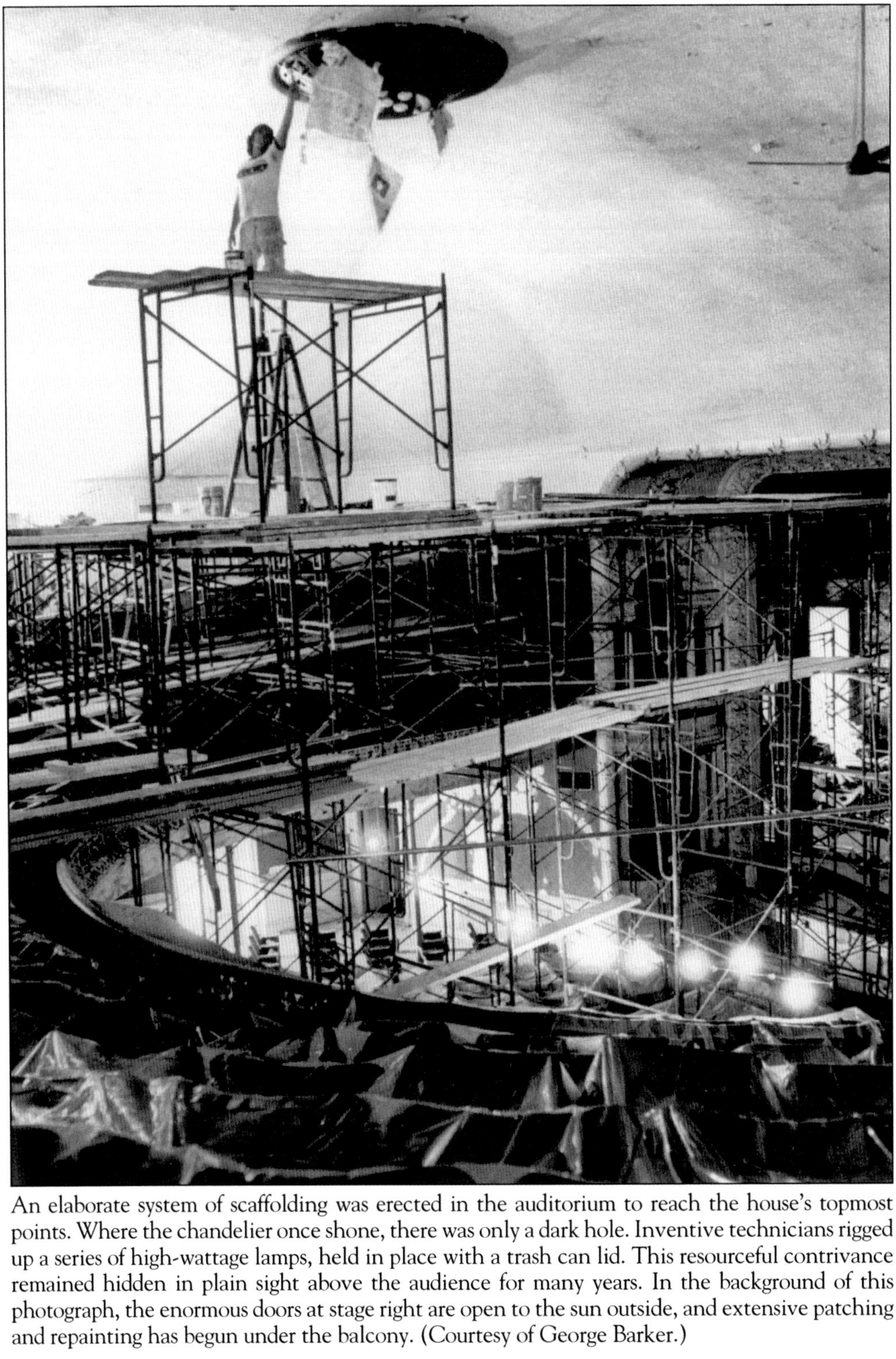

An elaborate system of scaffolding was erected in the auditorium to reach the house's topmost points. Where the chandelier once shone, there was only a dark hole. Inventive technicians rigged up a series of high-wattage lamps, held in place with a trash can lid. This resourceful contrivance remained hidden in plain sight above the audience for many years. In the background of this photograph, the enormous doors at stage right are open to the sun outside, and extensive patching and repainting has begun under the balcony. (Courtesy of George Barker.)

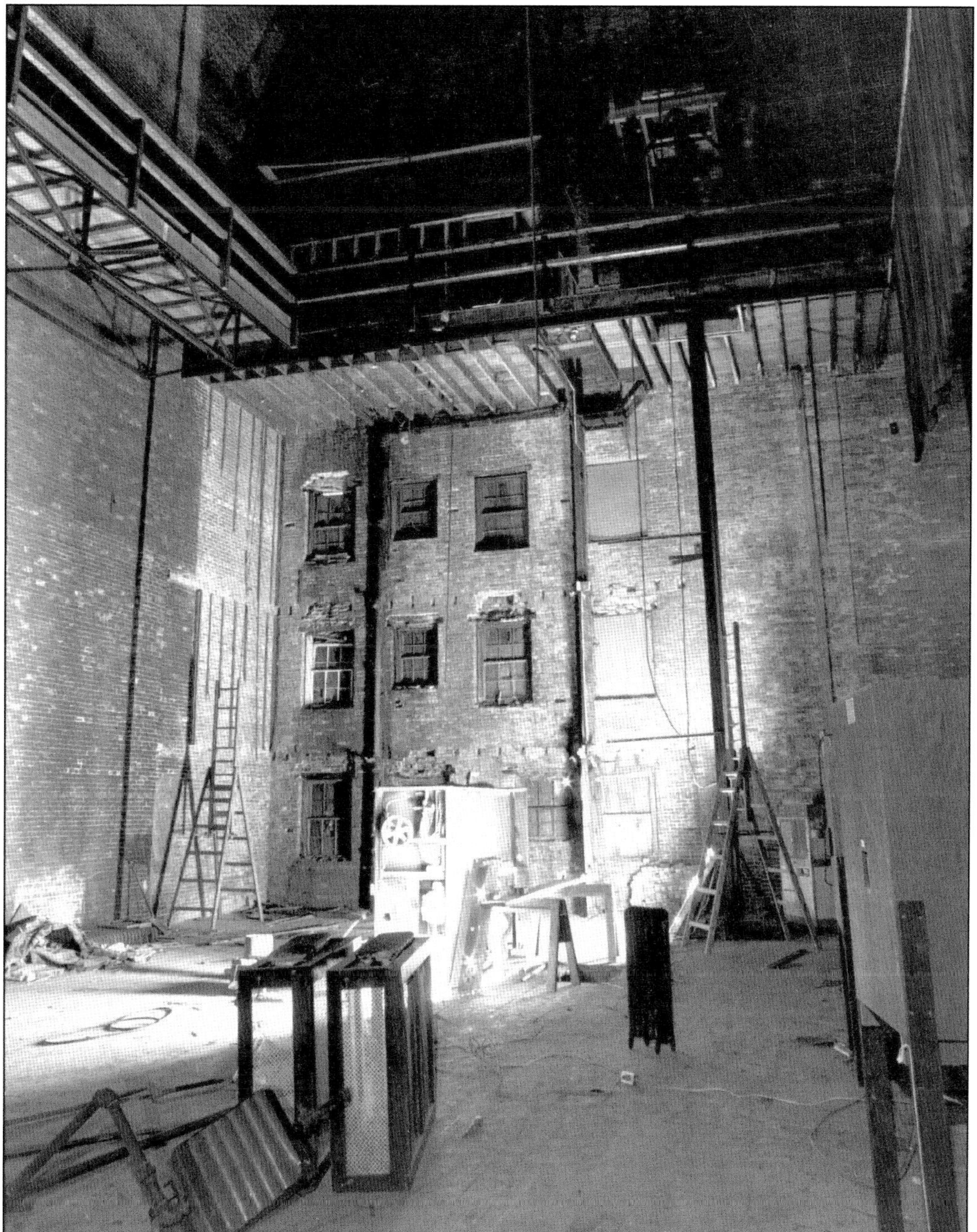

The original dressing rooms on stage left were found in a dangerous state of decrepitude. They were torn entirely out, and plans were drawn up for them to be rebuilt along the rear wall of the stage.

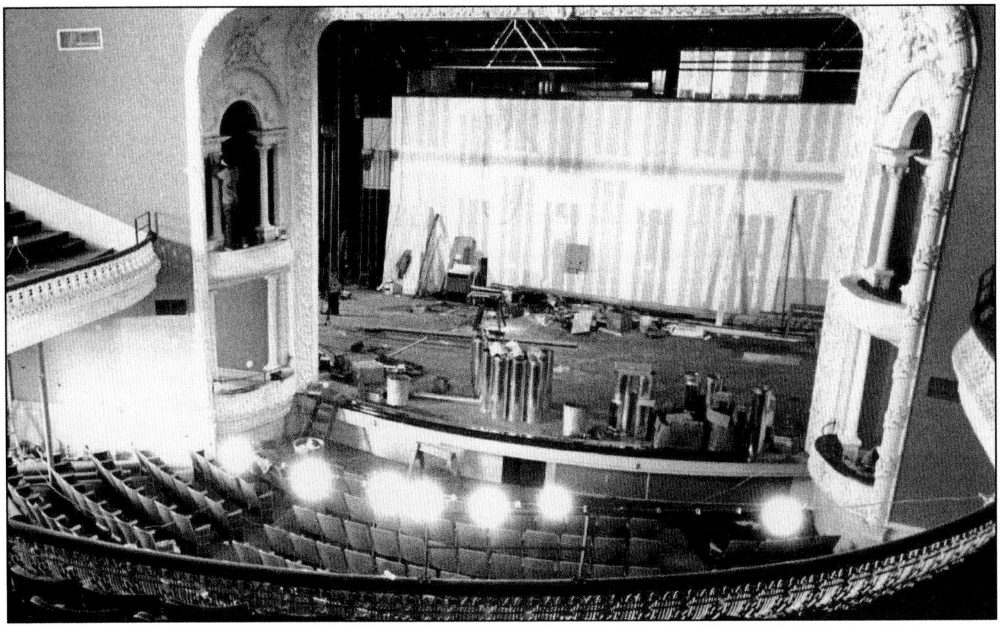

The new stage construction, seen here from the balcony as it was being built, would feature a production office, green room, and seven private dressing rooms on an upper level, with modern toilet and shower facilities below. Thought to be far more convenient and comfortable for the artists and crew, the new facility came at the cost of 15 feet of stage space, significantly restricting the area available for larger performances, such as opera, dance, and Broadway road shows. (Courtesy of George Barker.)

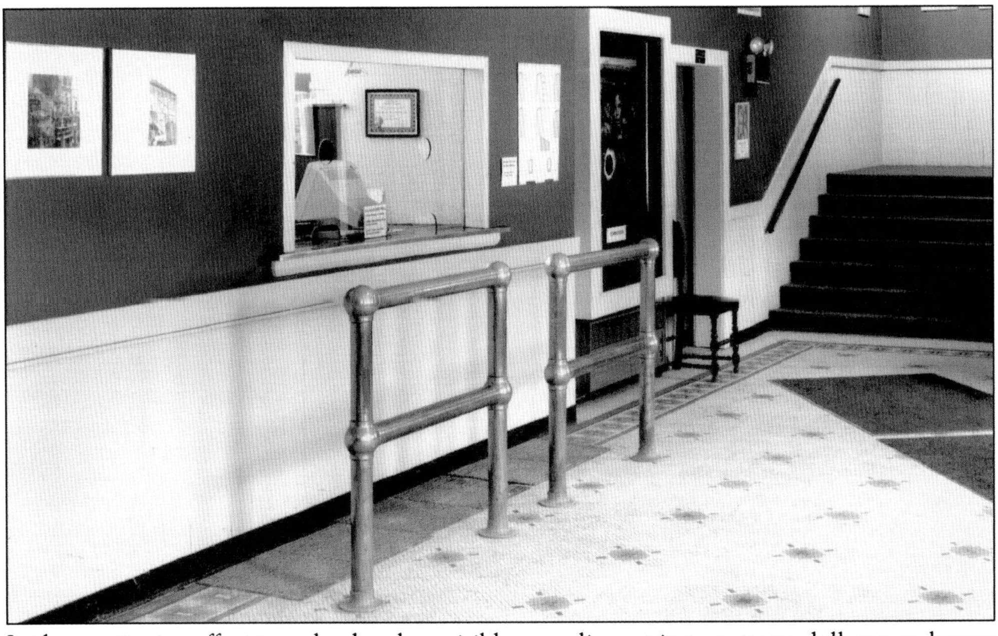

In the continuing effort to make the place visibly appealing again to patrons, dull orange-brown walls were repainted with a rich burgundy red. The century-old tile in the front lobby was scrubbed clean, and the brass rail at the box office was polished. Large oversized poster cases were built for both the interior and exterior. (Courtesy of George Barker.)

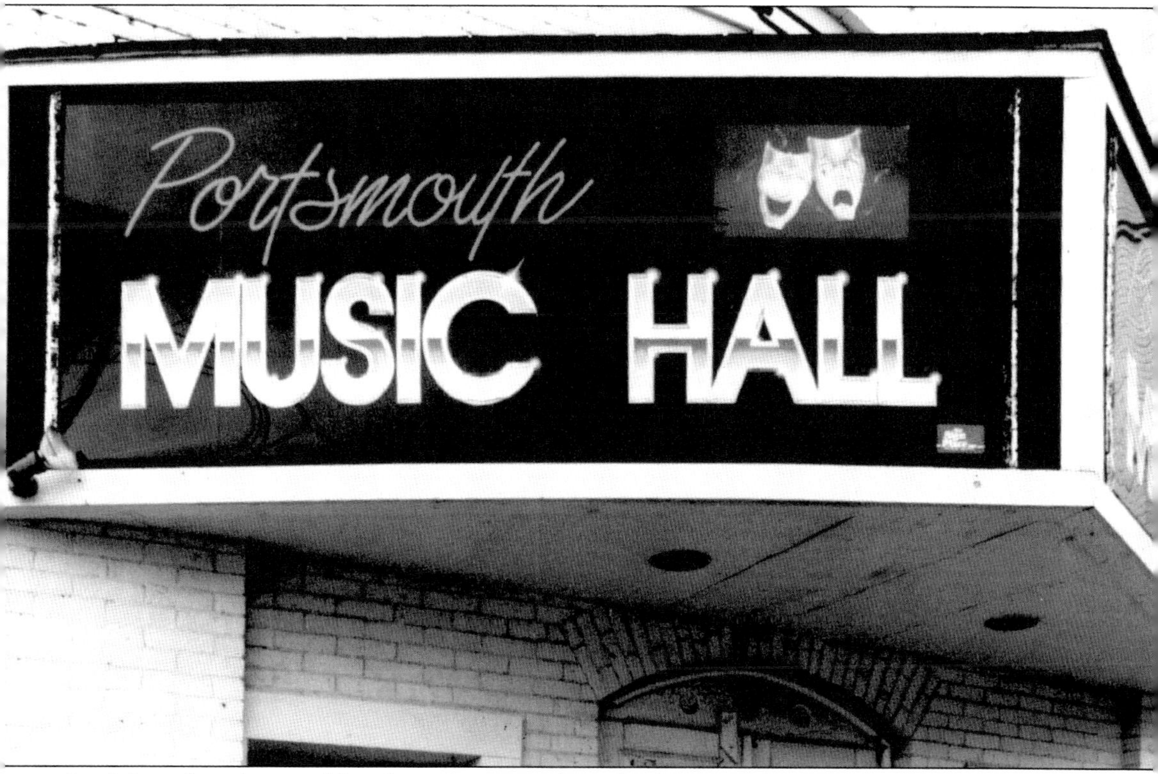

Confident that they could make a decent profit with their new downtown enterprise, Lewis Shaw and his group opened the Portsmouth Music Hall's doors for its first live performance season in almost half a century. (Courtesy of George Barker.)

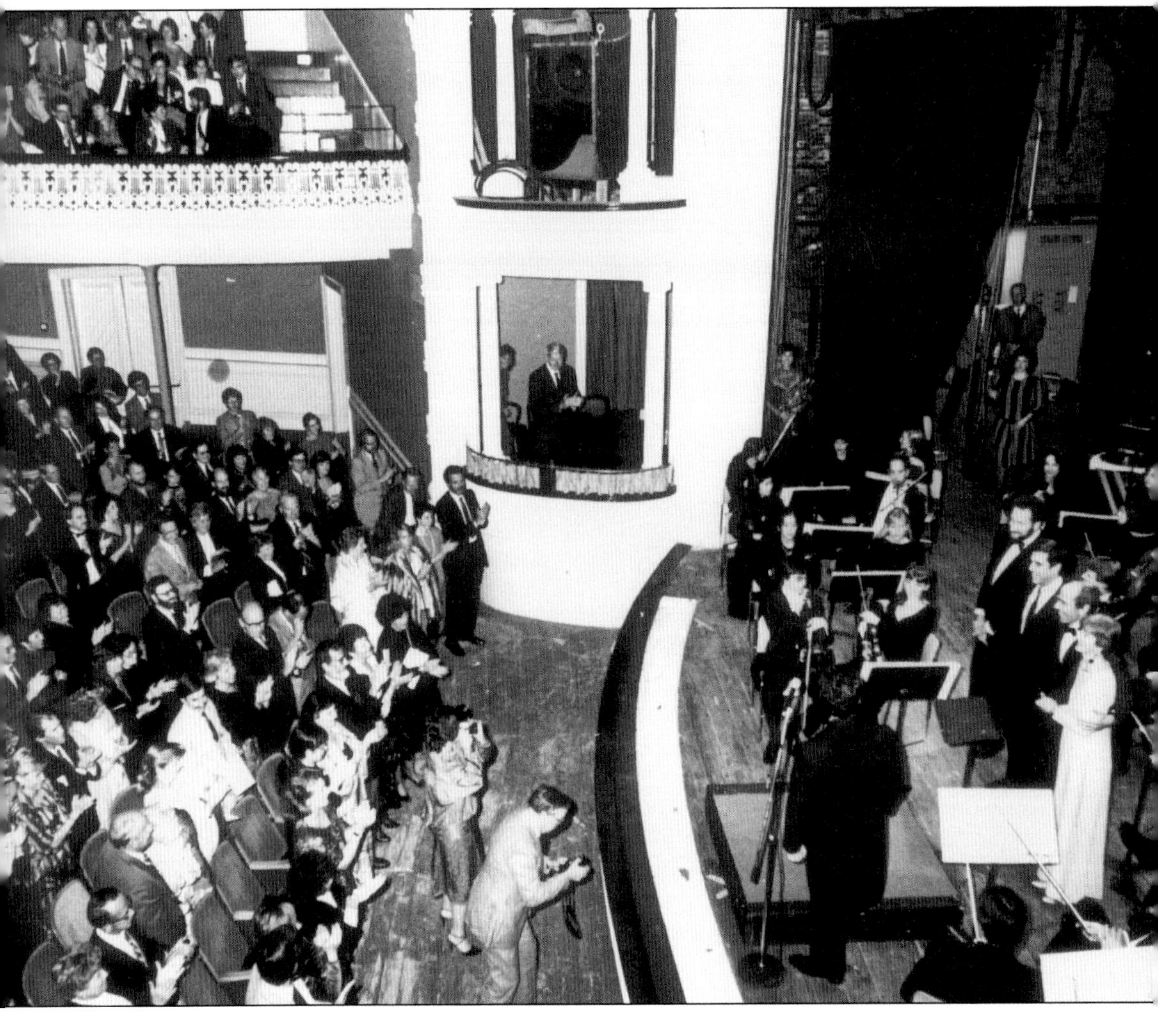

In a very auspicious beginning, the whole town showed up to celebrate the reopening. On Saturday, October 26, 1985, the new owners, Lewis Shaw, Jerry and Gretchen Weiss, and Ralph Brody, greeted the enthusiastic crowd from center stage, proudly kicking off their live events season with "An Overture to the Seacoast" by the New Hampshire Symphony Orchestra, conducted by maestro James Bolle. (Courtesy of the Harbor Arts Museum and the Richard Smith Collection.)

Over the course of the season, it became clear that more renovations would be necessary. The aging fly floor and hemp-rope rigging system needed to be updated to accommodate shows that required increasingly more elaborate lighting and stage effects. The brick in the back wall of the theater was rapidly deteriorating. The unforeseen costs of realistically maintaining a century-old theater, including staggering utility bills combined with the nearly prohibitive expense of attracting big name stars to the little Seacoast town, quickly began to wear through the pockets of the new owners. (Courtesy of George Barker.)

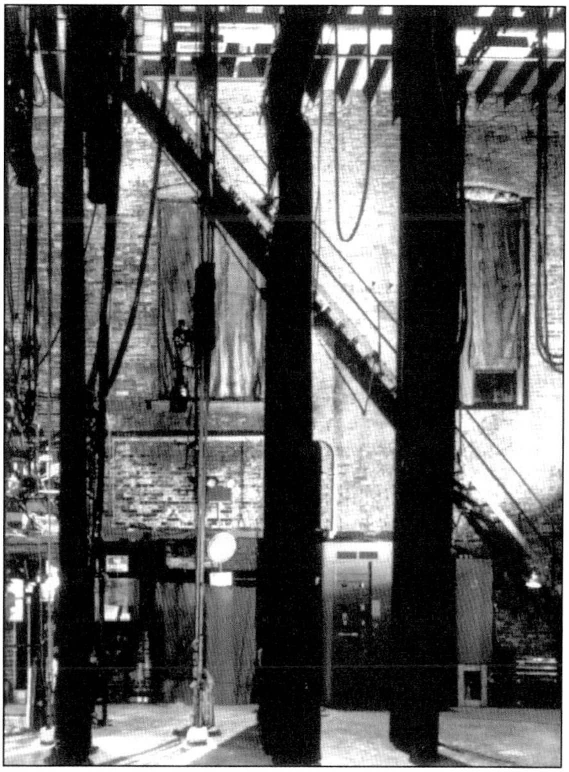

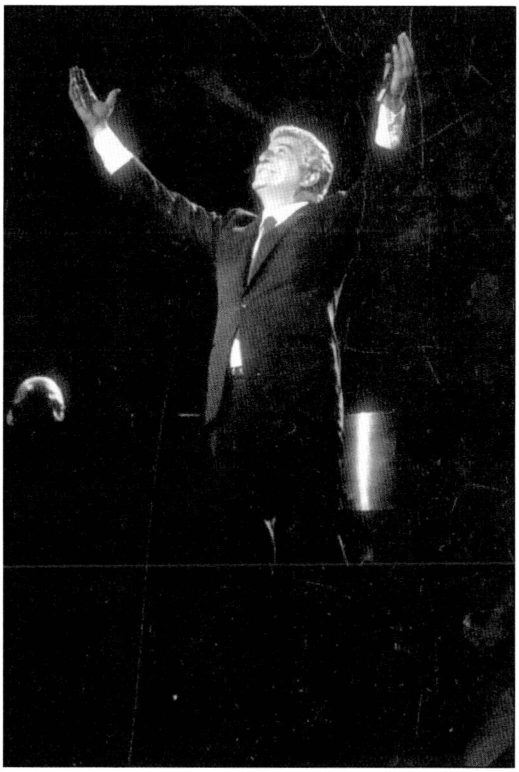

Bringing high-caliber class acts like Tony Bennett to the heart of the Seacoast did not come cheaply. Even if a show sold out completely, it would often just barely cover the expenses of the production. Many of the shows did not sell out, and bills started to go unpaid. It became apparent that ticket sales alone could not support a modern arts center of such proportions. In August 1986, at the end of their first and only season, the Portsmouth Music Hall filed for bankruptcy, and the lights went out once again. (Courtesy of Ralph Morang.)

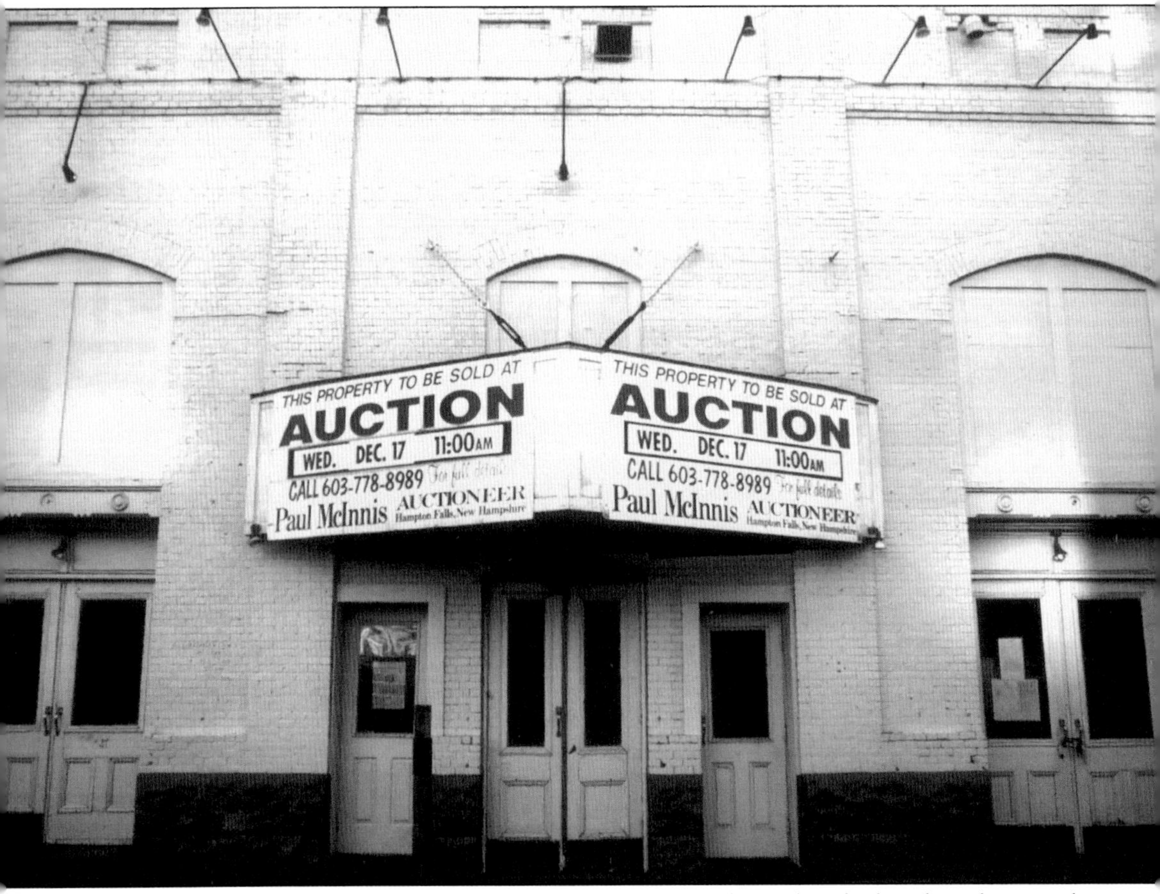

During this period, Bank Meridian assumed ownership and toyed with the idea of razing the building to clear some prime downtown real estate for potential development. In an odd stroke of luck for the Music Hall, the bank found it would be more expensive to tear down the building than the property would actually be worth. The wrecking ball was dodged. In what he described as a "purchase of the heart," Nashua developer Richard Cabral bought the theater from the bank at auction later that year. (Courtesy of Ralph Morang.)

Six

The Friends of the Music Hall 1986–Present

For a brief time, Richard Cabral kept the theater open for local charity events and occasionally rented the house out to host live performances produced by local promoters. Still, the hall was dark more nights than not. Without realizing an immediate profit, Cabral's enthusiasm for maintaining the building as a performing arts center waned. The central location and size of the structure posed some attractive alternative opportunities to a modern developer, and in a last effort to squeeze some profit from his purchase, he applied to the town council for a permit to gut out the building, with the intention of replacing the interior with a number of condominiums. Recognizing the danger surrounding the state of the Music Hall and having experienced a taste of the hall's old magic, a group of concerned local citizens banded together in the spring of 1987 in a grass-roots attempt to raise awareness of the theater's precarious position. Adopting the name the Friends of the Music Hall, they were granted non-profit status by the state of New Hampshire and launched a number of small campaigns aimed at raising funds to help preserve the theater. They sold "Save The Music Hall" buttons and attempted a "Buy a Brick" campaign. Formed specifically to insure that the facility not be converted into anything but a performing arts center, the group was incited to vociferous action by Cabral's threat to the future of the building.

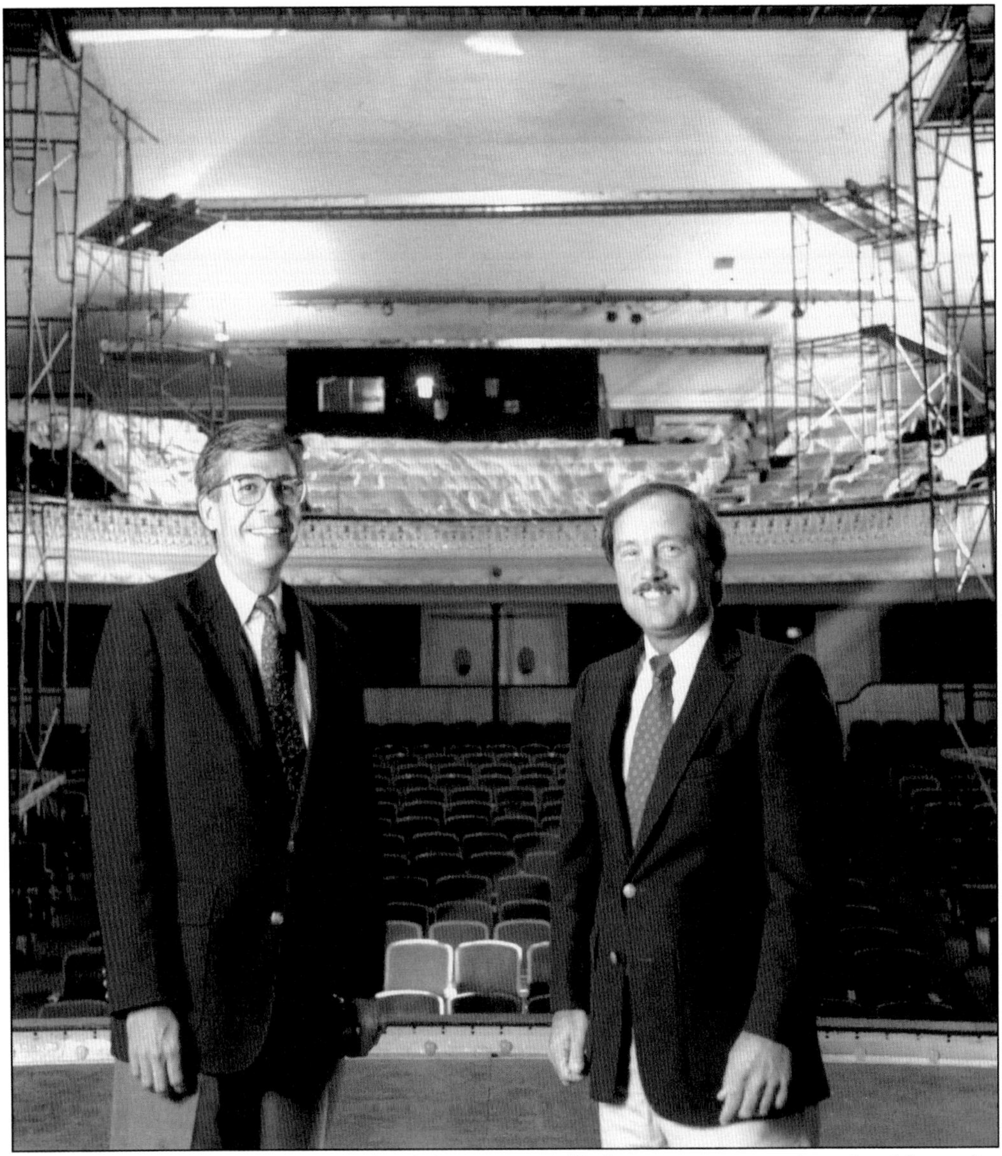

In the summer of 1988, the Friends of the Music Hall's bargaining strength and public cache significantly increased with the additions of David Choate (right), then manager of the Portsmouth-based Robbins Group of New Hampshire and president of the Prescott Park Arts Festival, and Jameson French, president of Northland Forest Products and member of the Greater Portsmouth Community Foundation's executive committee. Choate, a natural detail-orientated man and organizer who had worked with Richard Cabral on a number of other real estate ventures, was able to negotiate a deal with the developer. At a public press conference on September 19, 1988, it was announced that Cabral had agreed to sell the facility to the nonprofit group for what he had paid for it, plus the remaining debt from the earlier renovations. The price tag was $650,000. (Courtesy of George Barker.)

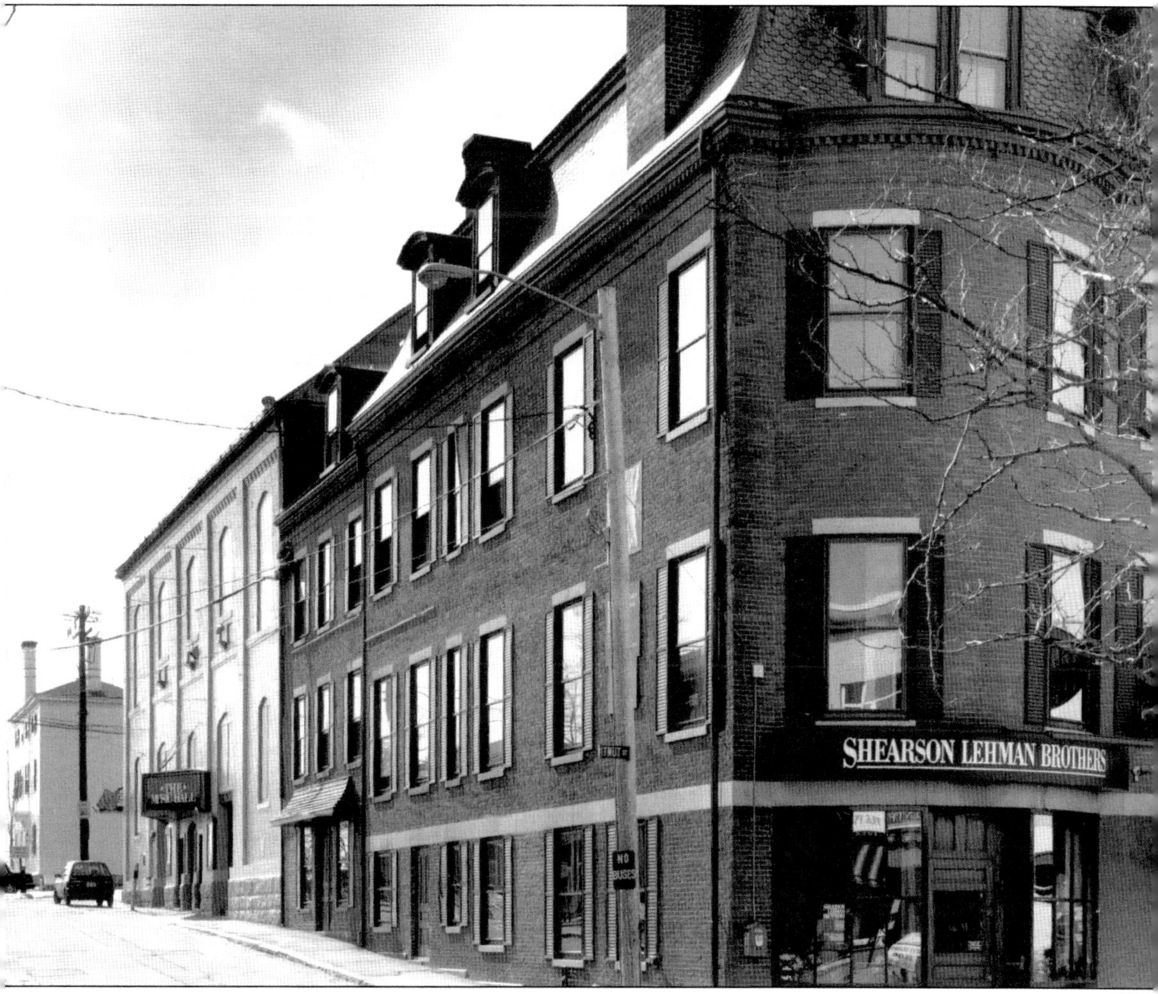

Bank Meridian, having had some experience with the risk involved with this very theater, agreed to provide the financing, but only if the Friends could prove public support by raising $200,000 of the money up front. With an established deadline of December 15, 1988, only three months away, the new board of trustees started making calls. Jameson French's personable demeanor and unmatched fund-raising skills resulted in a miraculous windfall of local support. With a last-minute extension to December 23 granted, they skidded over the finish line with $194,000 in donations. The bank accepted, the papers were signed, and by Christmas 1988, the Music Hall was officially in the hands of the community. (Courtesy of George Barker.)

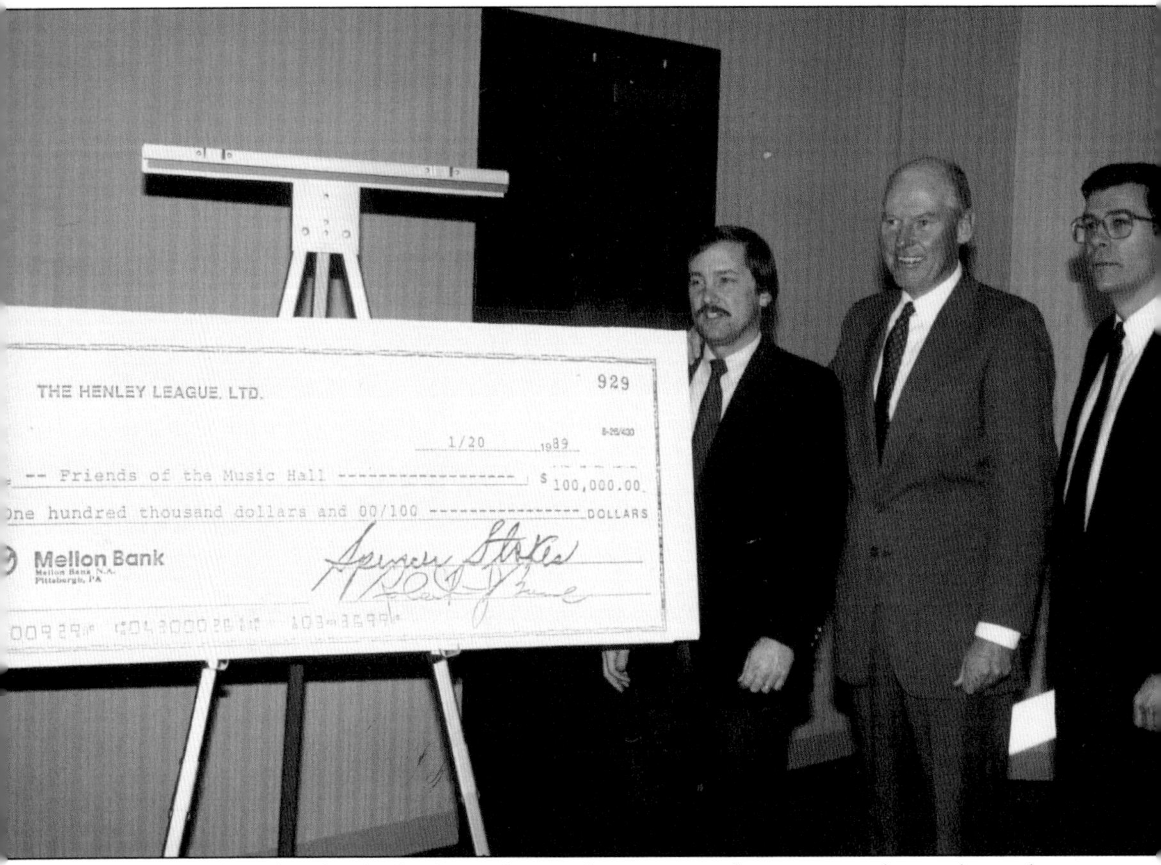

Understanding that they had only just begun, the group members continued to work to cultivate both small personal contributions as well as larger corporate support. In January 1989, after months of judicious pressure, David Choate and Jameson French secured the single largest donation they had seen: $100,000 from the Henley Group, presented by Mike Dingman. Overcome with enthusiasm at the press conference to announce the signing of this enormous check, Dingman spontaneously offered to additionally match all donations for the rest of the season up to a second $100,000. This unprecedented offer went a long way to prove the community's support for the preservation of the local arts scene and was a key element in the initial capital used to subsidize the Friends of the Music Hall's first "Celebrity Season" of events. (Courtesy of George Barker.)

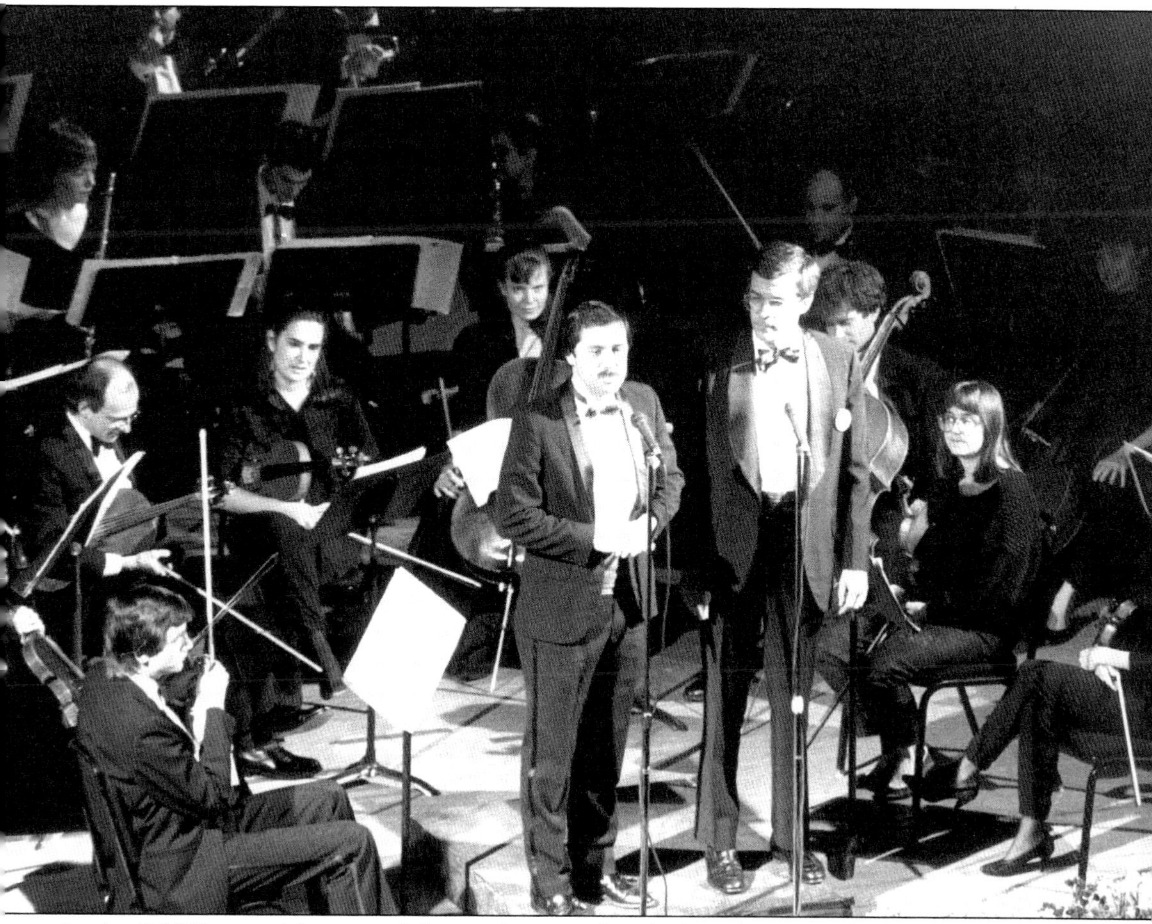

In April 1989, in celebration of the year's astounding luck and success, the New Hampshire Symphony Orchestra performed once again. David Choate and Jameson French put on their tuxes to introduce the show and to thank the community for its generosity, passion, and support. (Courtesy of George Barker.)

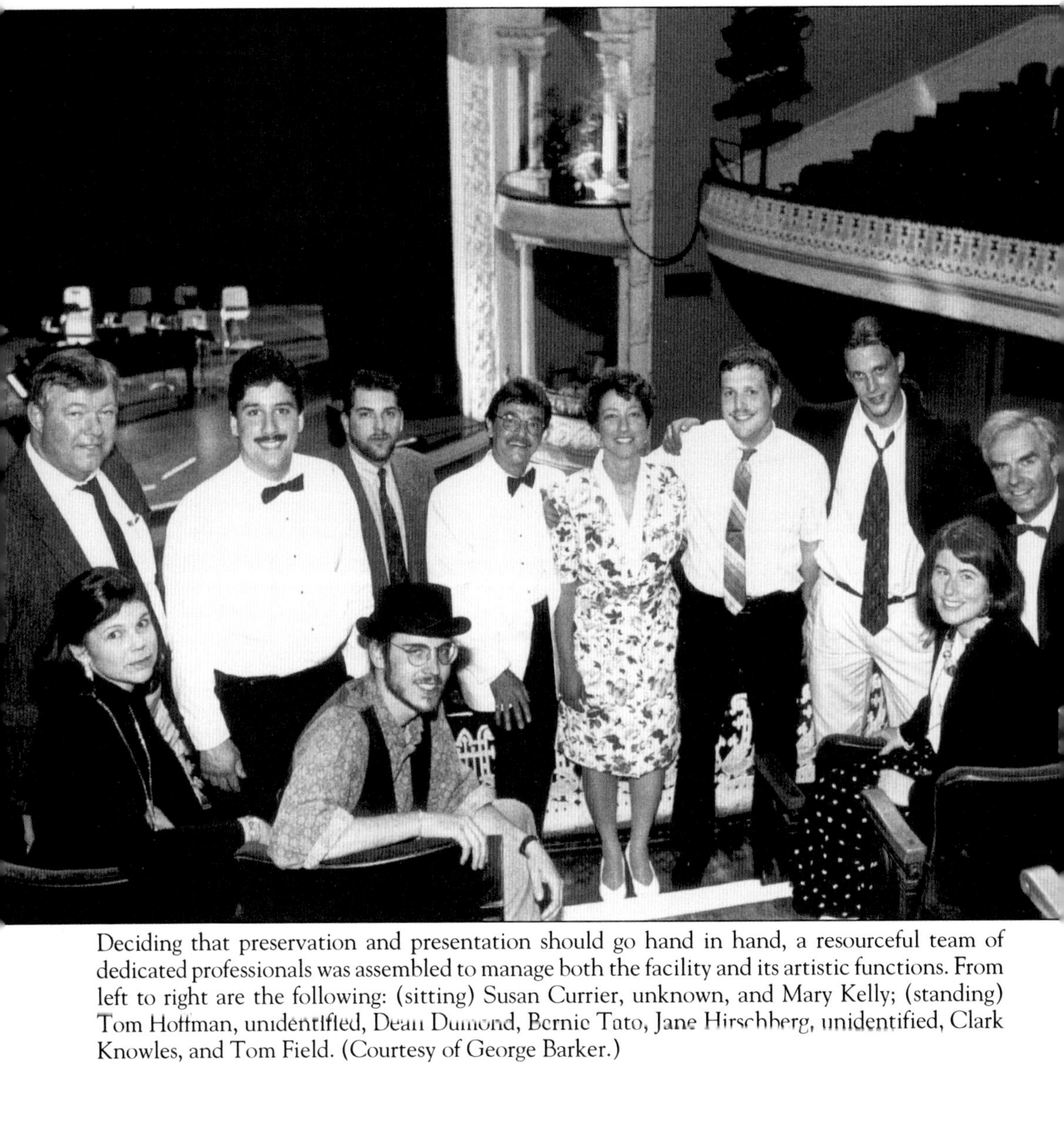

Deciding that preservation and presentation should go hand in hand, a resourceful team of dedicated professionals was assembled to manage both the facility and its artistic functions. From left to right are the following: (sitting) Susan Currier, unknown, and Mary Kelly; (standing) Tom Hoffman, unidentified, Dean Dumond, Bernie Tato, Jane Hirschberg, unidentified, Clark Knowles, and Tom Field. (Courtesy of George Barker.)

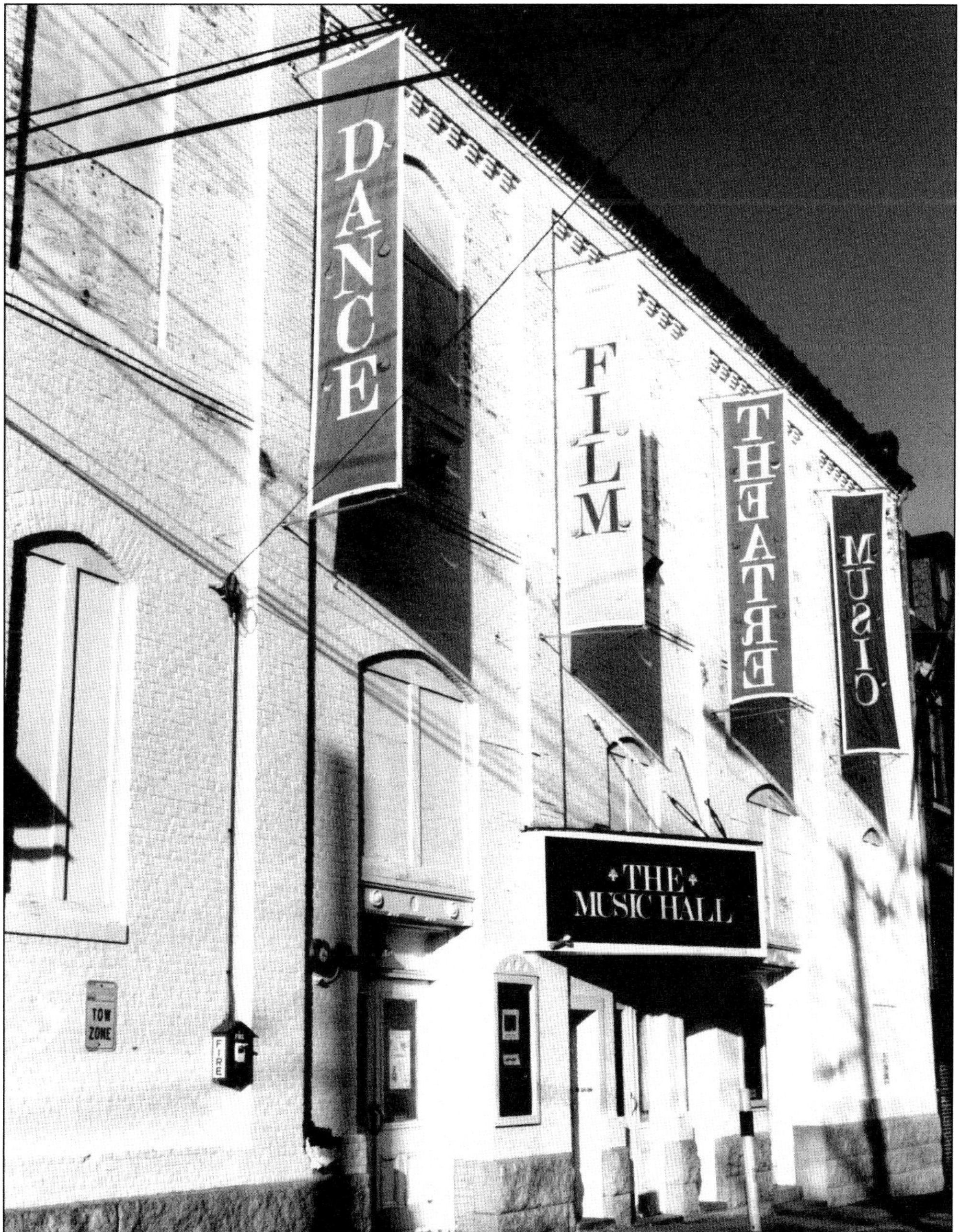

The name on the marquee was updated once again, and banners were hung to celebrate the amazing variety of events possible in the versatile Music Hall building. (Courtesy of George Barker.)

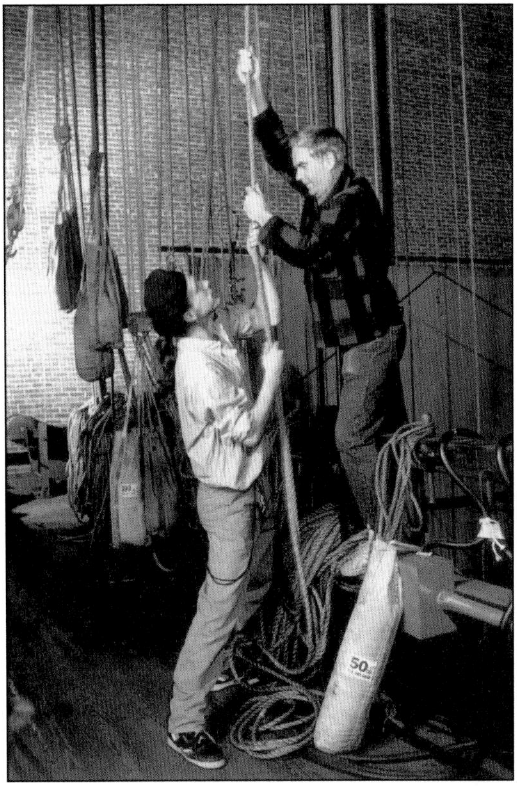

The stage rigging was overhauled, with new pulleys and ropes to replace the worn-out, old ones. Tom Field, early board member and associate of High Output (a Massachusetts-based theater and sound reinforcement supply company), played a key leadership role in refitting the Music Hall's technical capabilities. With help from Clark Knowles, he started a long tradition of meeting the challenge of incorporating cutting-edge technical upgrades within the theater's historical context. (Courtesy of George Barker.)

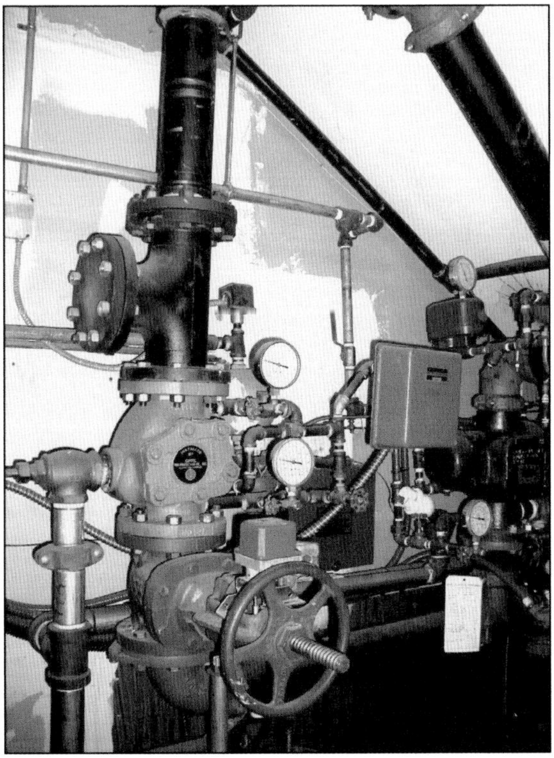

After a very dangerous (but lucky) 100 years, the building was finally brought up to modern fire codes. Fire alarms, a public-address system, and a full sprinkler system were installed. Sprinklers now protected all areas, including the lobby, backstage, and vast dome of the auditorium. (Courtesy of Chris Smith.)

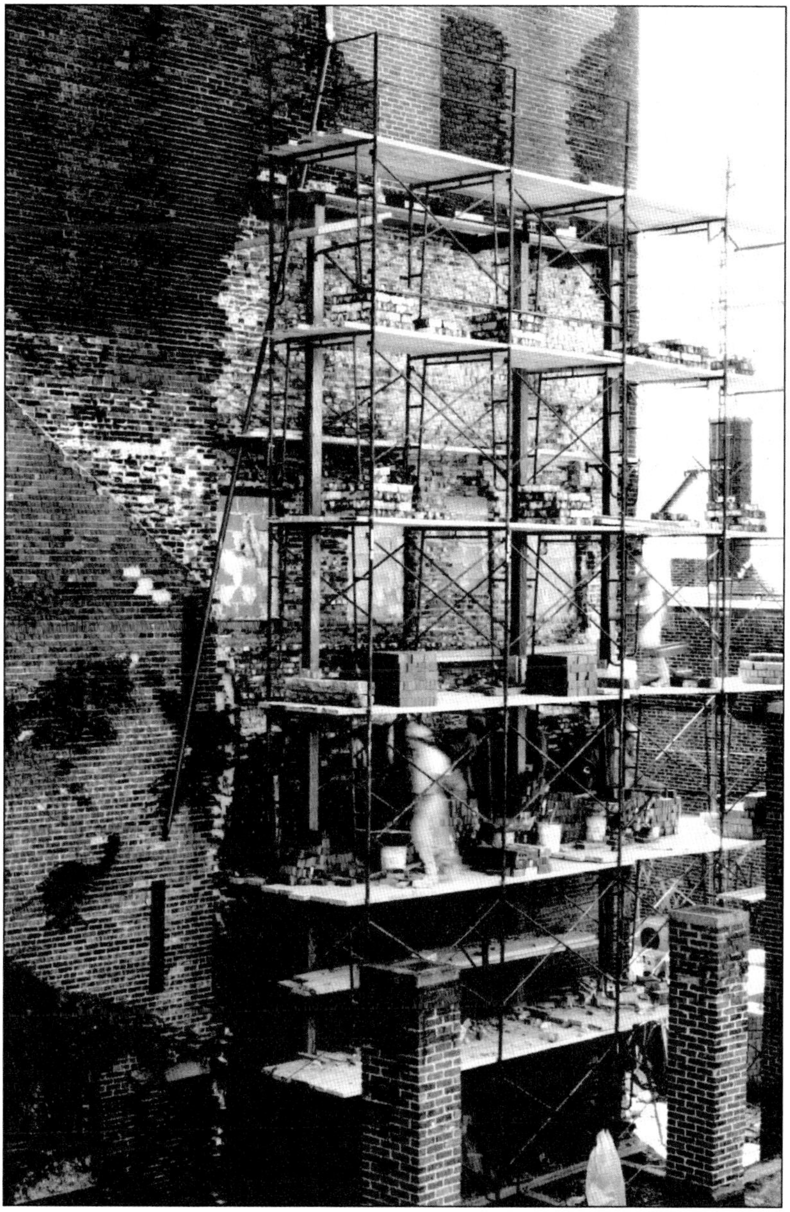

The back wall of the stage house was originally built against another building and was therefore built out of interior bricks. When that building came down (leaving its silhouette visible on the side of the Music Hall), the interior brick was exposed to the elements and began to slowly disintegrate. Great pains were taken to replace the crumbling wall, saving it from a devastating collapse. (Courtesy of George Barker.)

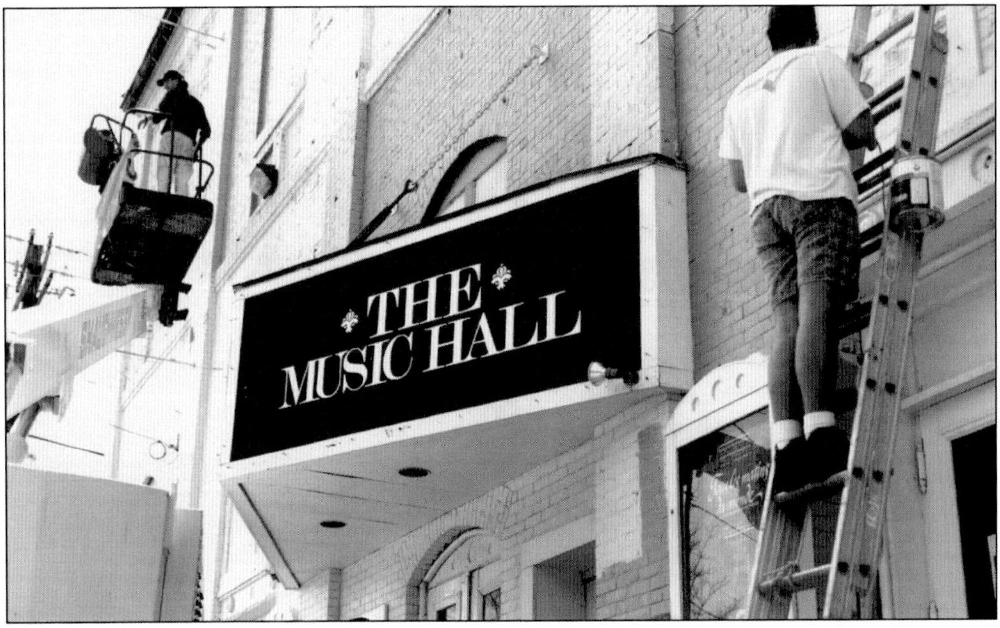

The building's plain white street-front paint job was covered over in 1990 with a salmon and cream theme, which was picked by popular vote out of three "historically plausible" color combinations presented to Music Hall members in the lobby before events. (Courtesy of George Barker.)

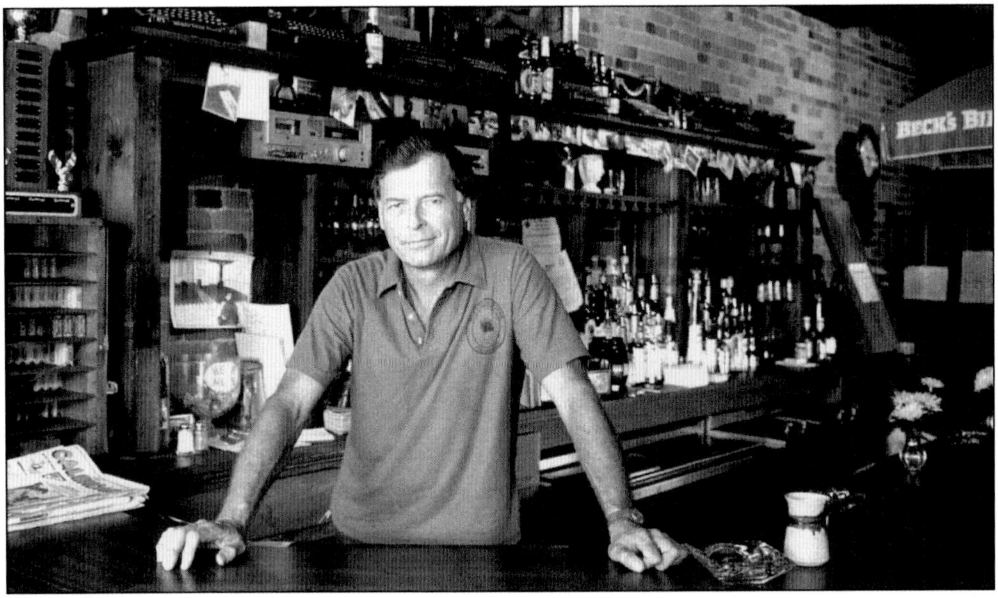

The Friends of the Music Hall was miraculously able to turn the national banking crisis of the early 1990s to its advantage. The failure of Bank Meridian allowed the Friends to strategically renegotiate the terms of the initial loan to roughly 30 cents on the dollar, but it had to be paid off immediately. Jay Smith, local entrepreneur and longtime arts supporter, gave a $200,000 loan (which remained anonymous to all but one original board member until Smith's death in 2002), paying off the mortgage, saving the day, and securing the Music Hall's potential for future success. (Photograph by Peter Randall, courtesy of the Press Room.)

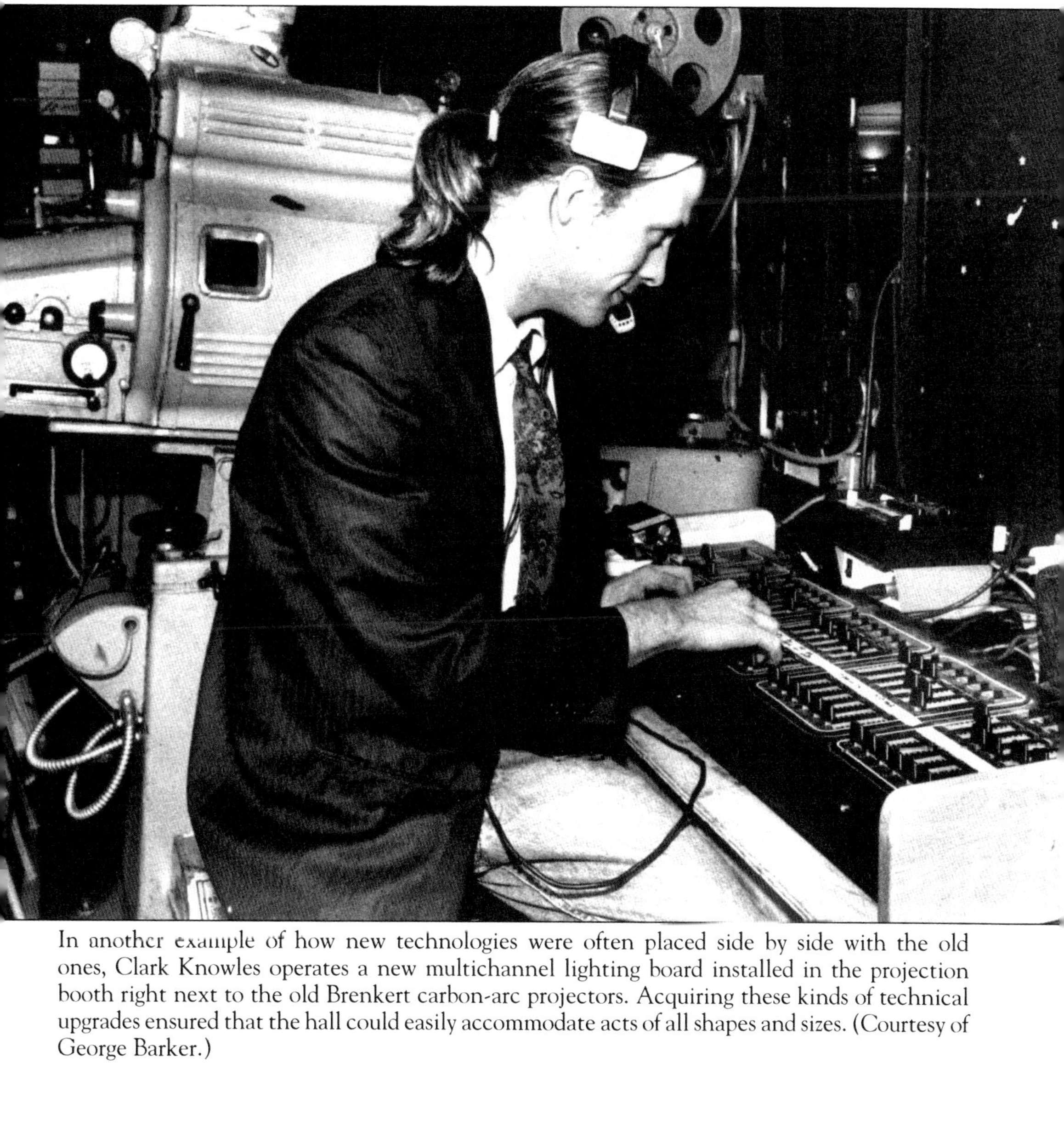

In another example of how new technologies were often placed side by side with the old ones, Clark Knowles operates a new multichannel lighting board installed in the projection booth right next to the old Brenkert carbon-arc projectors. Acquiring these kinds of technical upgrades ensured that the hall could easily accommodate acts of all shapes and sizes. (Courtesy of George Barker.)

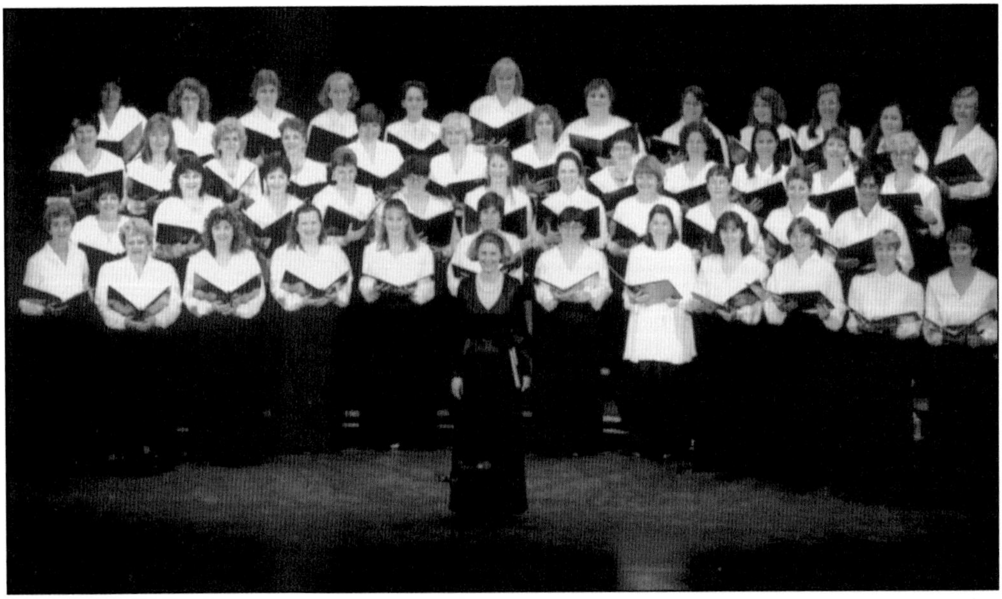

Community events featuring local talent have always been a mainstay on the Music Hall's main stage. Neighborhood artists, such as the Portsmouth Women's Chorus, led by Priscilla French, offered friends and family an otherwise rare chance to hear their loved ones perform in a dignified and acoustically superb setting. (Courtesy of George Barker.)

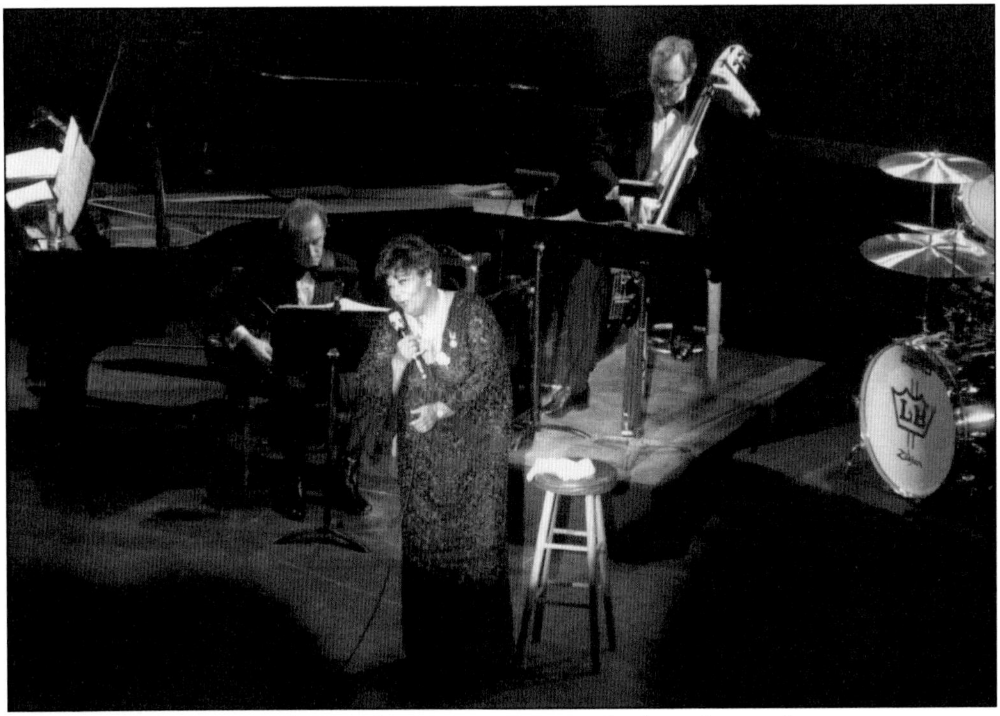

Supported by donations and grants from a growing network of members and corporate sponsors, the showcase of international, big-name talent was once again made possible. The Music Hall was fortunate enough to feature Pearl Baily, pictured here on the Music Hall's stage in one of her final performances, only months before her death in 1991. (Courtesy of George Barker.)

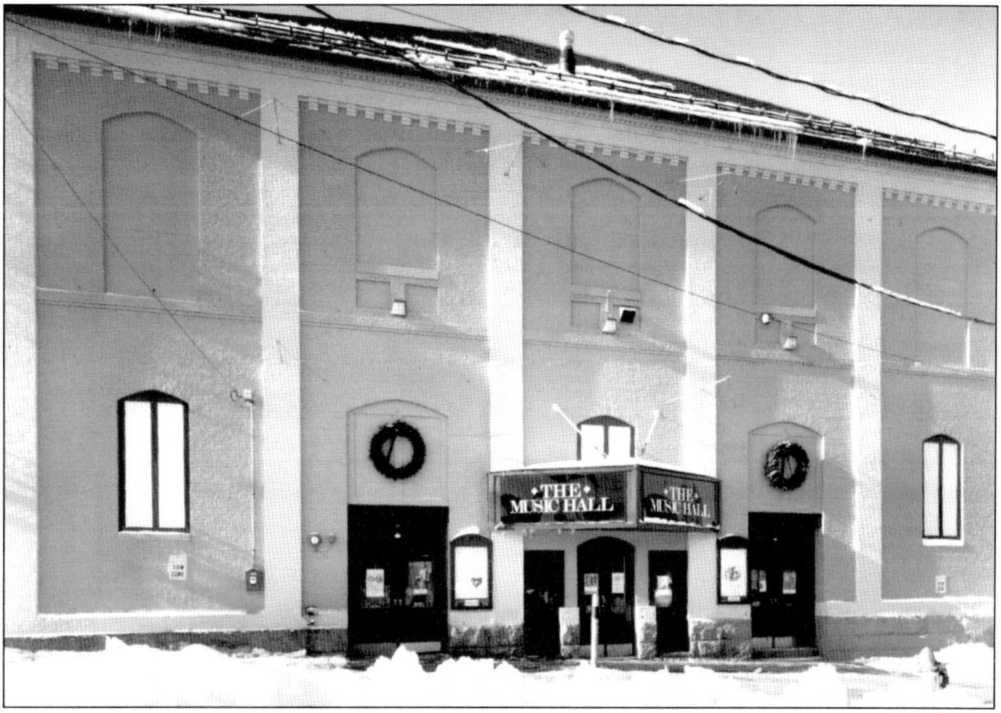

A new furnace and air-handling system helped keep the place warm in the wintertime. At the Music Hall the Christmas season bustled with holiday shows of all kinds, from the small traditions of *Nowell Sing We Clear* to the grand Handel's *Messiah*. (Courtesy of George Barker.)

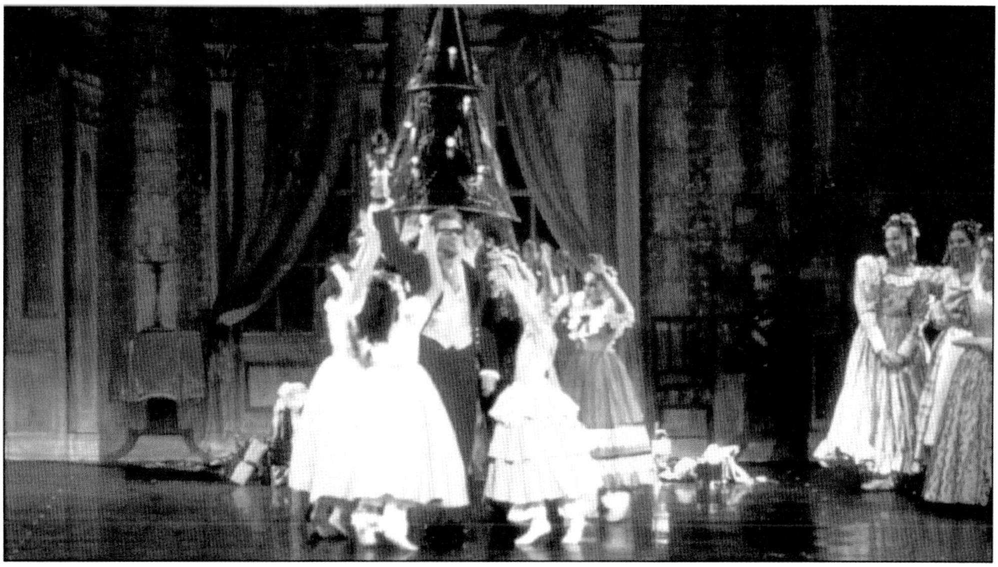

In what would become a Seacoast tradition, Ballet New England, a dance school with offices only blocks away, took over the building for the course of two weeks in December for their multiple performances of Tchaikovsky's *Nutcracker*. Choreographed by BNE's director, produced with the help of the Music Hall's staff and crew, and featuring local dancers ranging from ages 7 to 70, the *Nutcracker* became a popular annual favorite of families throughout the region. (Courtesy of Ralph Morang.)

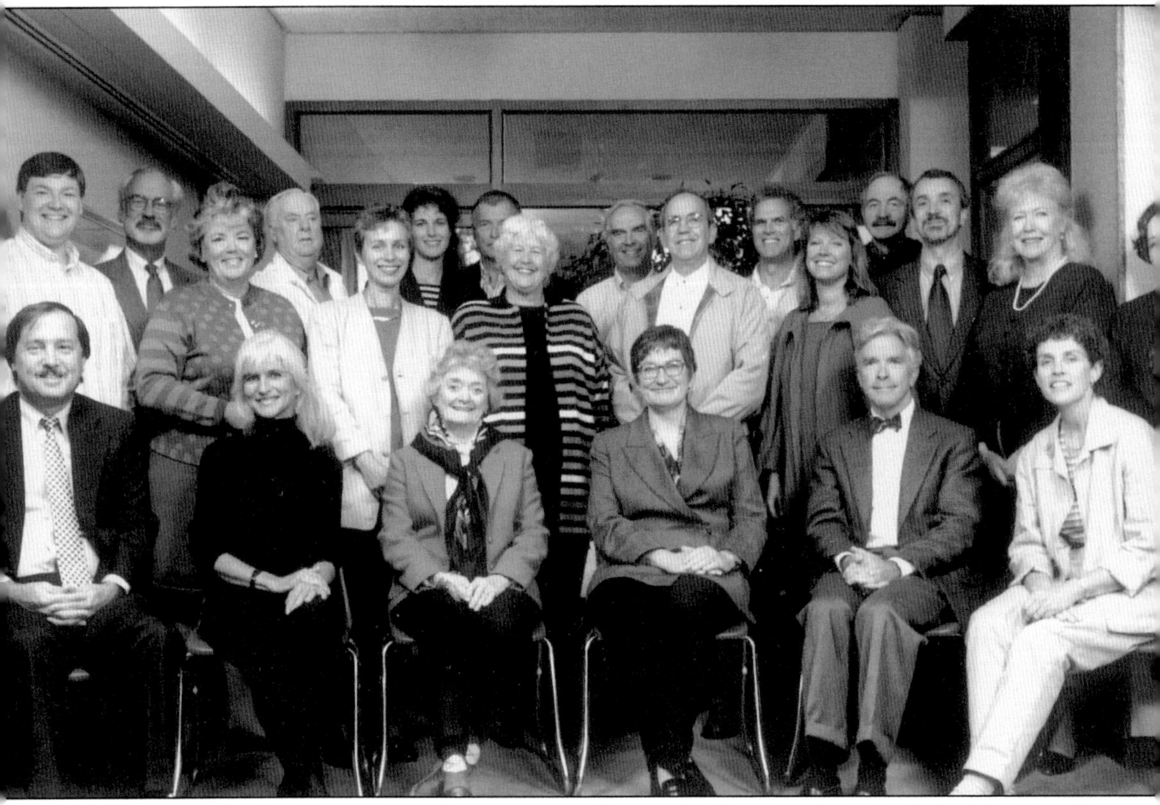

This photograph taken in 1996 features many dear and influential Friends of the Music Hall. With their support, community connections, and pure hard work, the Music Hall was able to break out of its back-street location and reach out to touch the lives of more and more people in the surrounding areas. Pictured from left to right are the following: (sitting) David Choate, Barbara Tsairis, Jean Cope, Christine Dwyer, Rick Miller, and Nancy Grossman; (standing) Rodney Rowland, Charles Manzella, Suzanne Hamblett, William Welsh, Karin Barndollar, Jennifer Cutshall, Jay Smith, Martha Fuller Clark, Thomas Field, Larry Lariviere, Frederick Thaler, Deborah Chag, Arthur Heard, Donald Tirabassi, Ann Dumaresque, and Edwinna Vanderzanden. (Courtesy of George Barker.)

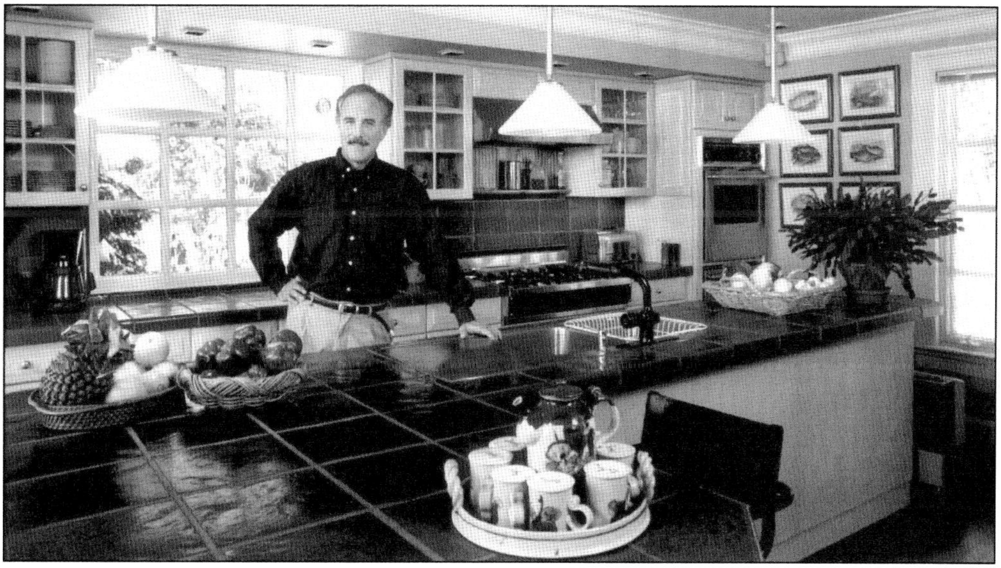

A special events committee was formed by effervescent spitfires, such as Debbie Chag, Jeanne Cope, and Karin Barndollar. With unmatched spirit and energy, they spearheaded a number of large, complicated, and often very lucrative off-site benefits for the Music Hall. The Kitchen Tour, a self-guided walk through some of the region's most fabulously designed kitchens, attracted thousands of people who may not have heard the Music Hall previously. Boston newscaster Randy Price (pictured here) was one of the first to graciously open his Kittery home to the roving crowds. (Courtesy of George Barker.)

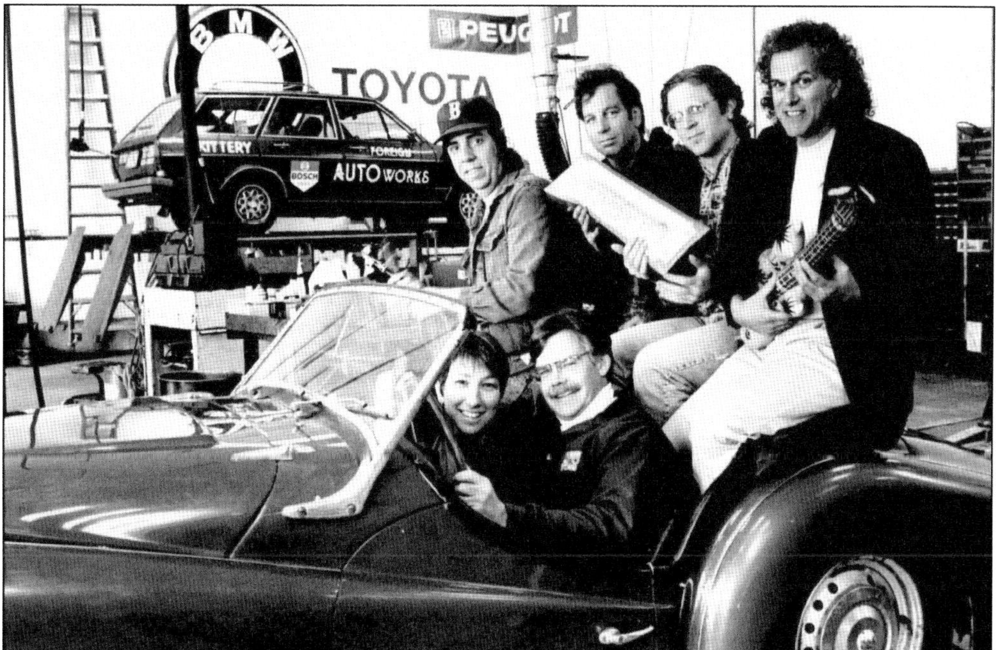

The Garage Dance took place at Autoworks, across the bridge in Kittery. Great fun for anyone who digs jazz and likes to dance, this function raised money to help support the Music Hall's continuing movie series. (Courtesy of George Barker.)

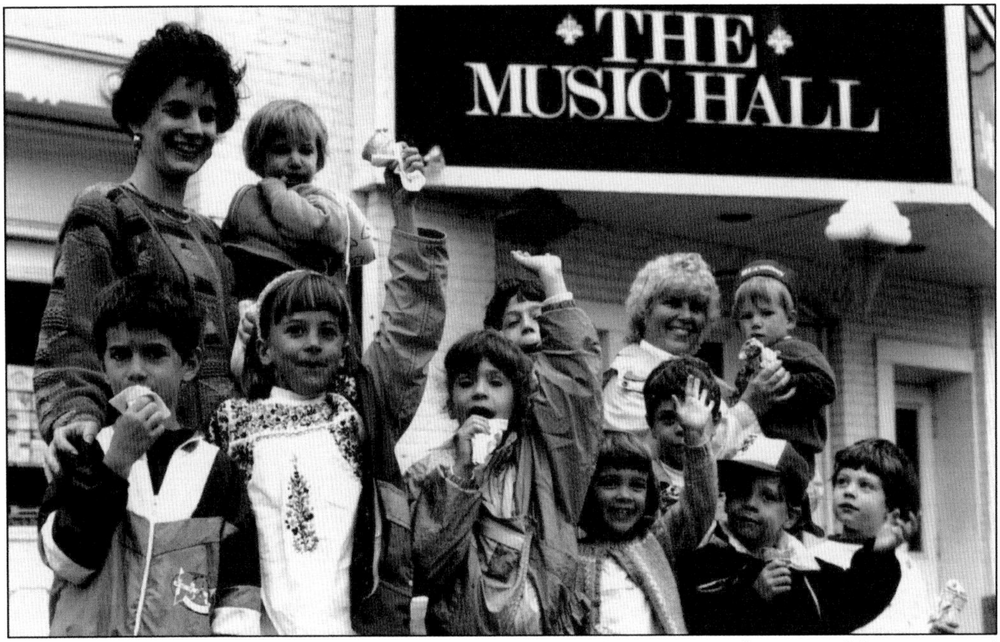

When the summer months got too nice to stay indoors, the Music Hall arranged for some cool outside entertainment with popular events like the Ice Cream Fest. Featuring live music, prizes, and all the ice-cream flavors in the rainbow, the Ice Cream Fest was an enormous hit. (Courtesy of George Barker.)

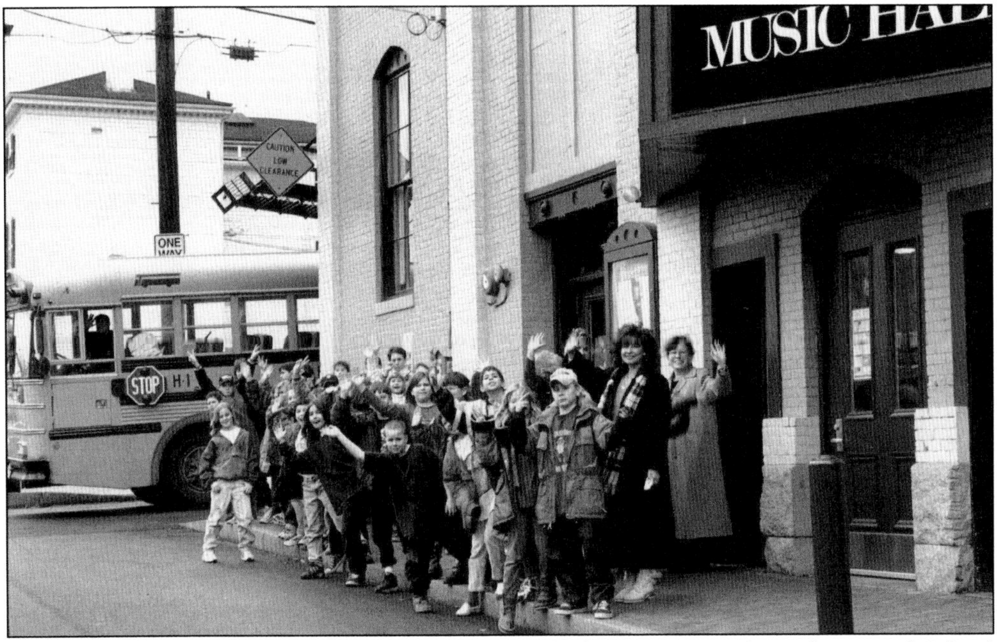

The Music Hall reached out to a new audience with the inception of its educational School Day series. Children were bussed in from schools from miles around for a series of terrific age-appropriate presentations. Herded into their seats and taught the p's and q's of theater etiquette, these youngsters often received their first experience of a real theater through this program. (Courtesy of George Barker.)

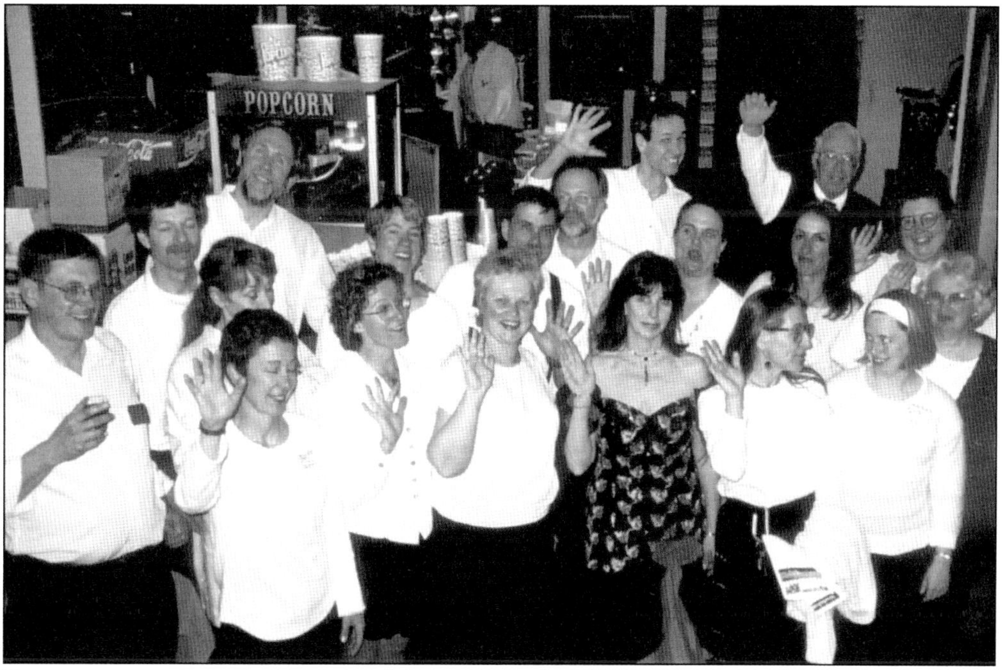

Donations came in many forms. In addition to needing financial support, the Music Hall could simply not function without its dedicated corps of volunteers. Giving freely of their valuable time and talent, the volunteers played key roles in many theater functions, from ushering patrons to their seats to carpentry to administrative support.

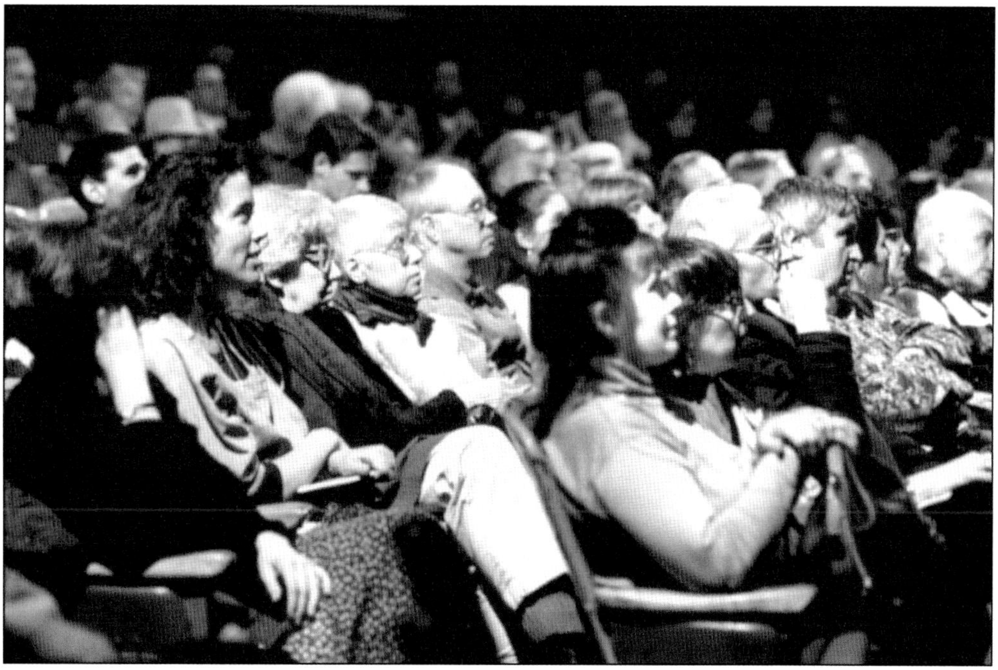

Members packed the house for show after show. The Music Hall had entered a new golden age of artistic relevance and community vitality unrivaled for generations. (Courtesy of George Barker.)

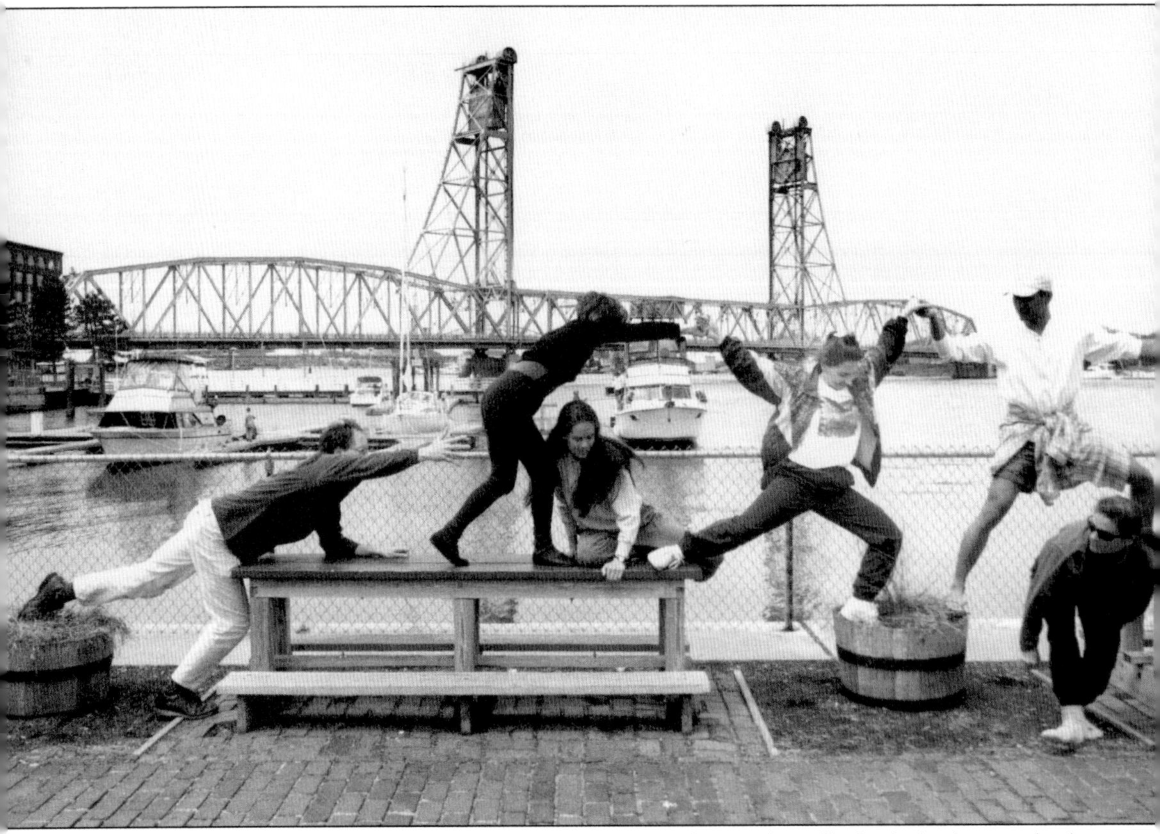

The internationally acclaimed Liz Lerman Dance Exchange literally built bridges with the community, celebrating the Seacoast's port town heritage, historical relationship with the sea, and shipbuilding trade through performance and interpretive dance with the *Shipyard Project* in 1994. (Courtesy of George Barker.)

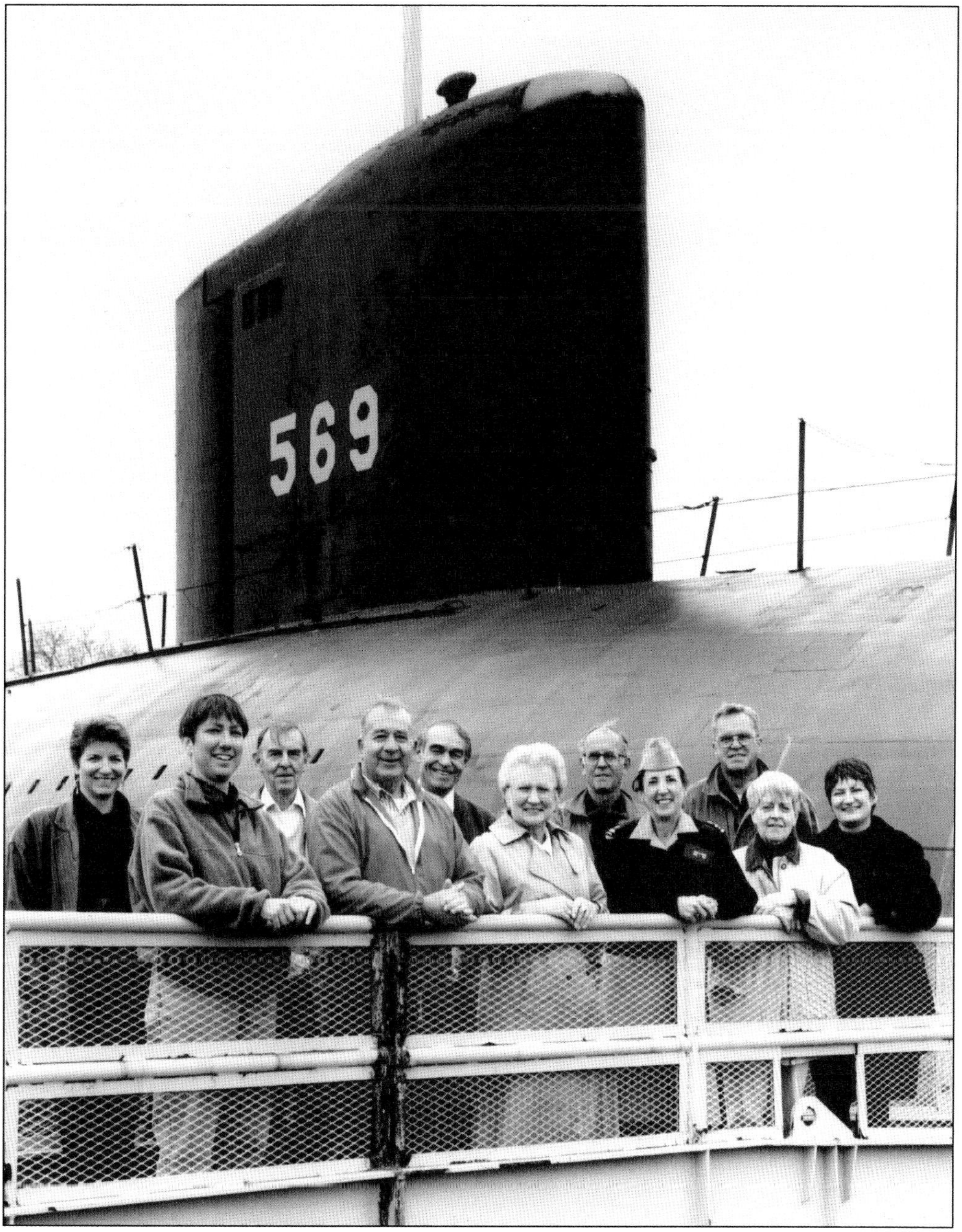

Jane Hirshberg (the Music Hall's director of development and education at the time) is pictured here with some neighborhood friends, colleagues, and one very large piece of equipment that helped make the *Shipyard Project* a nationally renowned endeavor. (Courtesy of George Barker.)

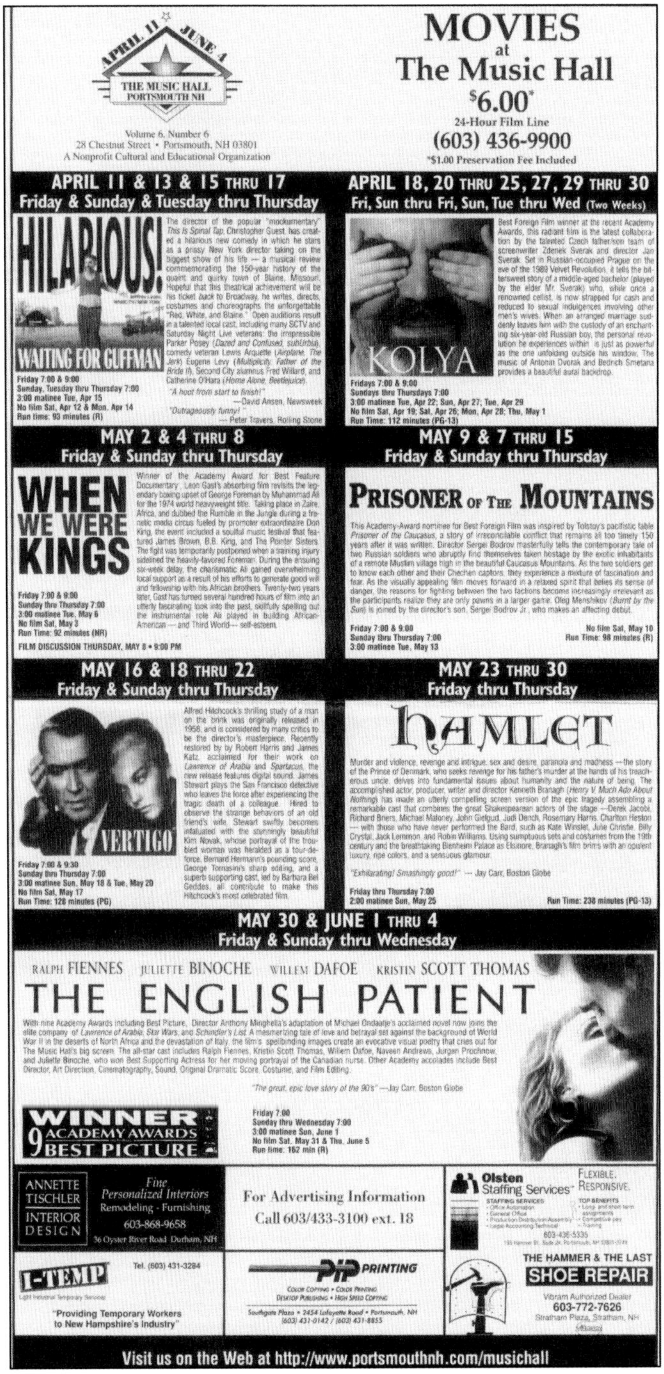

APRIL 11 · JUNE 4
THE MUSIC HALL
PORTSMOUTH NH

Volume 6, Number 6
28 Chestnut Street • Portsmouth, NH 03801
A Nonprofit Cultural and Educational Organization

MOVIES at The Music Hall
$6.00*
24-Hour Film Line
(603) 436-9900
*$1.00 Preservation Fee Included

APRIL 11 & 13 & 15 THRU 17
Friday & Sunday & Tuesday thru Thursday

HILARIOUS!
WAITING FOR GUFFMAN

The director of the popular "mockumentary" *This Is Spinal Tap*, Christopher Guest, has created a hilarious new comedy in which he stars as a prissy New York director taking on the biggest show of his life — a musical review commemorating the 150-year history of the quaint and quirky town of Blaine, Missouri. Hopeful that this theatrical achievement will be his ticket *back* to Broadway, he writes, directs, costumes and choreographs the unforgettable "Red, White, and Blaine." Open auditions result in a talented local cast, including many SCTV and Saturday Night Live veterans: the irrepressible Parker Posey (*Dazed and Confused, subUrbia*), comedy veteran Lewis Arquette (*Airplane, The Jerk*) Eugene Levy (*Multiplicity, Father of the Bride II*), Second City alumnus Fred Willard, and Catherine O'Hara (*Home Alone, Beetlejuice*).

"A hoot from start to finish!" —David Ansen, Newsweek
"Outrageously funny!" — Peter Travers, Rolling Stone

Friday 7:00 & 9:00
Sunday, Tuesday thru Thursday 7:00
3:00 matinee Tue, Apr 15
No film Sat, Apr 12 & Mon, Apr 14
Run time: 93 minutes (R)

APRIL 18, 20 THRU 25, 27, 29 THRU 30
Fri, Sun thru Fri, Sun, Tue thru Wed (Two Weeks)

KOLYA

Best Foreign Film winner at the recent Academy Awards, this radiant film is the latest collaboration by the talented Czech father/son team of screenwriter Zdenek Sverak and director Jan Sverak. Set in Russian-occupied Prague on the eve of the 1989 Velvet Revolution, it tells the bittersweet story of a middle-aged bachelor (played by the elder Mr. Sverak) who, while once a renowned cellist, is now strapped for cash and reduced to sexual indulgences involving other men's wives. When an arranged marriage suddenly leaves him with the custody of an enchanting six-year-old Russian boy, the personal revolution he experiences within is just as powerful as the one unfolding outside his window. The music of Antonin Dvorak and Bedrich Smetana provides a beautiful aural backdrop.

Fridays 7:00 & 9:00
Sundays thru Thursdays 7:00
3:00 matinee Tue, Apr 22; Sun, Apr 27; Tue, Apr 29
No film Sat, Apr 19; Sat, Apr 26; Mon, Apr 28; Thu, May 1
Run Time: 112 minutes (PG-13)

MAY 2 & 4 THRU 8
Friday & Sunday thru Thursday

WHEN WE WERE KINGS

Winner of the Academy Award for Best Feature Documentary, Leon Gast's absorbing film revisits the legendary boxing upset of George Foreman by Muhammad Ali for the 1974 world heavyweight title. Taking place in Zaire, Africa, and dubbed the Rumble in the Jungle during a frenetic media circus fueled by promoter extraordinaire Don King, the event included a soulful music festival that featured James Brown, B.B. King, and The Pointer Sisters. The fight was temporarily postponed when a training injury sidelined the heavily-favored Foreman. During the ensuing six-week delay, the charismatic Ali gained overwhelming local support as a result of his efforts to generate good will and fellowship with his African brothers. Twenty-two years later, Gast has turned several hundred hours of film into an utterly fascinating look into the past, skillfully spelling out the instrumental role Ali played in building African-American — and Third World— self-esteem.

Friday 7:00 & 9:00
Sunday thru Thursday 7:00
3:00 matinee Tue, May 6
No film Sat, May 3
Run Time: 92 minutes (NR)
FILM DISCUSSION THURSDAY, MAY 8 • 9:00 PM

MAY 9 & 7 THRU 15
Friday & Sunday thru Thursday

PRISONER OF THE MOUNTAINS

This Academy-Award nominee for Best Foreign Film was inspired by Tolstoy's pacifistic fable *Prisoner of the Caucasus*, a story of irreconcilable conflict that remains all too timely 150 years after it was written. Director Sergei Bodrov masterfully tells the contemporary tale of two Russian soldiers who abruptly find themselves taken hostage by the exotic inhabitants of a remote Muslim village high in the beautiful Caucasus Mountains. As the two soldiers get to know each other and their Chechen captors, they experience a mixture of fascination and fear. As the visually appealing film moves forward in a relaxed spirit that belies its sense of danger, the reasons for fighting between the two factions become increasingly irrelevant as the participants realize they are only pawns in a larger game. Oleg Menshikov (*Burnt by the Sun*) is joined by the director's son, Sergei Bodrov Jr., who makes an affecting debut.

Friday 7:00 & 9:00
Sunday thru Thursday 7:00
3:00 matinee Tue, May 13
No film Sat, May 10
Run Time: 98 minutes (R)

MAY 16 & 18 THRU 22
Friday & Sunday thru Thursday

VERTIGO

Alfred Hitchcock's thrilling study of a man on the brink was originally released in 1958, and is considered by many critics to be the director's masterpiece. Recently restored by by Robert Harris and James Katz, acclaimed for their work on *Lawrence of Arabia* and *Spartacus*, the new release features digital sound. James Stewart plays the San Francisco detective who leaves the force after experiencing the tragic death of a colleague. Hired to observe the strange behaviors of an old friend's wife, Stewart swiftly becomes infatuated with the stunningly beautiful Kim Novak, whose portrayal of the troubled woman was heralded as a tour-de-force. Bernard Hermann's pounding score, George Tomasini's sharp editing, and a superb supporting cast, led by Barbara Bel Geddes, all contribute to make this Hitchcock's most celebrated film.

Friday 7:00 & 9:30
Sunday thru Thursday 7:00
3:00 matinee Sun, May 18 & Tue, May 20
No film Sat, May 17
Run Time: 128 minutes (PG)

MAY 23 THRU 30
Friday thru Thursday

HAMLET

Murder and violence, revenge and intrigue, sex and desire, paranoia and madness —the story of the Prince of Denmark, who seeks revenge for his father's murder at the hands of his treacherous uncle, delves into fundamental issues about humanity and the nature of being. The accomplished actor, producer, writer and director Kenneth Branagh (*Henry V, Much Ado About Nothing*) has made an utterly compelling screen version of the epic tragedy assembling a remarkable cast that combines the great Shakespearean actors of the stage —Derek Jacobi, Richard Briers, Michael Maloney, John Gielgud, Judi Dench, Rosemary Harris, Charlton Heston — with those who have never performed the Bard, such as Kate Winslet, Julie Christie, Billy Crystal, Jack Lemmon, and Robin Williams. Using sumptuous sets and costumes from the 19th century and the breathtaking Blenheim Palace as Elsinore, Branagh's film brims with an opulent luxury, ripe colors, and a sensuous glamour.

"Exhilarating! Smashingly good!" — Jay Carr, Boston Globe

Friday thru Thursday 7:00
2:00 matinee Sun, May 25
Run Time: 238 minutes (PG-13)

MAY 30 & JUNE 1 THRU 4
Friday & Sunday thru Wednesday

RALPH FIENNES JULIETTE BINOCHE WILLEM DAFOE KRISTIN SCOTT THOMAS
THE ENGLISH PATIENT

With nine Academy Awards including Best Picture, Director Anthony Minghella's adaptation of Michael Ondaatje's acclaimed novel now joins the elite company of *Lawrence of Arabia, Star Wars*, and *Schindler's List*. A mesmerizing tale of love and betrayal set against the background of World War II in the deserts of North Africa and the devastation of Italy, the film's spellbinding images create an evocative visual poetry that cries out for The Music Hall's big screen. The all-star cast includes Ralph Fiennes, Kristin Scott Thomas, Willem Dafoe, Naveen Andrews, Jurgen Prochnow, and Juliette Binoche, who won Best Supporting Actress for her moving portrayal of the Canadian nurse. Other Academy accolades include Best Director, Art Direction, Cinematography, Sound, Original Dramatic Score, Costume, and Film Editing.

"The great, epic love story of the 90's" —Jay Carr, Boston Globe

WINNER 9 ACADEMY AWARDS BEST PICTURE

Friday 7:00
Sunday thru Wednesday 7:00
3:00 matinee Sun, June 1
No film Sat, May 31 & Thu, June 5
Run time: 162 min (R)

Visit us on the Web at http://www.portsmouthnh.com/musichall

For 10 years, movies at the Music Hall were booked by Jeffery Jacobs, a popular art house broker with offices in New York City. Much like E.M. Loew, he would often book the films into his primary venues, then pass them along to the Music Hall when they ran out of steam in the city. This movie mailer from 1996 exhibits a first-class selection of titles, but the films are all four to eight months behind their initial release dates. Film discussions would often follow the screenings, attracting a small but thoughtful group of movie enthusiasts.

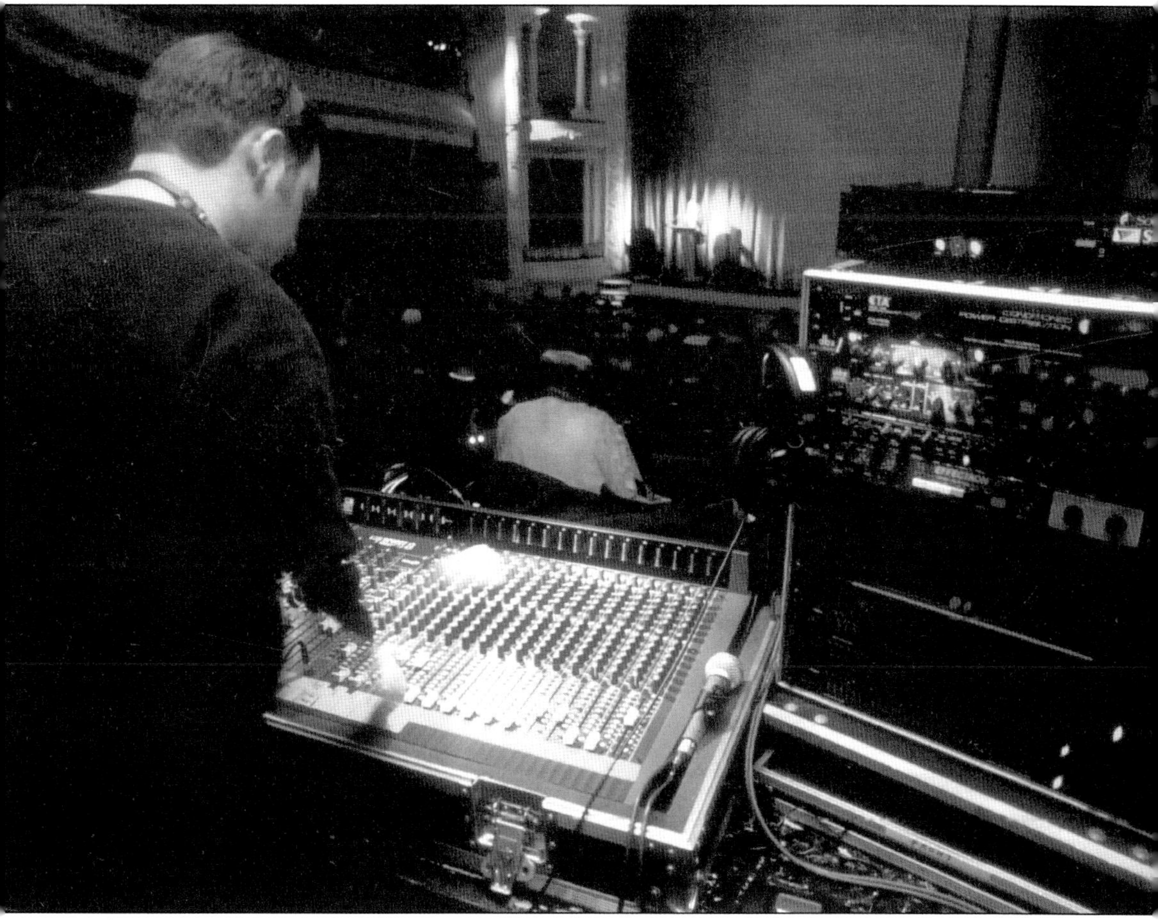

With state-of-the-art equipment, experienced technical engineers, such as Dean Clegg who is pictured here, could now retune the Music Hall to best fit the acoustics of any incoming production. (Courtesy of Ralph Morang.)

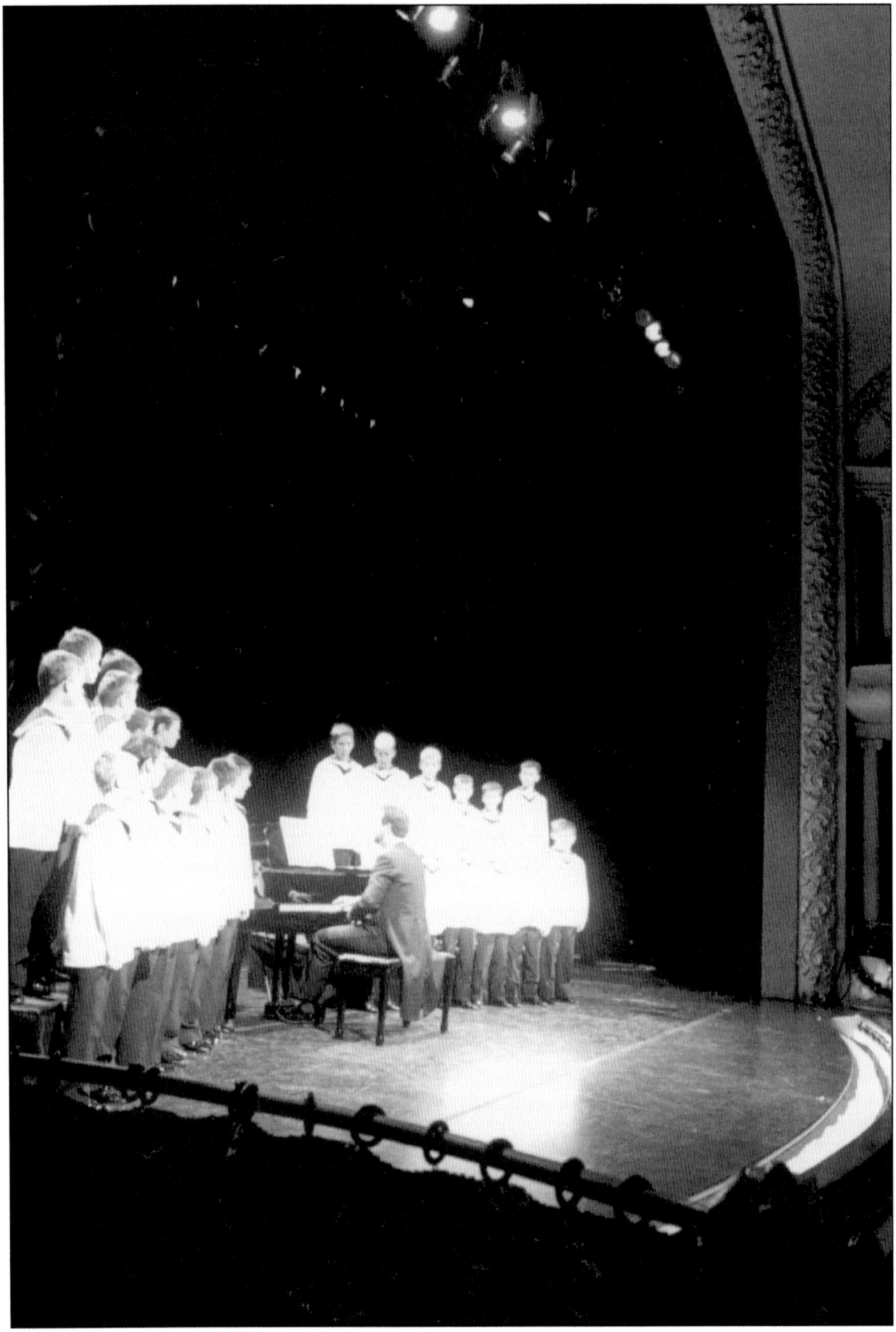

The soft, angelic voices of the Vienna Boys' Choir could be heard clearly in the back row of the sold-out hall. (Courtesy of Nancy Horton.)

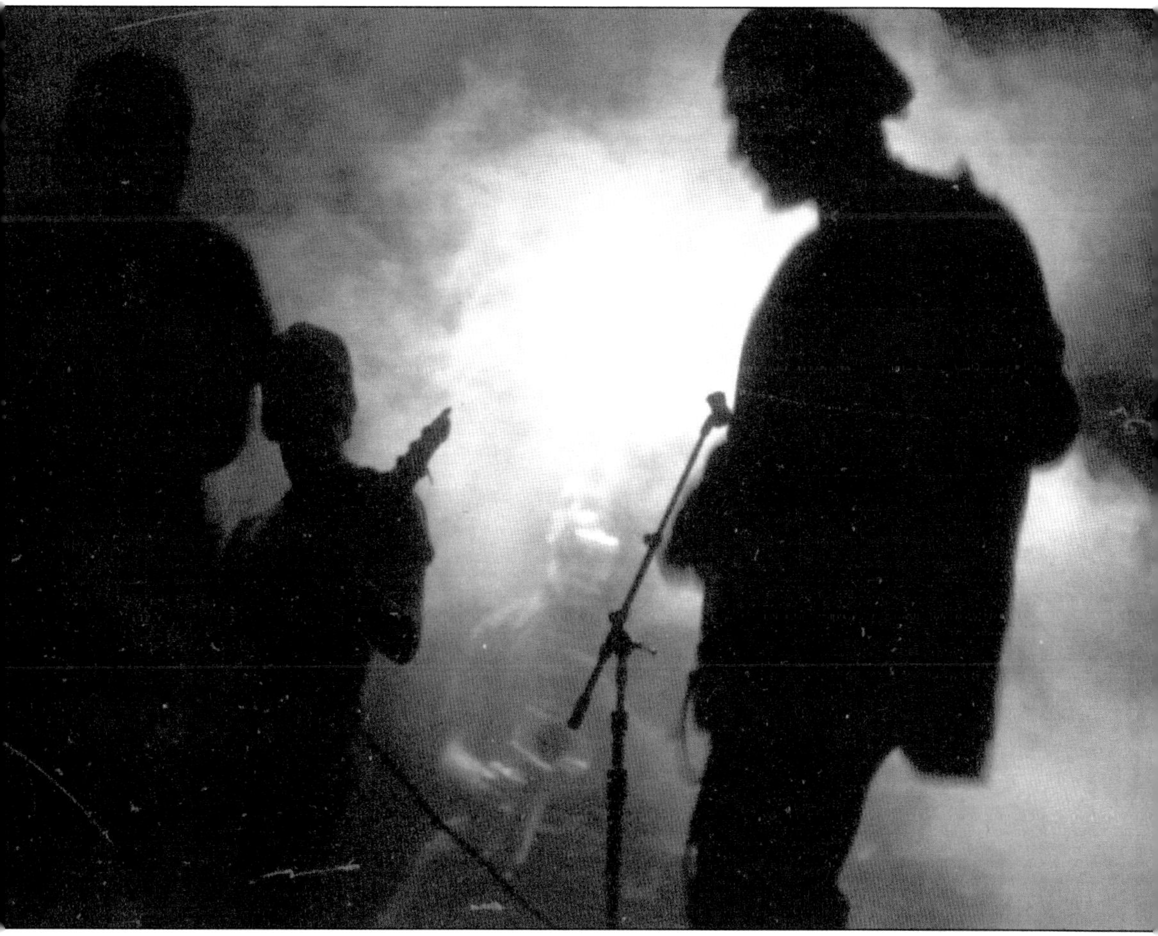

The Seacoast Music Awards gave many upcoming local bands a chance to rock in the biggest room in town; the bands reportedly could be heard clearly by the residents trying to sleep across the street at the Rockingham apartments. (Courtesy of Ralph Morang.)

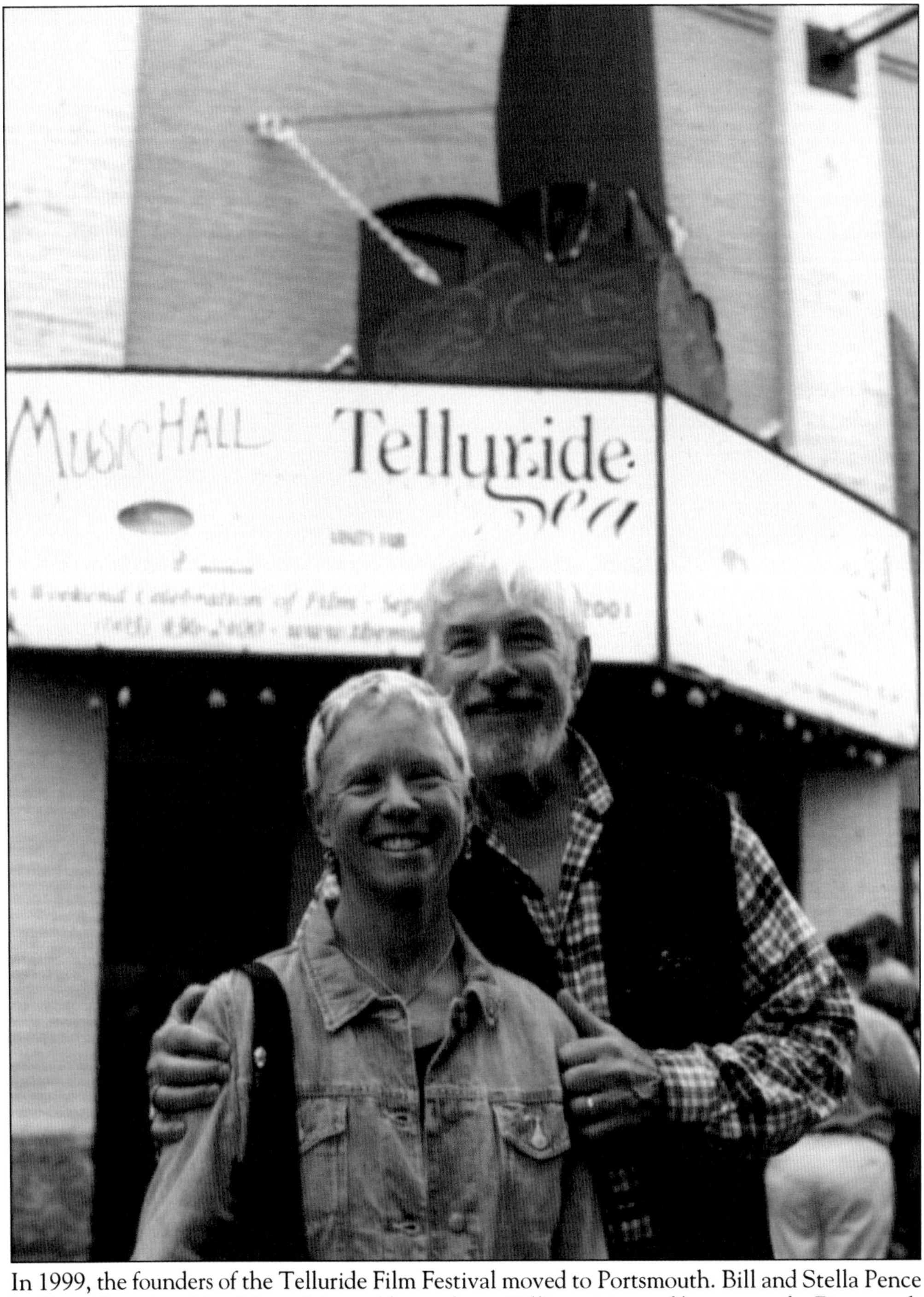

In 1999, the founders of the Telluride Film Festival moved to Portsmouth. Bill and Stella Pence had been longtime New Hampshire residents, due to Bill's position as film curator for Dartmouth University, but were attracted to the artistic spirit of the Seacoast region. With them they brought heavy film industry connections, a hands-on (or in this case, eyes-on) knowledge of upcoming films, and a history of experience with successful film event ventures that stretched back more than 30 years. (Courtesy of Nancy Horton.)

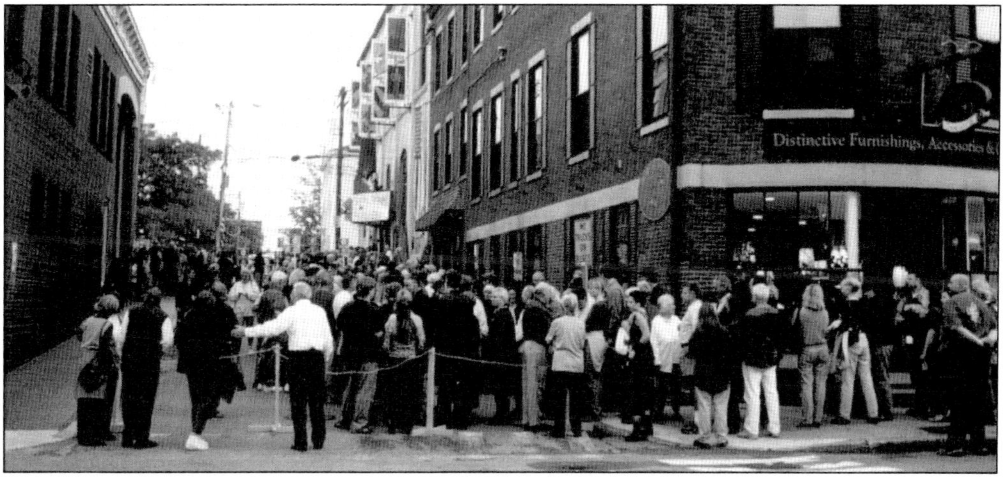

The Pences' first collaboration with the Music Hall was an immediate success. Telluride by the Sea was a smaller more intimate version of their internationally known Colorado event. Over the course of one weekend, the event featured six new films brought to the Seacoast directly from North American premieres in Colorado. The event earned instant recognition and touched a chord with local film lovers. Once again, lines stretched around the block for movies at the Music Hall. (Courtesy of Nancy Horton.)

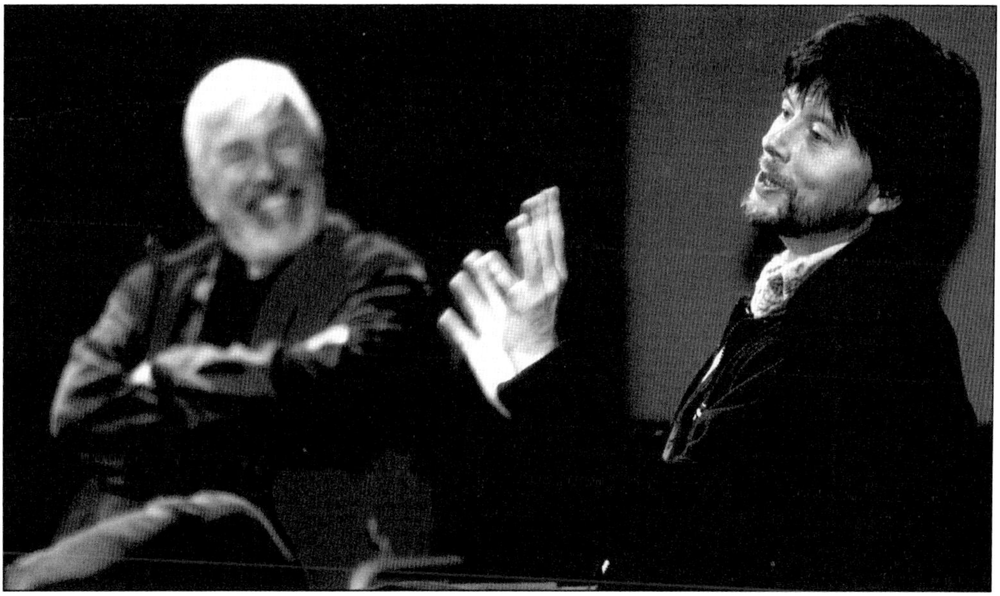

Acclaimed filmmaker, historian, and New Hampshire resident Ken Burns joined Bill Pence on stage to introduce and discuss his film *Jazz* in front of a sold-out audience. Donations included in the price of patron passes to the Telluride by the Sea weekend helped the Music Hall reach a longtime goal of raising funds for a full projection and film-sound overhaul. (Courtesy of Nancy Horton.)

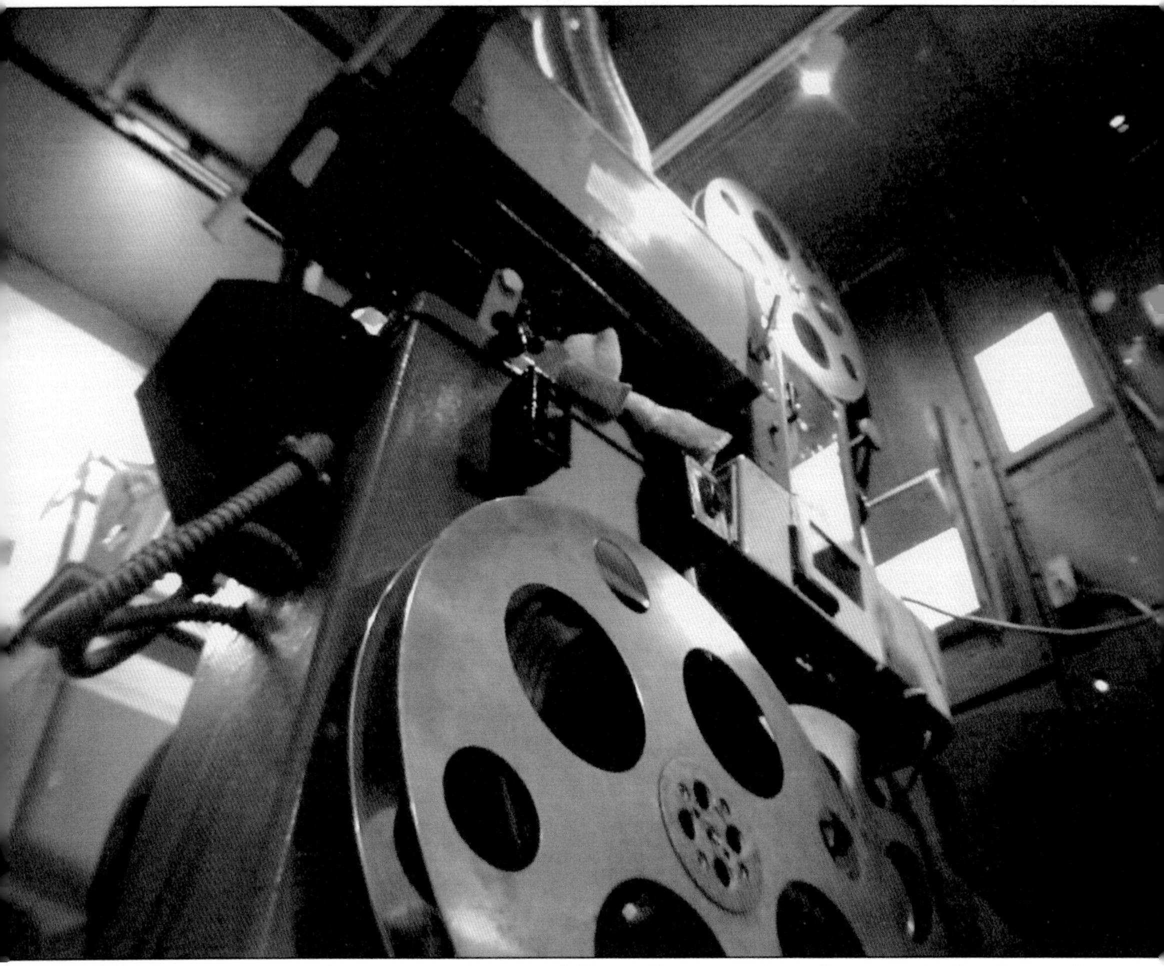

For a crisper, more vibrant screen image, a full set of new, cutting-edge, crystal-clear lenses for each projector was ordered, and the lamp house wattage was increased by 25 percent. (Courtesy of Rebecca Taylor.)

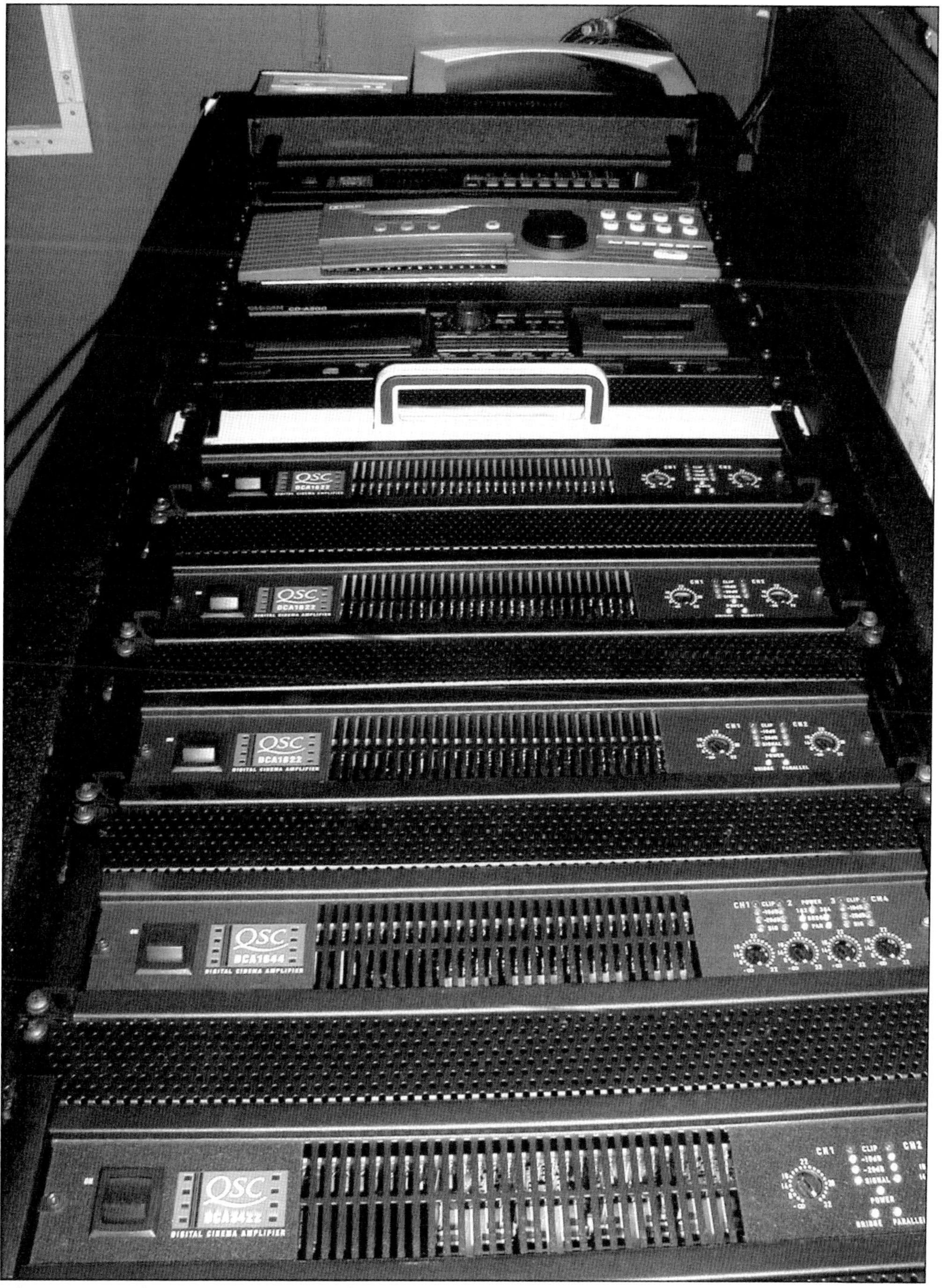

The new sound system was custom-designed to fit neatly into the Music Hall's charming historic architecture. The domed ceiling, curved rear wall, and lack of sound masking that produce the brilliant acoustics for a live performance posed a considerable challenge for the movie sound technicians. Meeting and exceeding all expectations, a dedicated 10-channel Dolby digital processor and system of focused JBL surround speakers were installed and calibrated. (Courtesy of Chris Smith.)

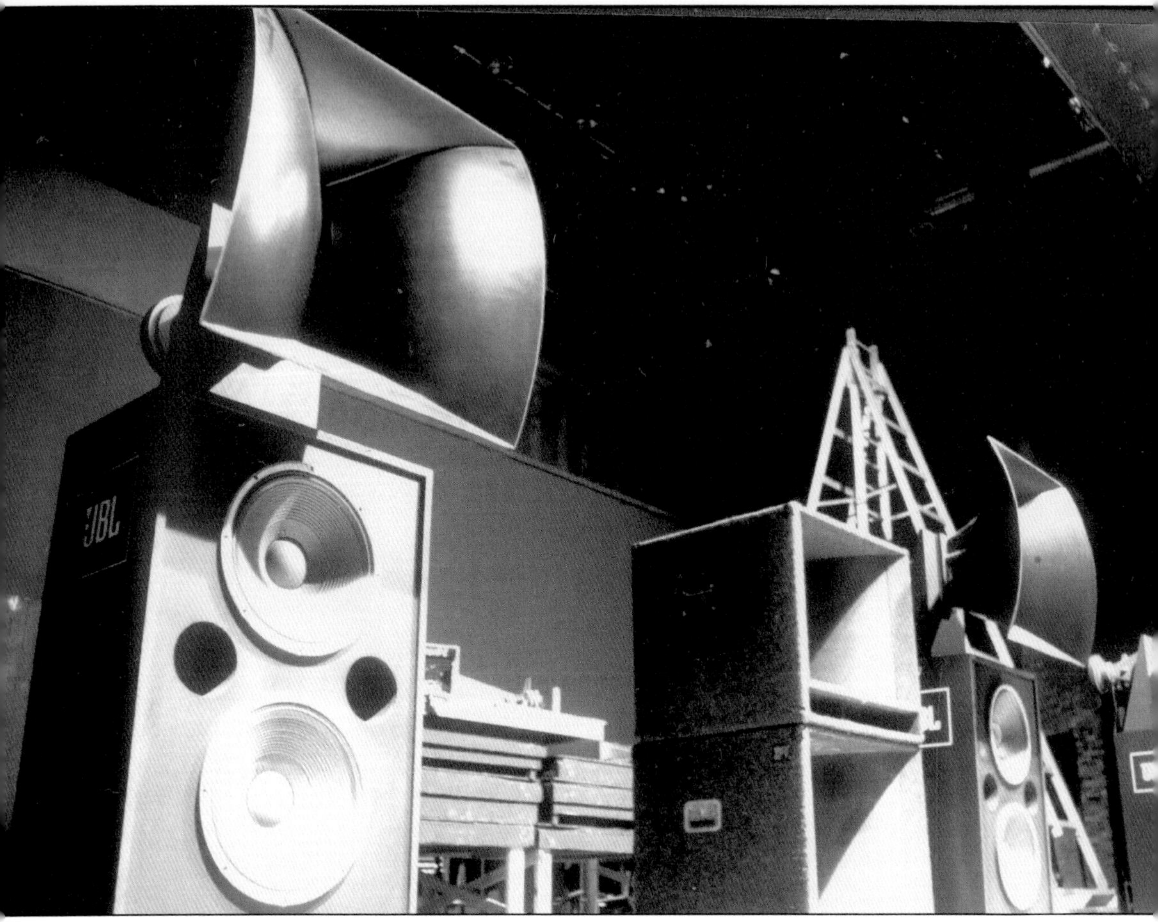

In what became a model for the whole upgrade endeavor, the existing speaker housings behind the screen were preserved, but all their tired internal components were traded for new state-of-the-art technology. A new high in resonance, depth, and tone was achieved.

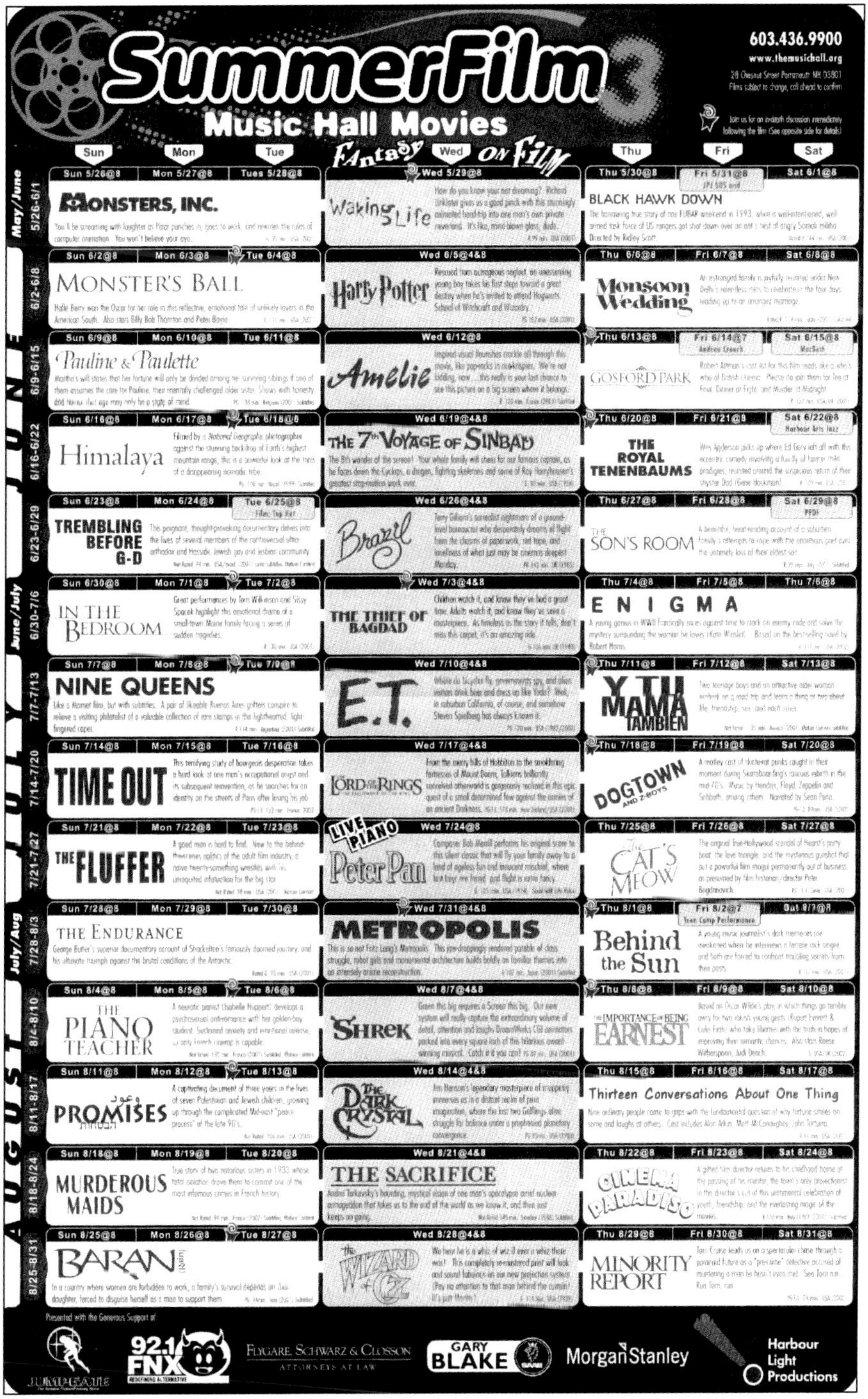

Bill Pence agreed to take the reigns of the Music Hall's film series. With a vigorous new program of classic, independent, and foreign features (and an occasional Hollywood blockbuster), movies at the Music Hall enjoyed a whole new level of public appreciation, and audiences began to swell. (Note the *Seventh Voyage of Sinbad* artwork, identical to that used in Loew's 1958 flyer advertising the same movie when it played at the hall as a first run.)

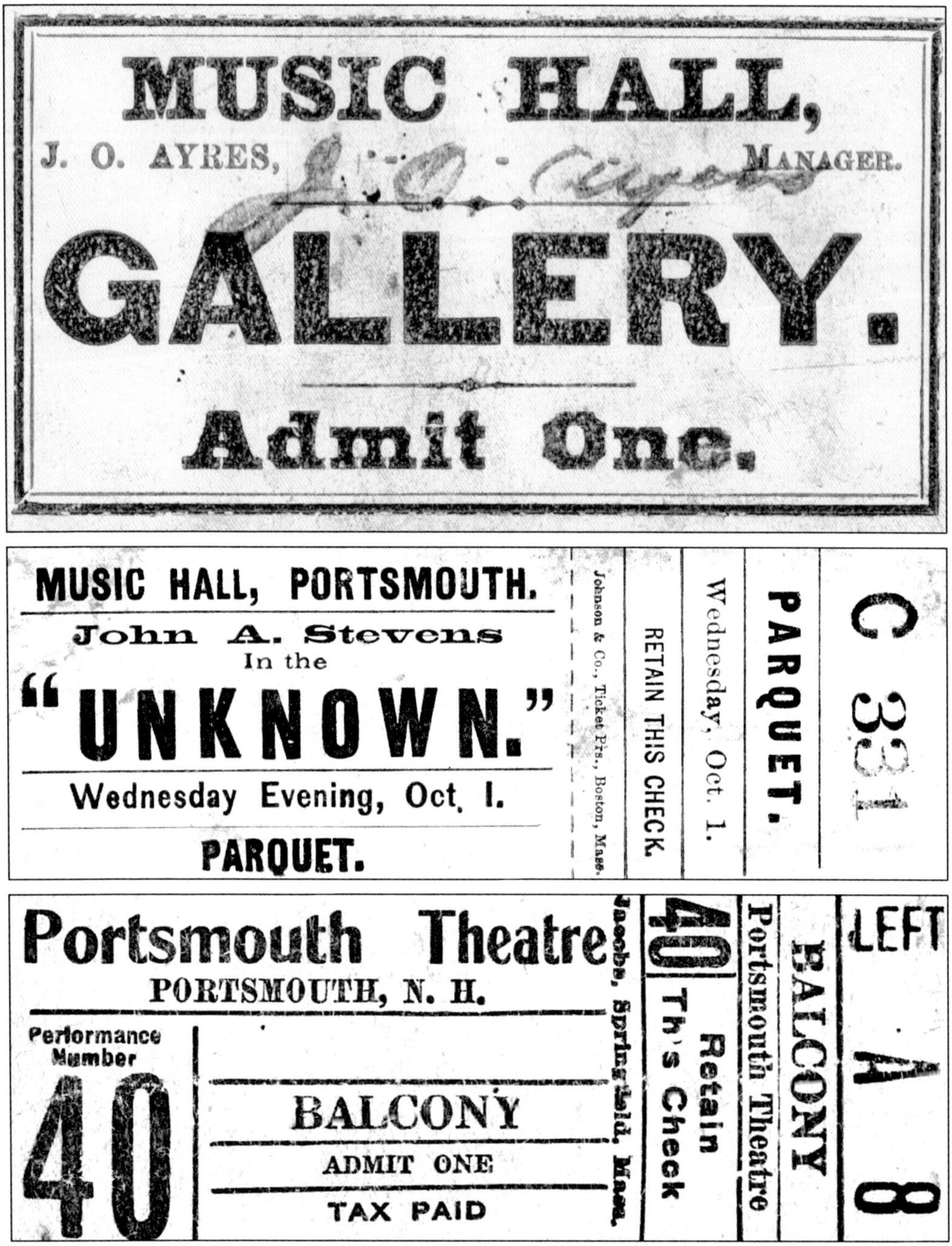

A brief look back at the lustrous history of the Music Hall can be illuminated by a series of tickets from popular events of years past. Our first ticket, signed by J.O. Ayers (predecessor to Hartford as manager under the Peirce family) is made of simple heavy cardstock and admits one into the gallery for any show. The ticket for *Unknown* remains a mystery in everything other than era. The theater was called Music Hall, without the word "the" until 1903, when F.W. Hartford renamed it the Portsmouth Theatre, as can be seen in the lower ticket, which also appears to be for a nonspecific performance. (Courtesy of the Harbor Arts Museum and the Richard Smith Collection.)

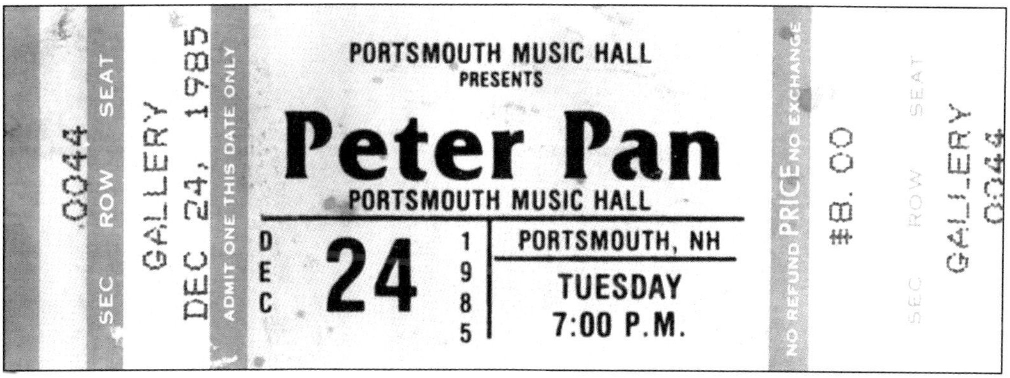

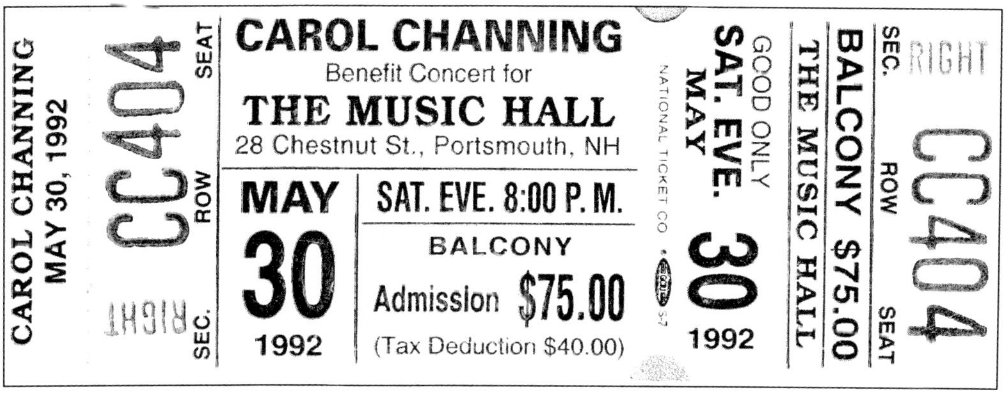

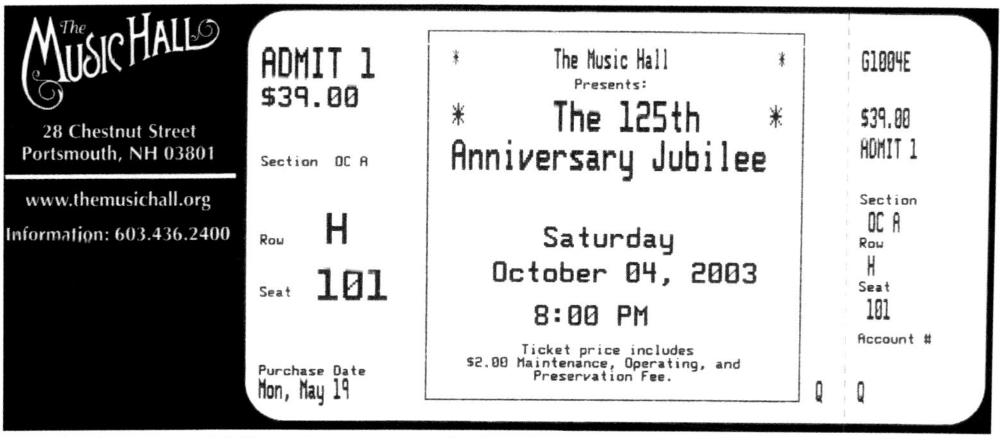

Decades later in 1985, *Peter Pan* was one the first large productions brought to the Music Hall in many years. This production was brought to Portsmouth by Roy and Eileen Rogosin, who soon afterward founded Seacoast Repertory Theatre, on the other side of town. Carol Channing arrived in 1992 to perform in a benefit to help the Friends of the Music Hall in their first few years. The lower ticket is from October of 2003, the celebration of the 125th anniversary of the beloved hall. On October 4, 2003, the Friends of the Music Hall celebrated the anniversary with a re-creation of the 1878 opening night performances. The show had patrons, staff, volunteers, and board members in period costume commemorating the impact of arts on local culture and applauding the strength of the community's resolve.

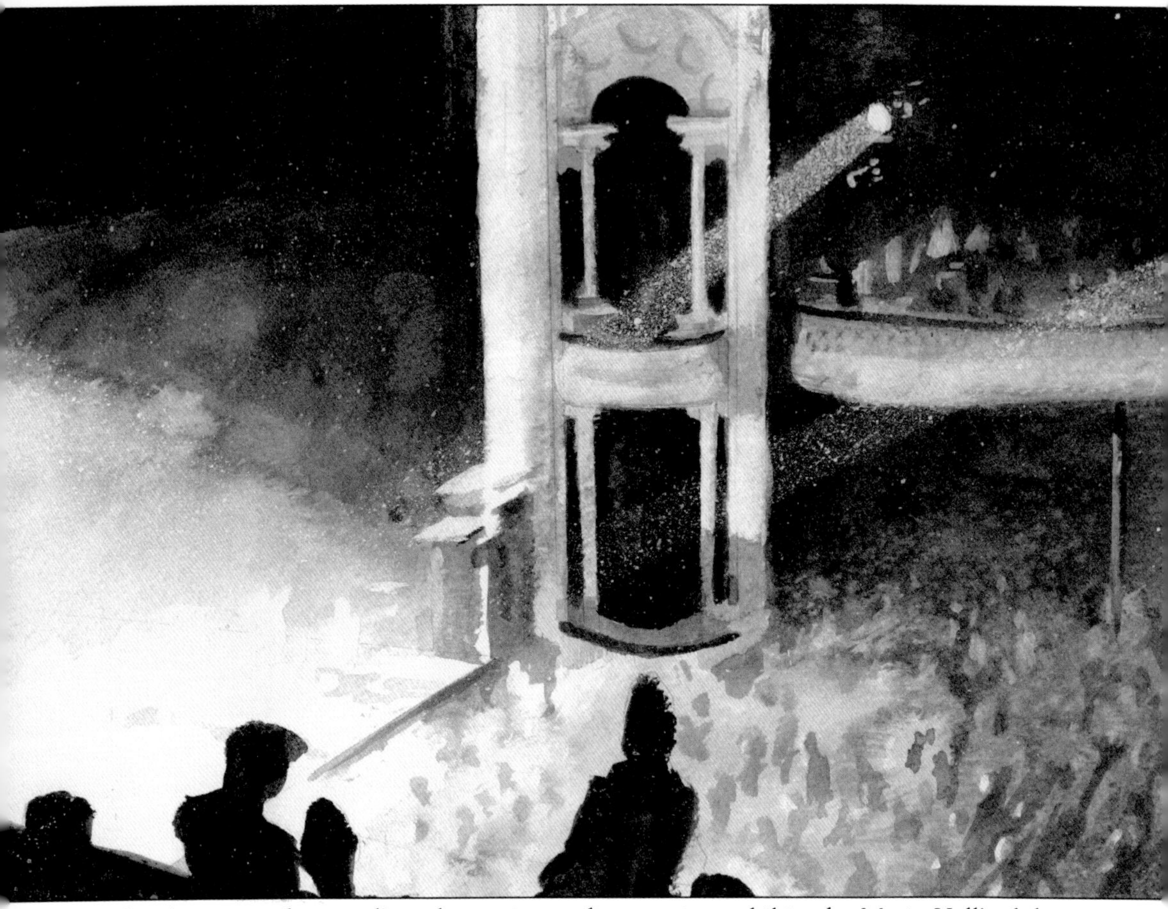

This depiction of a crowd's enthusiastic standing ovation exhibits the Music Hall's ability to inspire artists both on and off the stage. (Courtesy of Trevor F. Bartlett.)